THE CATSKILLS ALIVE!

Francine Silverman

HUNTER

Hunter Publishing, Inc.
130 Campus Drive
Edison, NJ 08818-7816
☎ 732-225-1900 / 800-255-0343 / Fax 732-417-1744
Web site: www.hunterpublishing.com
E-mail: hunterp@bellsouth.net

IN CANADA
Ulysses Travel Publications
4176 Saint-Denis
Montreal, Québec H2W 2M5 Canada
☎ 514-843-9882, Ext. 2232 / Fax 514-843-9448

IN THE UK
Windsor Books International
The Boundary, Wheatley Road
Garsington, Oxford OX44 9EJ England
☎ 01865-361122 / Fax 01865-361133

ISBN 1-55650-891-3
© 2000 Hunter Publishing, Inc.

All photos taken by author, unless otherwise indicated.
Maps by Kristine K. Costello & Lissa K. Dailey,
© 2000 Hunter Publishing, Inc.

4   3   2   1

About the Alive Guides

Reliable, detailed and personally researched by knowledgeable authors, the *Alive!* series was founded by Harriet and Arnold Greenberg.

This accomplished travel-writing team also operates a renowned bookstore, **The Complete Traveller**, at 199 Madison Avenue in New York City.

About the Author

Francine Silverman is a veteran feature writer for newspapers and magazines. She honed her skills as a reporter with Gannett Westchester Newspapers in Yonkers, New York, and as a freelancer. These days her passion is travel writing and this book marks the capstone of her career. Her travel articles have appeared in *The Inquirer* (Philadelphia), *The Record* (N.J.), *New York Post*, *River*, *Camperways*, *Travel Smart* newsletter, *Travel Agent Magazine*, *MotorHome*, and inflights *Kiwi*, *Mabuhay*, and *Passport Sabena*.

Bookmark the author's Web site at http://hometown.aol.com/fsilver767/myhomepage/index.html to keep abreast of news and events in the Catskills.

www.hunterpublishing.com

Hunter's full range of travel guides to all corners of the globe is featured on our exciting Web site. You'll find guidebooks to suit every type of traveler, no matter what their budget, lifestyle, or idea of fun. Full descriptions are given for each book, along with reviewers' comments and a cover image. Books may be purchased on-line using a credit card via our secure transaction system. All online orders receive 20% discount.

Alive Guides featured include: *Aruba, Bonaire & Curaçao; Jamaica; Buenos Aires & The Best of Argentina; Venezuela; The Cayman Islands; Cancún & Cozumel; St. Martin & St. Barts; The Virgin Islands*; *Nassau & The Best of The Bahamas*; and *Martinique, Guadeloupe, Dominica & St. Lucia*.

Check out our *Adventure Guides*, a series aimed at the independent traveler who enjoys outdoor activities (rafting, hiking, biking, skiing, canoeing, etc.). All books in this signature series cover places to stay and eat, sightseeing, in-town attractions, transportation and more!

Hunter's *Romantic Weekends* series offers myriad things to do for couples of all ages and lifestyles. Quaint places to stay and restaurants where the ambiance will take your breath away are included, along with fun activities that you and your partner will remember forever.

*To Ron and Amy with everlasting
love, and to the memory of my
mother-in-law, Ada, who always
said I had a book in me.*

Acknowledgments

Writing a guidebook requires the cooperation of hundreds of people. I've met so many wonderful folks in the Catskills – residents, merchants, proprietors, government employees – that it's impossible to name them all. I'm especially grateful to those who opened their homes and hearts to me.

Special thanks go to these individuals for graciously sharing their expertise along with their time and enthusiasm for my project: Richard Caraluzzo, Carolyn Bennett, Melanie Carpenter, Stefania Jozic, Trish Kocialski, Cora Schwartz, Carla Smith, Mike Tancredi, JoAnn Gallagher, Liz Callahan, and Edward Sidote.

Finally, I'd like to express my deep appreciation to my publisher, Michael Hunter, and editors, Lissa Dailey and Kristine Costello, for their continued support and patience.

We Love to Get Mail

This book has been carefully researched to bring you current, accurate information. But no place is unchanging. We welcome your comments for future editions. Please write us at: *The Alive Guides*, c/o Hunter Publishing, 130 Campus Drive, Edison, NJ 08818, or e-mail your comments to hunterp@bellsouth.net.

Contents

Maps

Introduction

Of all the scenery of the Hudson, the Kaatskill Mountains had the most witching effect on my boyish imagination.
— Washington Irving

This book took root during the summer when my husband and I spent a weekend in Forestburgh, New York. I was awed by its ineffable beauty – only two hours from home. I was also struck by the scarcity of tourists at the Delaware River, not far from our inn. Some feel gambling will save the Catskill Mountain area, which lost it cachet with the advent of air travel. Others believe casinos will destroy its rural charm. The point has been moot since the New York State Legislature voted it down. The issue has now resurfaced.

However, whether casinos become a reality or not, the region is showing some signs of recovery. Many hotels are reopening or are under renovation, and the famed Woodstock site has been staging Day in the Garden concerts, drawing thousands to Bethel. In preparing an article on the Catskills for *Travel Smart* newsletter, I discovered many wonderful outdoor activities and unique attractions nestled in the mountains, some newly opened. The heyday of those mega-resorts may be gone, but the sleeping giant is beginning to stir.

Like the famed author Washington Irving, I've always been captivated by the Hudson Valley region. And although I haven't seen any headless horsemen in my drives through the Catskills, I have seen deer, turkeys, a bear cub and stray horses. Still, legends remain and not just of Rip Van Winkle. Each county has its own folklore, and for the treasure hunters among us, I've included some.

To the many New Yorkers who once summered in Sullivan County, including myself, "the mountains" meant the Catskills. We never knew these were only the foothills – that even more spectacular sights lay beyond the Borscht Belt.

I wrote this guidebook not only to share my affection for these mountains, but also to correct some of the misconceptions I've heard, such as "Monticello is the Catskills," or "Woodstock isn't in the Catskills," and "There's nothing to do in the Catskills anymore." One author even asked in a rather disapproving tone why I chose to write about the Catskills in the first place. But most people, upon learning of my forthcoming book, have related their own fond memories of summers in bungalow colonies or working as hotel busboys.

Carved by wind and water, the Catskills seem somehow gentler and more mysterious than volcanic mountains.

Part of my fascination about the Catskills is due to their geology. Meta Lilienthal, in her book, *Dear Remembered World* (1947), contrasted them to the cold and forbidding snow-covered mountains of Switzerland: "Not so the Catskills," she wrote. "Their wooded slopes and softly curving summits, their graceful lines and close connection one with another, as if they were all holding hands, and not too great aloofness from the life of the valleys below, suggested a gay companionship, an understanding friendship."

This guidebook also addresses a problem pinpointed by Stephanie Ross of the Sullivan County Historical Museum. There is no single visitor's center, so unfortunately, it's easy for tourists to miss attractions. To help you avoid the time-consuming problem of getting lost, this book uses landmarks (such as a Mobil station), with approximate distances, to identify hard-to-find sites or routes. This book assumes you'll find your way on the highways and then helps with directions closer to your destination. In some cases, I omitted directions because they are best given by the site manager, are already written in the brochure, or require too much instruction. In such cases, I included the details that were omitted from directions given to me that caused me to overrun my destination. My aim is to help you find your way on the first shot, even on deserted mountain roads.

How To Use This Book

This guidebook is divided into the four counties that make up the Catskills region – Sullivan, Ulster, Greene and Delaware. While you and I may see the Catskills as one whole entity, these counties are generally promoted separately.

Sullivan County, the southernmost county, has been synonymous with the Borscht Belt for about half a century, although it would like to change that image in people's minds and move on. Its thousand square miles offer countless treasures, and new resorts are certain to brighten the economic landscape.

Geographically, **Ulster County** is the most varied. It's shaped something like a pitcher, with New Paltz to Saugerties the handle, the Town of Hardenburgh the spout, and everything else the belly. Politicos, in fact, see the county in at least two parts as Ulster begins the process of seeking dual designation. Everything east of the Catskill Park (which encompasses some Hudson River towns) would be officially designated the Hudson Valley and every place west of the Park, the Catskills. The big question is – if Ulster is

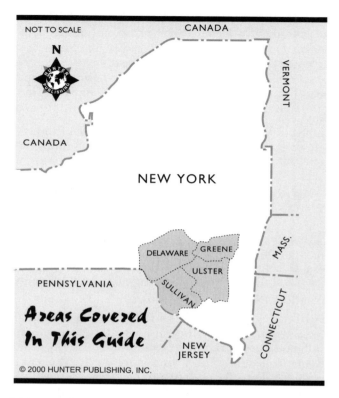

NOT TO SCALE

N

CANADA

CANADA

VERMONT

NEW YORK

DELAWARE · GREENE

ULSTER

SULLIVAN

PENNSYLVANIA

MASS.

Areas Covered In This Guide

NEW JERSEY

CONNECTICUT

© 2000 HUNTER PUBLISHING, INC.

bifurcated, will the Catskills then have five counties?

Delaware County spans the far western Catskills. It is larger than the state of Rhode Island, but has a population density of only 21 people per square mile. Roughly half of its 1,460 square miles are made up of trout streams. It was among these waters that Theodore Gordon, the father of American fly-fishing, introduced the techniques that changed the sport of fishing altogether. This rural county is also hunters' heaven, with thousands of acres of game habitat and an abundance of deer, turkeys and gamebirds.

The northernmost county, **Greene County**, is ski country and home to Kaaterskill Falls, the most celebrated site in the Catskills for its enduring beauty to generations of artists, writers and just plain folk.

Any less than glowing comments about places mentioned in this book are not meant to detract from the site or proprietor, only to give them a more personal touch. If you're like me, you consider the innkeeper or restaurateur as important as the inn or restaurant. Like a CEO of a company, they set the tone of the establishment.

The "Works in Progress" callouts found throughout the book represents significant projects that may or may not materialize. Habitues of the Catskills have heard so many empty promises from so-called benefactors over the years that they are understandably skeptical. Readers will ultimately know which developers fail to fulfill their promises.

Catskills Alive! is geared toward anyone seeking a weekend – or a week – away. Often a short vacation close to home is in order. But where to go? If you live in the New York metropolitan area, the Catskills is ideal for a weekend vacation, or even for a day trip. It's only two or so hours from Manhattan, borders Pennsylvania, and is close to New Jersey, Connecticut and Massachusetts. If you're a visitor to the Big Apple and have extra time, why not get away from the hustle and bustle of the city for a relaxing and inexpensive few days in the country?

Enjoy fresh air, scenic views and fun times in the Catskills!

Reasons to Visit

People still think of the Catskill Mountains as the Borscht Belt. That's because for most of this century the Sullivan County hotels served only kosher food and spawned the careers of countless Jewish comedians, actors and singers. Aside from this, few are aware of the gems beyond the Borscht Belt.

Mountains, lakes, streams and reservoirs are all here for your pleasure.

Immigrants who once sweltered in New York City's congested Lower East Side breathed easier in the mountains, some becoming its first farmers and inn-keepers. People with tuberculosis flocked to the region's sanitariums to help clear their lungs. Travelers continue to come to the Catskills for fresh air and clean water.

Winter weather here is slightly colder than in New York City, 90 miles south of Sullivan County. The region also gets more snow. Naturally, it's cooler in the mountains than in the towns, but the summers can get hot, especially in the valleys.

While billboards still shout Kutsher's and Nevele Grande, other beautiful inns and B&Bs abound. Several are located on streams or are nestled in the shadow of a mountain range. Unlike the mediocre meals at most large resorts, some restaurants provide a wonderful dining experience. The mood is generally casual, whether you're savoring a lakeside seafood dinner or are singing along with the pianist at a family-style eatery.

Activities such as fishing, mountain climbing and watersports are the usual pastimes, but horseback riding, mountain biking, golf and tennis are equally popular. Hotels and inns are sometimes affiliated with a local stable, golf course or canoe concession.

History buffs can learn local history in the little museums or may discover a relic while walking in the woods. Long-ago authors and artists were the first to record the magnificence of the region and some of their homes are now open to the public.

There are animal farms open to the public, private breeders with inns that welcome guests, and enough deer and small animals around to soften the child within us all.

Animal lovers will find a virtual menagerie here.

A child and deer become friends at Hull-O Farms in Greene County.

The scenery is breathtaking in so many areas. A 1991 *I Love New York Travel Guide* brochure cited 14 "Spectacular Views" in the state. Only the Catskills and the larger Finger Lakes areas had four citations each – more than any other state region.

Introduction

Geology & Geography

Geologists describe the Catskills as flat-lying plateaus dissected by streams, with deep gorges ("cloves" to the Dutch). To the rest of us, however, they are simply called mountains. Who ever heard of a plateau inspiring legends, folk heroes or diabolical names like Devil's Kitchen?

"Some of the greatest scenery would not be there except for the work of the glaciers," says Catskill geologist Robert Titus.

While I hate to admit it, technically the Catskills *are* a plateau since they are almost uniform in height with little bare rock. In the Devonian Epoch (405-365 million years ago), the Catskills were beneath a shallow ocean. As continents moved, they were uplifted and the sediment and life forms at the bottom of the sea converted to sedimentary stone. During the Ice Age (two million to 14,000 years ago), these sandstone-encrusted plateaus were eroded by rivers and melting glaciers to form peaks and valleys.

★ DID YOU KNOW?

The 100 gently-rounded peaks were sometimes called the Blue Mountains because of the thick canopy of hemlock trees. Even now, from afar with the sun glistening, the peaks appear pastel blue and pink.

Continuing Debate

The definitive area of the Catskills differs greatly among historians, geologists, residents and outsiders. Some say only the area within the Catskill Park is the Catskills; others say anything within the bounds of Greene County. For the purposes of this book, the four counties – Sullivan, Ulster, Greene and Delaware – comprise the Catskills.

Environment

Reservoirs

Toward the end of the 19th century, it became evident that the Kensico and Croton Reservoirs, constructed in the early 1800s in Westchester County, could not sustain a growing New York City population. Today, the Catskill reservoir system provides NYC with nearly 90% of its drinking water. From 1907 to 1964, the city bought 57,619 acres of Catskill land, razed towns and farms, and moved almost 5,000 people in order to scoop out six reservoirs: Ashokan (completed in 1919), Schoharie (1927), Rondout (1945), Neversink (1945), Pepacton, the longest, at 18.5 miles (1955), and Cannonsville (1962).

Forests

*Let us permit nature to have her way;
she understands her business better
than we do.*
– Michel de Montaigne, French
philosopher and essayist (1533-1592)

The 300,000-acre **Catskill Forest Preserve** is the state land within Catskill Park. It was created in 1885 to protect the area's water resources and to provide public recreational opportunities. The preserve is protected by law from being sold or destroyed under an 1894 amendment to the New York State Constitution directing that "the lands of the State now owned or hereafter acquired, constituting the forest preserve... shall be forever kept as wild forest lands." Within the preserve are wild forest areas for hiking, horseback riding and snowmobiling, and wilderness areas for primitive camping and solitude.

The **Catskill Park** encompasses all four counties and is designated by a green line on official maps. Sixty percent is privately owned and is home to nearly 50,000 year-round residents. Almost all the notable mountain summits are within the boundaries of the park.

In general, summits above 3,500 feet are covered with virgin red spruce and balsam fir. Between 1,200 and 3,500 feet is a beech-birch-maple layer also containing hemlock. Below that is a forest of oak, hickory, chestnut, black gum, tulip and flowering dogwood.

Wildlife

> *I believe all animals were provided by God to help keep man alive.*
>
> – Iwao Fujita

Black bears tend to avoid open spaces and shy away from contact with humans.

A diverse assortment of wildlife roams the wilderness. The last inventory of animal life in the Catskills was compiled in the early 1980s and counted some 44 species of mammals, 98 species of birds, and 37 species of reptiles and amphibians. These included black bear, white-tailed deer, coyote, bobcat, wild turkey, pheasant, mink, red squirrel, porcupine, snowshoe hare, beaver and rattlesnake. No known endangered species is among them.

Black bears are found in three separate ranges in New York State: the Adirondacks (9,300 square miles), the Catskills (1,270 miles) and the Allegheny region (450 square miles). The state's total bear population is about 400, most of which live in the more mountainous, heavily forested northern part of the range, including much of the Catskill Forest Preserve.

Contemporary Catskills

In 1950, half a million people spent their holidays in the Catskills. Although most of the big hotels are gone, and with them most of the visitors, some things have not changed in the last half-century – a profusion of dude ranches, freshwater streams, invigorating air, historic shrines and monuments, and reasonable room rates.

Today's residents are a blend of two basic groups – natives and transplants. The latter are mostly second homeowners from New York City or New Jersey, but some have left the rat race to permanently smell the flowers. Foreign-born residents are largely from eastern and western Europe and Ukraine. There are pockets of ethnic groups, including Hasidic Jews around the old Borscht Belt region; the French in Shandaken; Ukrainian in Glen Spey; and German and Irish in East Durham.

Although I've heard some moans and groans from residents about the economy in the Catskills, none has mentioned leaving. The pull of the mountains is too great, I guess. Bob Steuding, the Poet Laureate of Ulster County, tells a wonderful story in his book, *A Catskill Mountain Journal*, which the city slickers among us can really appreciate. About a century ago, a mountain man had to journey to New York City. It took a whole day to walk out of the hills. He then took the train from old West Shokan (now under the waters of the Ashokan Reservoir) to Kingston, then rode a trolley car through Kingston down the hill to Rondout to board a steamboat. It took a few hours to land in Manhattan. When he returned home some days later, the townspeople were bursting to learn what he saw. The man thought for a moment and then replied, "I can't tell you much about the place. There were so many buildings in the way, I couldn't get the lay of the land."

Nearly every village has a post office and a general store. In some cases, that's the whole village!

Of late, locals are worrying about radical changes in their lifestyle. Will gambling ruin the rural flavor and increase traffic? Will the "beautiful" people who are abandoning the Hamptons for the Catskills kill the leisurely pace? (Top models and musicians have been scooping up old farmhouses for a song in Ulster County, around Woodstock, Stone Ridge and High Falls. They claim to have rejected their old lifestyle, trading "the scene" for scenery and parties for privacy.)

Population by County (1998)

Sullivan	69,111
Ulster	166,351
Greene	47,807
Delaware	46,086
TOTAL	329,355

Nightlife 🎵🎶🎼

Unless you're a barfly or are staying at a resort, you won't find much to do after hours in most areas of the Catskills, especially off-season. (If you're like me, the mountain air will make you too sleepy to care.) Although there are many creative people involved in community theater, they are scattered about and their timetables tend to be erratic. If you can't catch a show, an appealing option is a leisurely dinner in a country restaurant.

✎ *TIP*

At many of the smaller resorts you'll find nothing more than a band or DJ. If you're a night owl, inquire about the local entertainment options before booking reservations.

Getting Here & Getting Around

Navigating the Catskills

Don't get confused, as I did, when looking for a village. You might see the sign, think you're there, and suddenly there's another sign for a different village. The counties in the Catskills are divided into towns and the towns into hamlets or villages. Their names are often the same names as the towns. The village of Bethel is in the Town of Bethel, the village of Liberty is in the Town of Liberty, and so on. If, for example, you're driving north on Highway 97 heading for the village of Cochecton and see a sign for Cochecton, it's probably for the town. The next sign may be for Skinners Falls, but don't panic. The village of Cochecton is up ahead. That said, I'd suggest you purchase a Catskills map at one of the convenience stores. At least you'll know how lost you are!

Admittedly, it's frustrating when signs are hardly visible on roads or restaurants or when signs and billboards advertise businesses that are long gone. So many times I've been disappointed to find that a restaurant or attraction announced on the road was shut down. It's also annoying when certain commercial establishments keep a low profile. What I've learned is that zoning boards in some towns have strict regulations about signs and that sometimes new business people are resented by their village elders, forcing them to quietly welcome visitors. Keeping a balance between retaining the old ways and supporting the local economy is sometimes tricky.

One last caveat. Don't leave eating to chance. You might find yourself driving for miles with nothing in sight but silos. See *Best Places to Eat* under each county for area restaurants, diners and cafés.

I hope you'll enjoy this book as much as I've enjoyed researching it. If you discover places I've overlooked or misrepresented, please write to me c/o Hunter Publishing, 130 Campus Drive, Edison, NJ 08818, or e-mail me at fsilver767@aol.com.

Driving

Most visitors arrive by car; thankfully, gas stations are abundant. Sullivan County is accessible from the New York State Thruway (Interstate 87) at exits 16 and 17, Ulster County exits are 18, 19 and 20, and Greene County exits are 20, 21 and 21B.

Mileage From NYC Line to Catskill Region via Thruway*

Exit 16, Harriman 45
Exit 17, Newburgh, I-84,
    Stewart Intl. Airport 60
Exit 18, New Paltz 76
Exit 19, Kingston, Rte. 28 91
Exit 20, Saugerties, Rte. 32 101
Exit 21, Leeds, Catskill, Cairo, Rte. 23. . 113
Exit 21B, Coxsackie, Rtes. 81 and 9W. . 124

The Major Deegan Expressway becomes the Thruway at the Bronx/Yonkers line and runs north to the Canadian border. From Albany it's called the Northway. An extension (I-90) also runs west from Albany.

Car Rentals & Cabs

Daily rates for a mid-sized car originating in Sullivan County (rates subject to change):

Budget; unlimited free mileage, $49. ☎ 914-794-4424/6303.

M&M Ford Lincoln Mercury, 127 Mill St., Liberty; gives first 75 miles free; 10¢/mile thereafter, $39.95. ☎ 914-292-8600; 800-452-2217.

Yellow Cab Co. serves Monticello and surrounding areas; airport service; 24-hours daily. ☎ 914-794-1120/4040.

National Mountain Transportation has door-to-door daily service to Sullivan, Ulster and Greene counties from all five boroughs of NYC. $50 per person. ☎ 718-884-9400.

Catskill Shuttle – Van pick-ups in midtown Manhattan, JFK and LaGuardia airports, three days a week. ($35 one way; $65 round trip). Pick-ups in other parts of NYC are $6 extra. Stops in Sullivan County (Liberty, Monticello, Roscoe) and Delaware County (Downsville, Walton, Delhi). ☎ 800-607-2753. Pets are welcome.

If you're already in Sullivan County and need a ride, call **Ronnie's Taxi & Car Service** out of South Fallsburg. ☎ 914-434-6550.

Bus Service

All listed bus service originates from Port Authority at 41st and 8th Avenue in Manhattan. **Short Line,** ☎ 800-631-8405; 212-736-4700, which also has terminals in New Jersey (☎ 201-529-3666), stops in Ellenville, Wurtsboro, Liberty, Loch Sheldrake, Monticello and Sullivan Social Service, and also has a limited Kingston run.

Adirondack Trailways, ☎ 800-858-8555, goes to Kingston and Saugerties via Palenville, Hunter, Tannersville and Windham (Route 23A), and will drop off anywhere on request.

Pine Hill Trailways provides service to New Paltz, Rosendale and Kingston with connections west to Woodstock, Phoenicia, Pine Hill, Andes, Delhi,

Fleischmanns and Margaretville (Route 28). ☎ 800-858-8555.

Train Service

Sadly, only tracks are left from the glory days of the railroads. Passenger trains ceased running in the Catskills long ago. **Amtrak** (☎ 212-532-4900) runs along the Hudson River as far as Poughkeepsie. ☎ 800-724-3322; 212-532-4900 for Metro North Railroad/Amtrak information about connections north and west.

Air Service

Stewart Airport serves the Catskills (Thruway Exit 17). Airlines serving the airport include:

American Airlines . . . . ☎ 800-433-7300
Delta . . . . ☎ 800-221-1212
Midway . . . . ☎ 800-446-4392
US Airways . . . . ☎ 800-428-4322
United Express . . . . . ☎ 800-241-6522

Where to Stay

*A*ccommodations of all shapes and sizes are scattered throughout the Catskills, from simple motels to mega-resorts and from small hotels to mini-palaces.

Most resorts serve three meals a day. Whether they are in the Borscht Belt or not, the food is Catskill-style – plentiful. If you prefer savoring the charms of the Victorian era while enjoying the comforts of home, you'll discover that most of the B&Bs and inns in the Catskills were built in the 19th century and have been lovingly restored. It's easy to turn back the clock when artifacts enjoyed by your great-grandparents envelop you.

The majority of inns and B&Bs in the Catskills provide bathroom toiletries, while hotels, resorts & motels usually do not.

In choosing accommodations, think about your interests and needs. B&B owners, especially in the Hudson Valley (where many guests come from New York City), tell stories of people who drive up to the B&B only to discover to their dismay that the proprietors sleep in the same house. The owners of Evelyn's View in Milton have solved this problem by living in separate quarters, but most innkeepers are not in a position to reside elsewhere.

I've also heard that many guests, especially young people, have no interest in socializing with the owners. The Seupels of Whispering Pines in High Falls try to gauge a guest's comportment before launching into conversation. Says Celia Seupel, "What do you go to a B&B for? You want to really feel at home – to feel really comfortable." Still, some proprietors might not be as sensitive, and it's a good idea to call the innkeeper beforehand to assess their manner.

We take for granted that everybody is familiar with B&Bs, but in reality, they've only become popular in this country in the last 20 years. Joyce Barber, proprietor of Breezy Acres Farm in Hobart, has been running a B&B for 16 years. She considers herself "a real old timer in this business, even for the United States." When she started, people asked, "What's a B&B, anyway?" Just five years ago, there were only 19 B&Bs in Ulster County compared to more than 100 today.

According to *Bed & Breakfast Encyclopedia*, a publication of American Historic Inns, a country inn generally serves both breakfast and dinner and may have a restaurant associated with it. Also, the inn-keeper is usually less visible than in a B&B. A bed & breakfast may have three to 20 rooms or more and the proprietors often live on the premises. Breakfast is usually the only meal served.

⊚ TIP

Don't become victim to an errant alarm clock set by a previous guest. Check the clock-radio before retiring.

Seasonal Considerations

Be aware that April 1, May 1 and right before Thanksgiving are the opening dates of trout and hunting seasons, and inns in Sullivan and Delaware counties fill up quickly. Also, old houses generally do not have, or need, air conditioning. Some have ceiling fans or freestanding fans. If you're traveling in the hot summer and are concerned, ask the owner what to expect.

These figures for hotels, B&Bs and inns are based on figures in high season on weekends. Where there are ski slopes, winter is the busiest time. Inns generally raise their rates and motels that normally charge between $35 and $55 sometimes raise the price. (A good reason to visit out of season.) The recommended motels in this book are a cut above the cookie-cutter establishment, with cleanliness, safety factors and the proprietor's demeanor taken into consideration.

$ Alive Guide Price Scale

Lodging

The following price scale is intended as a guideline to help you choose lodging to fit your vacation budget. It is based on the cost of a double room, two people per room, and does not include the 15% service charge or 7.75% state tax.

ALIVE! PRICE SCALE	
Inexpensive	Less than $100
Moderate.	$100-$200
Expensive	$200-$300
Deluxe	More than $300
Price scale for resorts that include three meals a day	
Inexpensive	Less than $200
Moderate.	$200-$250
Expensive	$250-$350
Deluxe	More than $350

Restaurants

Beef and fish dominate most Catskill menus.

I leave it to the reader to rate a restaurant. Since taste in food is subjective, meal preparation often inconsistent, and because I'm not a food critic, I've only highlighted meals that were outstanding. That doesn't mean the other food was bad. The worst meals I've had in the Catskills could be termed so-so.

In some cases, I've given the actual price of my meal since a scale sometimes has its limits. Most of the restaurants are open year-round, but do call ahead.

There's not much price difference among restaurants in the Catskills. In most cases, an entrée with a glass of wine and coffee is $20-$25 per person, plus tip and tax (7.75%).

ALIVE! PRICE SCALE
Price scale reflects one entrée, glass of wine and coffee.
Inexpensive . . . . Less than $20
Moderate . . . . $20-$35
Expensive. . . . . More than $35

Shopping Best Buys

*E*very day we read about a small-town store being swallowed up by a big chain. Hopefully, this will never happen in the Catskills, where nearly every store is family-owned and the owner greets strangers with a smile.

With the exception of Apollo Plaza, the new Wal-Mart in Monticello, the mall in Kingston, and some scattered boutiques, the Catskills is not exactly a fashion mecca. What it does have are antique shops – ubiquitous in towns and on country roads – worthy of their own book. A peek at the Ulster County phone book reveals three times as many antique dealers as retail stores. Come to the Catskills for collectibles, crafts, fresh produce, breads, jams, honey, gifts and New York State wine.

Keeping Posted

In general, I've restricted the geographic scope of this book to the four counties, and for good reason. The east side of the Hudson River is heavily promoted, whereas the Catskills are treated as a stepchild to the Adirondacks. This isn't only true of the few guidebooks that exist on the region, but advertisements outside the area as well. Consider this – at the rest stop before NYS Thruway Exit 16 (gateway to the Catskills), the only ad is for Lake Placid, more than four hours north in the Adirondacks. The result is that vacationers from the country's most densely populated region, New York City, largely bypass the Catskills on their way upstate. What a pity!

The many free publications you'll find in the Catskills contain tons of info on events and attractions along with feature articles.

Within the Catskills, however, advertising abounds. Complimentary publications piled high in stores and restaurants put even New York City to shame. Problem is, you have to go to the Catskills to learn what's going on. And while I have tried to be as up-to-date as possible, that's an impossible task. So do pick up promotional materials wherever you find them – usually near the store entrance. Bear in mind that advertisers cross county lines.

After stopping at the Sloatsburg service area countless times on my way to the Catskills, I discovered a **New York State Travel Plaza** hidden in a back corner on the upper level. So before you even reach Exit 16 off the Thruway, think about stopping at one of the three service stops that have tourist centers: Sloatsburg (the largest), Plattekill or New Baltimore. The brochures are from all over New York and include many Catskills attractions.

In addition to the visitor's guide provided by each county's chamber of commerce or public relations bureau, I've found the following publications (most free) invaluable.

Brochures & Publications

Once you reach the Catskills, look for the following:

- ❖ *Hudson Valley Guide*, an annual comprehensive guide with maps.
- ❖ *Kaatskill Life* (www.kaatslife.com), a glossy quarterly magazine portraying a variety of topics, is sold by subscription and sometimes distributed free throughout the Catskills.
- ❖ *Sullivan County Cultural Directory*, an annual containing cultural events, restaurant reviews and historical nuggets.
- ❖ *Sullivan County Scene* (www.scsmag. com), a quarterly of events, listings and articles on topics such as health, retirement and wedding tips. The *Scene* also publishes a summer guide, *Sullivancountyny.com*, which serves as the county's magazine/Web site.
- ❖ *Catskill Shopper*, a seasonal guide with features about Sullivan County and a five-month listing of regional events.
- ❖ *Catskill Country*, a biannual guide to the entire region.
- ❖ *County Shopper*, published in two editions (Delaware and Catskill Park) covers nearly all of Delaware County.
- ❖ *Community Directory*, a comprehensive source of information on Delaware County.

❖ *Sidelines*, a new football guide with weekly schedules, statistics and trivia questions.

❖ *The Guide – Catskills Mountains & Hudson Valley* (www.theguidemagazine.com/index_.html), a monthly publication covering Ulster and Greene counties with informative features by Gene Ligotti about the history of towns and waterways.

❖ *Chronogram* (www.chronogram.com), a monthly calendar of arts, New Age events and classes, and a business directory.

❖ *Ulster*, published three times a year, with features and a guide to inns, art, antiques and dining in the county.

❖ *Options UnLtd.*, an annual lifestyle magazine devoted to food, including restaurant menus, events and accommodations in Ulster and Greene counties.

❖ *About Town*, a tabloid-size listing and events calendar in Gardiner, Rosendale, New Paltz, Stone Ridge, High Falls and Highland/9W Corridor, is published seasonally.

❖ *Catskills Travel Guide*, an undated brochure, cited as "Best Regional Travel Guide 1995-96" at the 1997 "I Love New York" competition.

❖ *Catskill Trumpet*, a quarterly tabloid focusing mainly on the northern Catskills, including parts of Ulster and Delaware counties.

❖ *Hunter-Windham Scene* (www.hunter windhamscene.com), a vacation guide published six times a year.

❖ *The Times Herald Record* prints a calendar of events in Orange and Sullivan counties every Friday. It also publishes several supplements distributed separately from the newspaper. I picked one up (called the *Answer Book*) in a real estate office. The first magazine-sized publication of *The Record*, it's geared to new homeowners, but has some listings that may be of interest to tourists, such as religious services and movie theaters. Check for it in Sullivan and Ulster county real estate offices.

❖ *The River Reporter* (www.riverreporter.com) is a comprehensive tabloid-size weekly published in Narrowsburg. It sells for 60¢, covers news and events in Sullivan County, as well as Wayne and Pike counties in Pennsylvania. The paper often includes inserts like Today's Business and The Source (a 40-page resource guide to Sullivan County, primarily for residents).

❖ Special interest publications include *I Love New York – Catskills Travel Guide*, containing a list and map of golf courses countywide, and *I Love New York – Ski the Catskills*. ☎ 800-I-LOVE-NY for these free guides.

❖ A family-oriented pamphlet of note is *The Catskill Adventure – Day Hikes and Paddles for Families*. Published by the New York State Department of Environmental Conservation (NYSDEC), it contains descriptions of 16 short hikes throughout the Catskills, lakes accessible to boats, and the best trails for children under five. A trip log is included, and those who complete seven of the listed outings receive a Catskill Adventure Patch. ☎ 914-256-3082/3083.

Additional Information

❖ **Sullivan County** – ☎ 800-882-CATS; Ofc. of Public Information, ☎ 914-794-3000, ext. 5010); www.scva.net or www.scsmag.com/index.html

❖ **Ulster County** – ☎ 800-DIAL-UCO

❖ **Delaware County** – ☎ 800-642-4443

❖ **Greene County** – ☎ 800-335-CATS; or www.greene-ny.com

Sullivan County

Overview

Sullivan County is just 90 miles from New York City and borders Pennsylvania on the west. Southernmost and closest to New York City, it's the most familiar of the four counties because of the old Borscht Belt and fly-fishing fame. Route 17, also called the Quickway, is its main artery, running from Exit 16 on the Thruway in a north-

westerly direction to Deposit, in Delaware County, and continuing toward Binghamton and beyond. Motorists on Route 17 pass through Orange County before reaching the eastern edge of Sullivan County at Bloomingburg. Mountains first come into view around Wurtsboro (Exit 113).

Although many attractions are closed in the winter, the Catskill Mountains are worth visiting any time of year. In the warmer months, Sullivan County is especially inviting. The Delaware River and all the lakes and streams are available for swimming, fishing and canoeing, and the county boasts some 17 golf courses.

You can stay at either an all-inclusive resort and leave your car parked the whole time, or stay at a

B&B and explore the county's little-known treasures. Included in this chapter are a few ideas. If you
discover any I've left out, please let me know.

Friendly Faces

Even the police are pleasant in the Catskills, providing you obey the law. I once
stopped on the side of the road to photograph the view. An officer stopped and I immediately wondered what I did wrong. I
explained what I was doing and he smiled
and said, "You should come back in the fall
when the colors change."

ⓢ TIP

A word of caution: Don't speed, especially on Route 17 where state police
are ever present. Once you exit the
highways, getting lost is a given.
The Catskill region is 4,000 square
miles, twice the size of the state of
Delaware, and many of the roads
are rural and unmarked. Locals are
frequently the tourist's best guides,
not official maps. This means stopping at every convenience store to
ask directions. Don't despair. The locals are helpful and you might even
find a friendly farmer to guide you.

Works in Progress

Signs recently installed on the Quickway read "Future 86," indicating that Route 17 will eventually become an interstate (outside of the Catskills, 177 miles of Route 17 from East Corning to the Pennsylvania border has already become Interstate 86). According to Dennis Wilson, resident engineer of the county's Department of Transportation, legislation has been approved by the state, but it's anyone's guess when work will begin on fixing exit ramps and so forth.

Besides the fact that the roadway from Harriman to Binghamton is the oldest portion of Route 17, the motivation for improvement is to encourage economic development in Sullivan County. "People expect certain standards when they ride an interstate," says Wilson. "The AAA will route them on an interstate. Businesses want to be located near an interstate." Regardless of when it happens, several road projects are planned for the very near future, including a ramp into Apollo Plaza and a welcome center/rest stop somewhere between exits 113 and 115.

Several new building projects in Sullivan County have recently been completed, including the gigantic 200,000 square-foot Wal-Mart in Monticello. About the size of five football fields, it's half department store and half supermarket, bank, hair salon and portrait studio.

Sullivan County

History

History repeats itself. That's one of the things wrong with history.
— Clarence Darrow

Early Days

Nestled in the foothills of the Catskills, Sullivan is the most publicized of the four counties. Its oldest town is **Mamakating**, formed in 1743. However, Sullivan County itself wasn't established until 1809, when it was carved out of neighboring Ulster County.

Sullivan County's 15 townships were created between 1743 and 1869.

Sullivan County's first known inhabitants were an **Algonquin** tribe, the **Lenape**, meaning "real men" or "genuine men." (Many anthropologists believe they were the ancestors of those who crossed the Bering Strait and first populated the North American continent.)

Algonquin Influence

The Lenape called the region Onteora – land in the sky. Many places in Sullivan and Ulster counties have been named after Algonquin words, such as Cochecton, Willowemoc, Mongaup, Ashokan, Kerhonkson, Shandaken and Shawangunk. Neversink, which comes from "Neya ink," meaning the place of the big rock, is the name of a river, hamlet, township and reservoir.

With the arrival of the Dutch, the entire region became known as the Catskills. Sullivan County was named for John Sullivan, a Revolutionary War general whose army chased away the Indians of western New York in 1779.

Prior to construction of the Newburgh-Cochecton turnpike in 1801 and the tanning industry in 1830, most of the population centered around the county's major waterways – the Bashakill, Neversink, Mongaup and Delaware rivers.

Industry

Before the hotel era, the prosperity of the Catskills was defined by three major industries – tanneries, lumber mills and quarries – all begun in the 1800s. With the construction of the Delaware and Hudson (D&H) Canal in 1828, coal boats drifted along at three miles an hour from Honesville, Pennsylvania to Port Jervis and then northeast to Kingston, New York, for passage on the Hudson to New York City or Albany. Mules hauled the boats 108 miles on a towpath alongside the canal, and the trip from end to end took a week. The 84 miles in the Catskills largely paralleled present-day Routes 97, 209 and 213.

★ DID YOU KNOW?

The D&H Canal was the first enterprise in the United States to cost over one million dollars. Service ended in 1898 due to the increased use of the railroad.

During the canal era, tanneries began sprouting throughout the Catskills. Hides from South America were shipped up the Hudson and carried by wagon to their destination. The industry brought prosperity to the region during the Civil War when it produced much of the leather, especially saddles, used by the Union army.

Vast tanneries were established near Palenville, Tannersville, Edwardsville (now Hunter), Prattsville, Phoenicia, Samsonville and Claryville in Ulster County. But Sullivan County had 39 tanneries, more than any location in the state. As James Eldridge Quinlan, author of *History of Sullivan County* (1873) wrote: "There's an old saying, 'The Civil War was won with boots tanned in Sullivan County.'"

Old Falls Tannery

Perhaps the most successful tannery was Old Falls, owned by Rufus Palen. After starting a tannery in Palenville in Greene County, he came to Neversink Falls in 1832. His partner was Nicholas Flagler, whose granddaughter started the boarding house that became the Flagler Hotel. Tanneries were firetraps, but because of Palen's intense fear of fire, safety measures prevented his tannery from suffering the fate of so many others. It stayed in business for 40 years.

The tanning industry ended after the war when the curing of animal hides practically depleted the hemlock trees. This deplorable stripping of nature did have some positive effects, however. Cut trees allowed more sunlight to come through, generating the growth of birch, maple, oak and other hardwoods. The tanning industry also led to the construction of roads and railroads. Great numbers of Italians came to work on the railroads and the reservoirs. Irishmen arrived, many from New England and Canada, to work in the lumber industry. In 1840, New York was the largest producer of timber in the country.

★ DID YOU KNOW?

A great deal of hemlock bark was required to obtain a small quantity of tannin. A cord of bark was needed to tan 10 hides, and hemlock bark could be peeled easily only when the sap flowed freely, between May and July. Bark peelers worked hard during these three months, but then left behind huge hemlock trunks to rot away.

Birth of Catskills Hotels

Even before the great wave of Jewish immigration to America in the late 19th century, some Jewish families were trying their hands at farming. As more Jews escaped from Manhattan's congested Lower East Side, with support from the Jewish Agricultural Society and others, farms proliferated. But the stony soil and short growing season forced the owners to become innkeepers. These rooming houses were the precursors of the Borscht Belt, named for the beet soup so popular among Jews.

The earliest "tourists" were hunters and fishermen from New York City who, in the 1830s, hired local farmers as guides and were lodgers in their farmhouses. (It wasn't long before the streams and lakes of Sullivan County became well known to fishermen.) Historians mark the arrival of the first real

The word Catskills is derived from the Dutch: "cat," meaning sloping walls of earth, & "kill," a creek.

tourists around 1873 with the completion of the New York and Oswego Midland Railroad. The coming of the Ontario & Western Railway (O&W) through Sullivan County in 1869 brought promotion of the region by the railway. Millions soon came to the mountains by rail. Initially, the Jews were not welcome by the Protestant and Catholics who rented rooms. But in 1899, *Summer Homes,* a series of guidebooks issued by the railroad, published its first advertisement for a Jewish-owned resort, Rock Hill Jewish Boarding House. John Gerson, the first known Jewish farmer to settle permanently in the Sullivan-Ulster County area, placed the ad.

Seasonal Visitors

A special report in a recent issue of *The Times Herald Record* placed the number of Hasidic Jews from Brooklyn who now come to the Catskills every July and August at 40,000. The article says that the Catskills are so well known among Orthodox Jews that some come from around the world to be with their kin, filling more than 100 camps and bungalow colonies that lie vacant for 10 months of the year. While these summer residents help the economy and are a tight-knit community, many local residents resent them for real and imagined reasons. It's not unlike the first Jews' reception in the mountains.

★ DID YOU KNOW?

Some Jews fled to the mountains for another reason. The crowded city tenements were near open sewers, breeding grounds for tuberculosis. In the ghetto, victims cried in Yiddish, "Air, give me air!" Because the town of Liberty had the highest elevation, it was the ideal setting for a sanitarium. The Loomis and the Workmen's Circle were among the most famous.

Present Day

Sullivan County is composed of abandoned hamlets and thriving towns, often worlds apart in mind and miles. Residents of one community are often unaware of attractions in the other. All take pride in their own county, though, and several movements are afoot to recreate Sullivan County as a tourist destination through clean-up and marketing efforts. Catskills' IDEA (Institute for the Development of Entertainment Arts) was founded in 1992 by retired Broadway producer Stan Raiff on the assumption that the old resort area has a great past and great future. In 1996, the organization received praise from the governor and members of Congress for bringing top-flight entertainment and historic bus tours to Sullivan County.

Still, many buildings are in shoddy condition and especially depressing to those who remember places like Liberty, Livingston Manor and Monticello in their heyday. Yet there are still hidden wonders to be discovered, and the mountains haven't lost their power to cast a spell.

As Washington Irving expressed it: "Whoever has made a voyage up the Hudson must remember the Kaatskill Mountains... Every change of season, every change of weather, indeed, every hour of the day produces some change in the magical hues and shapes of these mountains.... "

Bygone Borscht Belt

When I sat down to write this book, the report on the old Borscht Belt was grim. Since then the Concord and Grossinger's, the grand dowagers of the "Gilded Age" in the Catskills, have been sold to investors who plan to convert them into mega-resorts befitting the 21st century. In January 1999 the land once occupied by Laurels Country Club was sold for just over $1 million. And in May 1999 the Stevensville Hotel, closed a decade ago, re-opened as the Swan Lake Resort Hotel. The biggest prospect, however, is casino gambling at **Monticello Raceway**. The plan to approve a $500 million casino to be given in trust to the St. Regis Mohawk Indians awaits approval of the Federal Secretary of the Interior and Governor George Pataki.

All this news finally broke in a positive headline in *The New York Times* on Feb. 5, 1999, declaring "Investors Stir Hopes of Revival in Catskills."

Good news aside, the Borscht Belt as we remember it, is gone forever. In the 1920s before airplanes and air conditioning, Jews flocked to Monticello, Liberty, South Fallsburg, Ferndale, Swan Lake, Parksville, Ellenville or Livingston Manor for the fresh country air. The 100-mile car trip took 12 hours because the only thoroughfares on Old Route 17 were cow paths through the center of each hamlet with strictly enforced speed limits of four miles an hour.

★ FAMOUS FACES

"When I began coming up to the Catskills in the 1930s, the trip could take a whole day. Cars always overheated; we'd spend so much time filling the radiators. The hills were monstrous. Cars couldn't make it up. One summer I got as far as Wurtsboro Mountain, but then the car just wouldn't go any further. I sold it for $40 and hitchhiked the rest of the way." *– Opera star Robert Merrill*

Comic Joey Adams' family was too poor to own a car so they usually traveled by train. This involved a trolley trip from Brooklyn to a crosstown bus on 42nd Street to a ferry to Weehawken followed by a quarter-mile hike to the last railroad car for those traveling to Ellenville. After a grueling six-hour ride on the O&W passengers had to change trains in Summitville. (Before cars, hotel owners met passengers at the station in a horse and buggy.) Adams later worked as a waiter and entertainment director at several hotels and wrote a book aptly titled *The Borscht Belt*.

Poor Jews who couldn't afford a hotel or even a bungalow stayed in a kuchalayn, which literally means "cook alone." However, while each family supplied its own food and linens and cooked its own meals, food preparation and eating were communal. Too many cooks often led to squabbles over ownership and rights. Adams recalls that his mother would fight with the other women over food and sink space.

"Take the sink – and hold it!" was the perpetual battle cry. With spouses gone during the week the wives probably needed an outlet. Consider this: When the "husband train" arrived on the weekend it was sometimes met with a brass band!

★ FAMOUS FACES

When they weren't playing Grossinger's, Kutsher's or the Concord, most performers entertained at kuchalayns. Singer Julius La Rosa was among them. "I had a friend write a parody to *E Cumpari* – in Yiddish! As you can well imagine, it played like gangbusters," he wrote in an e-mail. "Early on, a senior lady called me Mr. La *Rosen*. Honest!"

Adams points out that while the Jewish Alps had no palm trees or polo, it had the hospitality of farmers. "And to folks who fed chickens, cows, horses, goats, family and neighbors' kids several times daily, what was so tough about having a few extra guests from the city?"

The hospitality is still there, but the hotels are too many generations away from the family farm. Just 20 years ago, there were more than 100 hotels and rooming houses in Sullivan County. By the time Grossinger's closed the numbers had diminished. Today there are only five large hotels in Sullivan and Ulster counties. In November 1998 the Concord closed its doors.

Simon Says More Nostalgia

Young and old alike seem to know Lou Goldstein. When I told my 27-year-old daughter Amy about my upcoming interview, I was startled that she knew him. "Oh, I love Lou Goldstein!" To my further amazement, she also learned the merengue and electric slide from Lou's wife, Jackie Horner, who was the inspiration for the 1987 hit movie *Dirty Dancing*, Amy's favorite film at age 16.

I met with these quintessential Borscht Belters at the Liberty Diner to rekindle fond memories and to catch up on the latest gossip. Lou and Jackie met at Grossinger's in 1953 and gained fame there, and were bursting with delightful anecdotes. The pair still lives in the shadow of the "G," surrounded by hallways of memorabilia. Both are still active at the Raleigh and other extant resorts. She still teaches dance seven days a week at the Raleigh and runs its theme-based senior weeks. Lou plies his humor and no-win Simon Sez in the Catskills and at sales conventions. "It teaches [salesmen] how to listen," he says (see photo on page 477).

Jackie, trained in ballet and Grossinger's dance director until it closed, performed with the June Taylor Dancers and Radio City Rockettes and appeared on the Milton Berle and Sid Caesar shows. The first time she came to Grossinger's, she met Lou, a member of its athletic staff. He'd been at Grossinger's since 1949.

According to the couple, Jennie Grossinger, "a kind, sweet lady," was not the force behind the hotel in the early years. It was run by Milton Blackstone and an excellent staff of people. Blackstone was responsible for bringing Eddie Fisher to Grossinger's to perform weekends.

Sullivan County

Eleanor Bergstein, the screenwriter of the movie
Dirty Dancing, was a guest at Grossinger's one
weekend when she met Jackie. She wanted to do a
movie about Grossinger's and found Jackie's story
inspiring. Jackie was the prototype of Penny Johnson, the dance teacher in the coming-of-age story set
in 1963, and the teenage girl who falls for Patrick
Swayze was patterned after one of Jackie's students.
The title of the film originated from Milton Blackstone's prudishness. He'd tell Jackie, "You know,
your students are dancing too close. Tell them to separate because they are dancing dirty."

The Borscht Belt's Heyday

Built around the turn of the century, these large hotels epitomized luxury and elegance to newly arrived immigrants who first endured hardships in
the ghetto and then in sweltering tenements and
sweatshops. As Stefan Kanfer writes in *A Summer
World*, "the drama that began in the shtetls of Rus-
sia unfolded in the Lower East Side and spilled out
into the Catskill Mountains of New York State."

The Borscht Belt was known as the Cradle of Show
Business, giving countless celebrities their start.
David Daniel Kaminski, a.k.a. Danny Kaye, discovered show business when he was 16 and hired as
tummler by the White Roe Lake House in Livingston Manor in the summer of 1929. (Loosely translated, tummler or "toomler" is a kind of social
director who keeps the guests busy and amused.)
Kaye worked there a few summers before being
hired by the President Hotel in nearby Swan Lake
for a whopping salary increase of $100 a week.

These resorts were also the creators of the all-
inclusive vacation package. Forty years ago, Borscht

Belt hotels were running four and five pages of ads in *The New York Times*. On June 7, 1959 the Concord ran a full page announcing its lineup for the summer: Milton Berle, Martha Raye and Billy Eckstine. An article in that same edition reported on a Catskills "revolution" in hotel improvements and installations, notably indoor pools and golf courses. (Two decades earlier there was a boom in construction of outdoor swimming pools. A decade earlier air conditioning was coming into fashion in the mountains.) Sadly, most of the hotels mentioned in the article and advertisements are gone.

"Sullivan County is not the Jewish Alps of yesterday," laments Irwin Richman in *Borscht Belt Bungalows*. "It is more diverse, and perhaps more bizarre, than the county of my youth. Even if increasing numbers of secular Jews 'rediscover' it, it will never again be the Borscht Belt of legend."

Borscht Belt Hotel Updates

Virtually every hotel in the former Borscht Belt is now a work in progress. Those under new ownership are either in the process of or contemplating renovations, and it takes time for them to get their properties in shape. All the lobbies look good but many of the guestrooms and hallways still have peeling paint, chipped furniture and worn carpets.

Improvements are costly and disruptive and must be done piecemeal. If no renovation is going on during your stay, try to ignore the flaws and have fun. If workmen are under your feet, consider it a good sign and forgive the inconvenience.

If for no other reason, you'll know the Borscht Belt is gone when you see the diversity in hotel guests –

young, old, white, black, Hispanic and Asian, just for starters.

Grossinger's, closed in 1986, was sold for $6 million in a bankruptcy auction to a partnership that includes Louis R. Cappelli, a leading builder in Westchester County. He's also a major contributor to Republican politicians, one of them being Governor Pataki, who is said to favor gambling to help the economy. All the old buildings are being demolished except the restaurant and club to make way for a much smaller 200-room, five-star golf, spa and tennis resort hotel to be operated under a major flag (Marriott, Hilton or Sheraton). Members of the Min family had previously bought the property in 1993 for $5 million. The family maintained the golf course but was unable to resurrect the hotel business, and filed for bankruptcy protection in 1998.

★ FAMOUS FACES

Actor Eddie Fisher was discovered at Grossinger's in 1949. It was also the setting of his marriages to both Debbie Reynolds and Elizabeth Taylor. The Ritz Brothers began in the Catskills as tummlers and clowns. Shelley Winters got her start as a member of Grossinger's social staff in the 1940s, and she and hubby Anthony Franciosa spent many a summer there. Other performers from the early days included Jerry Lewis, Danny Kaye, Milton Berle, Zero Mostel, Buddy Hackett, Henny Youngman, Alan King, Jackie Mason and Joan Rivers.

If Grossinger's was the king of the mega-resorts with its own airstrip and post office, the **Concord** in Kiamesha Lake was the prince. Under the steward-ship of the Parker family for 61 years, it was sold to Joseph Murphy, a Manhattan real estate developer, in January 1999. He was interested in buying the hotel months earlier but was unable to raise the $24 million asking price; he then won it in a bid in a bankruptcy auction for $10.25 million. The Concord was more than $20 million in debt when original owner Robert Parker filed for bankruptcy in 1997. (The hotel closed a year after.)

Murphy's company, Concord Associates, had planned to spend $52 million to renovate the hotel. The 400 people who lost their jobs when the Concord closed had hoped for new job opportunities with the new hotel, which planned to hire 1,500 people. But Murphy was slow to make the needed renovations. Back in bankruptcy court a few months later, Louis Cappelli bought out Murphy, and plans to tear down the one-time crown jewel and start over. Construc-tion is planned to begin in late 2000. The resort will have a hotel and conference center, golf village, spa ranch, entertainment center and wilderness area.

A Bittersweet Farewell

Lou Goldstein, famous for "Simon Sez" at Grossinger's since 1949 was asked how he felt watching all the old buildings go down. He responded: "It was something like watch-ing my mother-in-law go over a cliff – in my Cadillac."

Laurels Country Club in Sackett Lake was seized by Sullivan County in 1995 for non-payment of real estate taxes. The old resort was closed in the late

1980s and the original hotel was demolished. On January 26, 1999, the 300-acre lakefront property was sold for just over $1 million to New Horizon Recreation, a Clifton, New Jersey development company that plans to build a Las Vegas-style hotel and entertainment complex costing tens of millions of dollars.

Prior to the Concord and Grossinger's early years, the **Flagler** in Fallsburg was the place to be. Playwright Moss Hart became its social director, or tummler, in 1929, designed the hotel playhouse, and put on theatrical productions. The Flagler Theater, built in 1928, seated 1,500 and in Hart's words was "the pride of the Catskills." His chief assistant was Dory Schary who went on to become head of Metro-Goldwyn-Mayer. Everything changed around 1969 or 1970 when a group of shady investors bought the hotel, calling it Fountains of Rome. A year later they abandoned the site when gambling legislation was blocked. A branch of the Crystal Run School (now Village), a center for the developmentally disabled, has been there since 1973 but plans are to close that campus by March 2000.

The **Aladdin** in Woodbourne was acquired by Carrie Komito from her mother in 1932. It went into foreclosure for past due taxes in 1993. On March 15, 1999, Sullivan County acquired the 70-year old hotel and a month later the County Legislature passed a resolution to sell it to Sima Bernat of New York City for $437,000. The county will hold title until it is paid off. The Aladdin deal was brokered by Michael Offit, Carrie's grandson. Bernat told Offit she was involved with resorts in the past, and that she intends to run a (Hasidic) tax-paying resort colony/hotel at the Aladdin. The only physical change at the Aladdin is the fenced-in pool.

Some other hotels and their incarnations include:

❖ **Brown's**, the hotel that Jerry Lewis made famous, is now Grand View condos; **Hotel Leroy** turned into Sullivan County Community College; college dorms now occupy **Hotel Evans**; and **Green Acres** is now New Hope Community, a residence for developmentally disabled adults.

❖ **Homowack** in South Fallsburg and **Tamarack Lodge** in Greenfield Park both became glatt kosher. Herman Wouk was the children's waiter at Tamarack in the 30s. His beloved novel, *Marjorie Morningstar*, took place in an imaginary camp in the Catskills.

❖ Also in South Fallsburg, **Brickman's**, **Gilbert's**, and **Windsor** are now home of the Siddha Yoga ashram; **Nemerson** is now the Yeshiva Viznitz for Girls. In January 1996, the kitchen at **The Pines** collapsed. The 400-room hotel later reopened and then closed two years later. As Phil Brown points out, it doesn't take long for a property to deteriorate. "After one season [The Pines] looks so decrepit. You'd figure it's been there for at least a decade without human life."

❖ **Waldemere** in Livingston Manor (Transcendental Meditation Center); **Youngs Gap** in Parksville (torn down); **President** in Swan Lake (vacation homes), **Sha-Wan-Ga Lodge** in High View (demolished); **Brown's Hotel Royal** in White Lake (Bradstan Hotel); **Paramount Hotel** in Mountaindale (houses one of the biggest of the 50 or so Ortho-

Sullivan County

dox camps in Sullivan County); and **Tennanah Lake Lodge** in Roscoe (Foundation for a Course in Miracles). The 344-room **Granit** in Kerhonkson (Hudson Valley Hotel) abruptly closed its doors in July 1997, forcing some 350 guests staying there to find new accommodations. **Leibowitz's Pine View Hotel** in Woodbourne is now the Sullivan County Correctional Facility where David Berkowitz (Son of Sam) is incarcerated.

Resources for Catskill History

Nostalgia for the good old days is intense. Consider the number of memoirs published in the last 10 years on the Borscht Belt: *Remember the Catskills – Tales by a Recovering Hotelkeeper* by Esterita "Cissie" Blumberg (Purple Mountain Press, 1996); *It Happened in the Catskills* by Myrna Katz Frommer and Harvey Frommer (Harcourt Brace Jovanovich, 1996); *A Summer World – The Attempt to Build a Jewish Eden in the Catskills, from the Days of the Ghetto to the Rise and Decline of the Borscht Belt* by Stefan Kanfer (Farrar Straus Girouz, 1989); and *Catskill Rambles* by Kenneth Wapner (The Overlook Press, 1992). The latest, *Borscht Belt Bungalows – Memories of Catskill Summers* by Irwin Richman, and *Catskill Culture – A Mountain Rat's Memories of the Great Jewish Resort Area* by Phil Brown were both published in 1998 by Temple University Press.

There are also films that revolve around the Catskills. Mentioned earlier, *Dirty Dancing* (1987), has a backdrop of the Catskills, although it was filmed in North Carolina. *A Walk on the Moon* (1999), filmed in Quebec, focuses on life in a Jewish vacation spot in the Catskills in the summer of 1969 – the year of Woodstock and the first walk on the moon. In this touching movie, a working-class New York couple gets caught up in the times.

Hungry for Catskills nostalgia and humor? The annual **Catskills Conference** will satisfy your yearning. It's a wonderful way to recollect old memories and network with like-minded people. **The Catskills Institute**, an organization founded by Phil Brown to keep alive the Jewish Catskills legacy, presents the conference, and also issues newsletters to members (membership is $25 annually) and gives discounts on Catskill books.

Conference topics have included everything from Catskills politics to Jewish summer camps. Films, slide shows and guest speakers round out the schedule. Past attendees have been authors, researchers, filmmakers, children and grandchildren of hotel founders, offspring of parents who worked in the Borscht Belt, people who spent their childhood summers there, and former busboys and waiters. Many bring along spouses and elderly parents. The conference schedule offers plenty of opportunities for socializing – during meals, breaks and at wine and cheese parties.

The Catskills Conference is traditionally held in August in Sullivan County. For more information, contact the Catskill Institute, c/o Phil Brown, Department of Sociology, Brown University, Box 1916, Providence, RI 02912 or ☎ 401-863-2367. Or visit his Web site at www.brown.edu/Research/Catskills_Institute, which also includes lectures, updates on hotels, a list of former hotels, books about the Catskills and more.

Sullivan County

© 2000 HUNTER PUBLISHING, INC.

N

Sullivan County

NOT TO SCALE

1. Beaverkill Covered Bridge	13. Holiday Mountain
2. Beaverkill Valley Inn	14. Tomsco Falls
3. Catskill Fly Fishing Center & Museum	15. Wurtsboro Airport
4. Livingston Manor Covered Bridge	16. D&H Canal Locks & Park
5. NYS Fish Hatchery	17. Basherkill Wildlife Management Area
6. Grossinger's Golf Resort	18. Bald Eagle Observation Hut
7. Sullivan County Museum,	19. Eldred Preserve
Art & Cultural Center	20. Fort Delaware
8. Stone Arch Bridge Historic Park	21. Delaware Valley Arts Alliance
9. Skinners Falls	22. National Park Service Visitor Center
10. Woodstock Festival Site	23. Minisink Battleground Memorial Park
11. Monticello Raceway	24. Roebling Bridge
12. Kutsher's Country Club	25. Zane Grey Museum (PA)

Best Places to Stay

The price scale for lodging can be found on page 20.

Hotels & Resorts

The merry, but unlook'd for guest
Full often proves to be the best.
– William Combe, English adventurer
and writer (1741-1823)

ELDRED PRESERVE
Route 55, 8 miles south of Route 17B
Eldred
☎ 800-557-FISH
www.eldredpreserve.com
Inexpensive

An ideal option for the occasional fisherman or family, Eldred's 3,000 rustic acres are dotted with ponds, lakes and streams, a small swimming pool, and a 26-room motel with nicely furnished and spacious quarters with TV and telephone. There are two first-class eateries on the premises: a coffee shop and a restaurant.

In this sylvan setting, small trout (mostly one or two pounds) are stocked in two catch-and-keep ponds as well as two catch-and-release ponds with larger trout and catfish. This isn't to say the fish are easy to snare, but with a little patience most people come away with a bucketful. (A stream restoration project is currently underway to extend the fishing streams a half-mile to attract fly-fishermen as well.)

A middle-aged couple from Brooklyn staying over for a few days told me they first came to the Preserve when their children were small, and now consider it a respite from the hectic pace of the city.

To some folks, paying $3.90 per pound of fish, plus $2.50 admission (for walk-ins), is expensive. However, the Preserve cleans the fish and packs it on ice for you. The Brooklyn woman deems this fantastic, since she's "not into that stuff." Her husband likes that he can sit comfortably on land while fishing instead of "freezing" in some stream. Another man there with his large family provided this reasoning: "The kids love to fish." And as the brochure boasts, "Many a child has taken his first fish at Eldred!" Open all year except Monday and Tuesday in the off-season. Several packages are available, with motel rates starting at $65 per person mid-week.

A license, which Eldred Preserve can furnish, is required for bass fishing.

Bass fishermen and hunters are not forgotten at Eldred, which has two private lakes, bass boats for rent and five stand-sporting clays for target practice.

An angler tries his luck at Eldred Preserve.

BEAVERKILL VALLEY INN
Ten miles from Exit 96
Lew Beach
☎ 914-439-4844
Deluxe

Wealthy fishermen no doubt choose to stay at the Beaverkill Valley Inn, one of the prettiest and most expensive accommodations in the Catskills. About 10 miles from Exit 96, the 19th-century country inn straddles the border between Sullivan and Ulster counties on the Beaverkill River. It's understated and elegant, befitting a Rockefeller. In fact, it was Larry Rockefeller (Nelson's nephew), who purchased the property in 1981. He's still part owner and has worked hard to keep developers out of the area. A *Gourmet* magazine article (Apr. 97) stated that he's been selling off his thousands of acres with conservation easements attached – provisions that forever prohibit residential or commercial development. "In the eighties, old farms in the valley were being bought up and subdivided without regard for the land or for the feel of the area," Rockefeller said. "I wanted to preserve the valley's beauty, its uniquely 19th-century mood. And fortunately, I had the means to do it."

Guests have easy and private access to one mile of the Beaverkill River that runs along the magnificent grounds. Other activities include hiking, biking, tennis, or simply relaxing on the swings and rockers on the wraparound porch. For indoor activities, the swimming pool, billiard room and ice cream parlor are all under one roof. As described by one guidebook writer, the resort is "an informally elegant, privileged retreat for anglers and moguls alike who want to relax and fish in the wilderness."

Sullivan County

Tipping is discouraged at Beaverkill Valley Inn.

The Carter Influence

Other notables who have helped maintain
the region's integrity are Jimmy and Rosa-
lynn Carter. The former president and his
wife stayed at the inn and helped generate
funds to build a modern museum at the
Catskill Fly Fishing Center. Ed Van Put reports in his 1996 book, *The Beaverkill*, that
the Carters wasted no time in plying their
skills as fly-fishermen. Even Mrs. Carter, he
writes, "more than held her own on the Beaverkill and took a wily rainbow or two from
the Delaware River, under high water conditions veteran anglers would have found difficult."

Although I didn't stay overnight at the Beaverkill, I
did have dinner there. I arrived early and the staff
couldn't have been nicer. The receptionist suggested
I eat in the dining room because a family with lots of
noisy children was dining al fresco. So I happily had
my four-course dinner among the sedate oak tables
and floral Victorian wallpaper. The meal was fine,
and the chocolate cake with a layer of jam, which the
waitress couldn't name, was delicious. Saturday
night dinner was $33, with a choice of two entrées.
Other nights, a fixed menu was $28, $19 for lunch
and $12 for breakfast.

★ FAMOUS FACES

Irving Berlin was a resident of Lew
Beach during the last 60 years of his
life.

Learn to Fish Like (& From) a Pro

If you wish to improve your fishing and casting skills, explore programs at the **Wulff School of Fly Fishing**, a mile from the inn. Award-winning champion fly caster and author Joan Wulff, widow of the legendary fly-fisherman Lee Wulff, runs the school. In May and June, her students comprise half the guests at the Beaverkill Inn. ☎ 914-439-5020; www.royalwulff.com.

★ WHAT'S IN A NAME?

The fabled Beaverkill River derived its name from the numerous beaver colonies settlers found along its headwaters. It was at Junction Pool just west of Roscoe – where the Willowemoc and Beaverkill meet – that American fly-fishing was first developed.

VILLA ROMA

Callicoon
☎ 914-887-4880; 800-727-8455
Moderate

At Villa Roma, you'll find a lively, all-inclusive family (and time-sharing) resort (although some weekends are geared to adults). Nestled in a valley, it boasts a fitness club, game room, indoor and outdoor pools, racquetball courts, ski slopes, nightly entertainment, disco, bocce, and children's and teen activities. The 1,200 rooms are modern and functional, some recently refurbished and some with a Jacuzzi. Special theme weekends include Italian, Irish and country western.

Villa Roma is a perfect place for you and the kids to stay.

The meal service is seamless. Some dishes, such as ziti in vodka sauce, are excellent. For a memorable breakfast, try the oatmeal with raisins, apples, cinnamon and nuts.

Only golfers are allowed on the mountainous 18-hole course, which boasts the prettiest views of all. Happily, the **Club Restaurant** at Villa Roma overlooks the golf course and is open to the public by reservation. ☎ 914-887-5080.

Directional Info: When you see the Villa Roma sign in Callicoon and drive up the hill, you're not lost. The resort is 2.8 miles from the main road.

WESTERN HOTEL
40 Hill Street
Callicoon
☎ 914-887-9871
Open all year
Inexpensive

Callicoon is one of those places that wears its history on its sleeve – prominently displayed on the tops of old buildings in the business district is the year they were built – 1852, 1888, 1908, 1913. Railroad tracks run through the middle of Callicoon, and the huge station is shuttered – a harsh *Danger!* sentry warns the public to stay away. The town was once a main passenger terminal. These days, only freight trains rumble by.

If you are a heavy sleeper, you can't beat the $67.58 rate at the Western Hotel.

I never saw a train the day I visited, so when one came whistling by my window at 5am and another at 5:50am, I was twice startled from sleep in the venerable Western Hotel. The good news is that the Western has been nicely restored, in sharp contrast to the wreck of the Olympia Hotel across Hill Street. Western's owners, Joseph and Leona Naughton, bought the 1825-building in 1969 and have filled the taproom, lobby and dining room with antiques. The six guestrooms are rather plain in comparison, but spacious, with TV, air conditioning, and a shampoo dispenser.

NARROWSBURG INN
176 Bridge Street
Narrowsburg
☎ 914-252-3998
Inexpensive to Moderate

Eight rooms with shared baths and one suite with a private bath. Their restaurant is open Wednesday through Sunday.

Like the Western Hotel, the Narrowsburg Inn overlooks railroad tracks. When I related my midnight-jolt story to owner Tom Prendergast, his response was, "Some people find that to be the charm of it."

The Narrowsburg Inn is the oldest establishment of its kind in the county, built in 1840 to host raftsmen, railroad workers and soldiers. Sometime between 1860 and 1880, when the railroad track was put down, the 12,000-square-foot building was raised six feet higher so the front door wouldn't be six feet under water. Although it's been refurbished, the inn retains the charm of another era.

Local Lore

The Narrowsburg Inn is suspected of harboring ghosts. Tom's son, Tom Jr., believes the third floor once served as a brothel. He says that when people stay in the second floor suite they report hearing sounds from above like someone bouncing a basketball. "We decided that's the sound of headboards hitting the wall."

THE RALEIGH
South Fallsburg
☎ 914-434-7000; 800-446-4003
Moderate

The Raleigh is surprisingly well maintained throughout. The 320 guestrooms and hallways have new carpeting and unscarred walls. The Grecian-style indoor swimming pool complex works well with the high ceilings and floor-to-ceiling windows and the dark wood and shiny floor in the walkway over the pool are quite attractive. During the winter senior citizens are the most frequent guests, but in the summer and on school holidays families are common.

Directional Info: Exit 107 and bear right; continue for three miles.

⊚ TIP

When calling for a reservation ask if it's a special weekend and, if so, inquire about the size of the crowd. Large organizations are not uncommon at these mega-resorts and can occupy most of the rooms. These groups often plan their own activities and you may feel left out.

KUTSHER'S COUNTRY CLUB
Kutsher's Road
Monticello
☎ 800-431-1273; 914-794-6000
Moderate

Kutsher's hotel has been in the Kutsher family since 1907.

Kutsher's bustles with people of all ages. Some of them are grandparents with their grandchildren, as suggested by the children's clothing store in the hotel called Granny's Heaven. The lobby's backdrop is the swimming pool and beyond is a sandy beach and lake. While the lobby looks fine (they all do), the chipped paint and soiled carpets in the hallways tell the real story. While the rooms aren't exactly up to par, word is that the food is great.

BEST WESTERN PARAMOUNT
At Exit 98, turn right onto 85N
Parksville
☎ 914-292-6700; 800-922-3498
Three meals daily; nightly entertainment
Open year-round
Inexpensive

Those with kids might want to check out this family-run and kosher 180-room hotel. A full-service hotel, it caters to groups and organizations at discount rates but individuals are welcome and it's child-friendly. (The clientele is largely retirees of mixed ethnicities.) All buildings are connected and wheel-chair accessible. The lake offers fishing and boating and a golf course and riding stable are nearby.

SWAN LAKE RESORT HOTEL
450 Brisco Road
Swan Lake
☎ 914-292-8000; 888-254-4194
www.swanlakeresort.com
Moderate

Interested in riding? Saddle up to Arrowhead Stables located just north of Best Western Paramount hotel.

If you've ever stayed at the Stevensville Hotel, you won't recognize its reincarnation. Dr. and Mrs. Victor Gallo, a Long Island couple, and Hyung Chin Park, the hotel vice president and pro at its golf course, have transformed this hotel into what general manager Steve Weiss calls "a cruise ship on land." (Weiss was activities director at the Pines Hotel for 12 years and has cruise ship experience.) From the looks of it, Mr. Park may well fulfill his dream of owning the most beautiful, glamorous and luxurious hotel in Sullivan County.

Sullivan County

Opened in the spring of 1999, the $3 million property has 355 renovated guestrooms (24 suites), an American Plan cuisine and a Japanese/Korean restaurant, a night club, conference rooms, tennis courts, and an 18-hole, par 72 championship golf course complete with golf school and pro shop. If that's not enough, there's also indoor and outdoor swimming pools, a fitness center and health club, a state-of-the-art game room, and an outdoor ice skating in winter. And, of course, the beautiful Swan Lake is great for boating and fishing.

The elegant lobby is graced with Italian and Oriental furnishings and sculptures. The hotel plans to cater to American, Korean and Japanese families, groups and corporate clients. Since the 400-acre property doesn't have a ski slope (it does have snow tubing and ice-skating), ski groups are shuttled to Holiday Mountain.

Catskills Legend

When the Syndicate held sway over the Catskills in the 1920s many a victim was executed and tossed into the deep lakes in Sullivan County. In fact, entertainer Joey Adams had a pinochle partner – known as a sweet, soft-spoken man – who was actually a killer. The man's body was later found at the bottom of Swan Lake with a slot machine tied around his neck.

Inns/B&Bs

All happiness depends on a leisurely breakfast.
— John Gunther, author (1901-1970)

GRIFFIN HOUSE

Exit 104 to Route 17B West
Jeffersonville
☎ 914-482-3371
www.griffin-house.com
Moderate

For the romantic among you who love music, this B&B in the well-preserved hamlet of Jeffersonville is the ticket. The American chestnut interior is cheerfully decorated in holiday décor, flowers, dolls and frilly fabrics, and the four themed guestrooms have compellingly plump beds. All this adds up to a cozy weekend.

Innkeeper Irene met "me husband" Paul Griffin while both were members of Fred Waring's Pennsylvanians and they've been filling the century-old mansion with musical reminders since purchasing it in 1990. She's a singer and native of northern England and he's from Manhasset, Long Island. Paul was a lead trumpet player until an accident on stage rendered him unable to continue playing. Fortunately, he also composes music and has a flair for science and technology.

Irene serves a full breakfast and opens the house to outsiders for dinner (six courses with wine is $45 and seating capacity is 35). She often sings for the diners and brings in guest performers. "We hope that every weekend different artists will do their own show," she says.

Sullivan County

An engaging couple, the Griffins claim that so many guests have become friends that they hate to charge them! The Griffins are expanding their empire to Griff-Inns, a consortium of bed and breakfasts in the area. Members will have to meet their high standards. As part of this, the Worthington (the former Lake Jefferson Hotel) is in the middle of a $2 million renovation, staged by its new owners, the Griffins.

Directional Info: Exit 104 to Route 17B. West until Fosterdale (14 miles from Hwy 17); right at blinking light to Route 52N until Stone Arch Bridge Park in Kenoza Lake. Turn right and continue four miles; make left at the First National Bank (Maple Avenue). It's the sixth house on the left.

THE MAGICAL LAND OF OZ
Shandelee Road
Livingston Manor
☎ 914-439-3418
www.bestinns.net/usa/ny/oz.html
Inexpensive

Seven guestrooms, shared baths, hot tub, exercise machines, badminton court, hammocks, TV room, petting farm. Country breakfasts served family-style. Theme weekends. Open all year.

Look out back and you can indeed tell you are at The Magical Land of Oz – there's the yellow brick road!

Whether you're off to see the wizard or fleeing a wicked witch, staying at Oz is like coming home to Kansas. If you're a recluse or misanthrope, forget it. Rumi, a German shepherd/corgi mix will run to your car gleefully barking at your arrival. You'll barely have space for your bags in any of the seven small rooms, furnished with little more than a bed, hooks and hangers. The rooms and two big bathrooms are on either side of a narrow hallway, promoting socialization. It's not unlike a college dorm, except the occupants range from infants to thirty-something singles and long-married couples. Though small, the rooms are clean, carpeted and frilly, each devoted to a character from the beloved film.

This three-story century-old farmhouse was last named Auntie Em's, and when the three partners bought it two years ago, they decided to continue the theme. Posters, pottery and wall hangings of Dorothy, the cowardly lion, and other Oz characters are scattered about.

Weldon Calloway, Terry Shirreffs and Jeff Skaar divide their time between running this B&B and Dawn Manor, a retreat catering largely to the gay community. Terry and Jeff were our hosts and could not have been more hospitable. They clearly love to cook and each breakfast is a new concoction, either of their own making or culled from a Web site shared by B&B owners. Breakfasts begin with a fresh fruit cup. One morning it was followed by spiced apple pancakes. Sunday's *pièce de résistance* was a rich pastiche of eggs, cheese and vegetables. "We don't want to do cold cereal kind of stuff," explains Jeff, "unless somebody begs for it."

Borrow a book from the library nook, relax in the sunroom, chat with your hosts, or stroll the flower-filled 10-acres. Blueberry bushes are there for the picking and two hammocks hang languorously between two sturdy trees. A rooster crows from somewhere over the rainbow and a bird chirps uninterrupted from a stand of tall balsam fir planted long ago as either a Christmas tree farm or enchanted forest.

Magical Land of Oz welcomes children of all ages & accepts well-mannered small dogs (call in advance).

Directional Info: Exit 96. Turn right at ramp and left at stop sign. Make first right onto Main Street and continue about 3½ miles to the top of mountain. Look for the Oz sign on your left.

Sullivan County

More lodging is listed on the Web site of the B&B Association of Sullivan County at www.bba-sc.org or ☎ 800-882-CATS.

A Refreshing Idea

Shandelee Lake is a short walk away and Oz has two rafts for the asking. The water is nice for swimming and it's quite shallow until you get way out, so it's perfect for kids. The old Waldemere Hotel looms large across the lake.

INN AT LAKE JOSEPH
400 St. Joseph Road
Forestburgh
☎ 914-791-9506
10 guestrooms, some with whirlpool baths
Moderate to Expensive

If driving around doesn't excite you, you can more or less stay put at this secluded Victorian mansion and former retreat of Cardinals Hayes and Spellman. Nestled in the woods, it's about eight miles south of Monticello and a few miles from the Delaware River. An outdoor pool is on the premises and the 250-acre lake is a four-minute walk through the woods – or a longer walk on the road.

The nearby lake is private and clean, despite the dark color from tannic acid (harmless). No motor boats are allowed and the inn has a limited supply of rubber rafts. Ivan is a laissez-faire host, and guests are free to raid the refrigerator at any time. It's a very relaxing and social place for couples or families. Dinners have been discontinued, but the inn will recommend local restaurants.

Famous Faces

Stephen Crane's family built a crude summer camp on the Mongaup River in Forestburgh when he was six years old. His writings about the wildlife and the people who claimed their woodlands have become an important part of county history. In fact, Crane's series of sketches about Sullivan County printed in the *New York Tribune* in 1892 were among his first published works. Many of them are included in a book entitled *Stephan Crane: Sullivan County Tales and Sketches* (Purple Mountain Press, 1968).

A reconstructed cabin with an inscription on a rock notes that while living in scenic Hartwood, Town of Forestburgh, Crane wrote three books, including his most famous *Red Badge of Courage* (1896), a Civil War novel. Crane died in 1900 of tuberculosis at age 29. You can find the Crane cabin off Route 42, on King Road, near a swimming pool.

Spas

NEW AGE HEALTH SPA
Route 55
Neversink
☎ 914-985-7600; ☎ 800-NU-AGE-4-U (for reservations and personal services scheduling)
Moderate to Expensive

New Age has consistently been rated best value in North America by Zagat's consumer surveys.

Spa includes pool, hot tub, solarium, sauna and steam, exercise room and yoga studio. Spa services include massage, hydrotherapy, body treatments and facials. Accommodates 70 guests. Cigarettes and alcohol are prohibited.

The only stress is trying to fit everything in. A full schedule begins at 6:30am with meditation, followed by a brisk walk in the woods and an endless array of activities: step classes, water aerobics, tai chi, tai boxing, stretch classes, and lectures. The day ends way beyond most people's endurance – with a 9pm movie.

At New Age there are plenty of easier classes – like gentle yoga – to satisfy even the most unfit guest.

You don't have to participate in anything, of course, but you'll miss the essence of the place: to help you feel good about yourself. You'll also miss the inherent intimacy that develops when people are sweating and chanting side by side. The staff is excellent and the atmosphere pressure-free and non-competitive.

We arrived late on Friday night and found peanut butter and jelly sandwiches in our room. (Boxed meals are provided for late arrivals and early departures.) Though small and modest, our room had a walk-in closet, alarm clock, and coco-mango bath gel in the soap dispenser that smelled good enough to eat. Robes are provided for your stay, and you'll spend much of your time in them. Leave your fancy clothes, candy and caffeine behind. Forget the TV and telephone.

Direct mini-van service to New Age leaves from Madison & 72nd Street in Manhattan on Fridays, Sundays and holidays.

The Ultimate Spa Book, published a decade ago, rated the food at New Age as very bland and referred to an absence of lockers in the changing rooms. Neither statement holds true today. The vegetarian meals are tasty, fresh, and nutritious (only de-caf coffee is available) and lockers are abundant. Counting calories is not paramount, although nutritionists are available to guide you if desired. Optional dishes listed on the flip side of the menu (with calorie count) can be ordered separately or with the main entrée. Saturday night we had an herb-encrusted salmon that was superb.

New Age is a cluster of bungalows on 155 acres bordering Catskill Park that includes five guest buildings, spa, outdoor pool, greenhouse (where many of the delicious salad greens are grown), tennis courts, and new yoga studio. Opened subsequent to our stay, the large, open space can accommodate more levels of classes and intensives. Along the groomed trail is a freestanding, 50-foot alpine tower that really tests your mettle.

Like the spa itself, the attractive gift shop sells what you would expect at a place called New Age – meditation candles, aromatherapy products, New Age books – and you don't have to stay at the spa to shop there.

Times have changed from the days of the "fat farm." However, once you sign up for spa services, which are well worth the price, it can get costly. Also added to the bill are a 17% service charge, spa service charge, and an 8% sales tax. The good news is that, unlike other spas, the staff doesn't push guests into trying expensive services they're not interested in.

Motels & Lodges

HENDRIX MOTEL & REYNOLDS INN
Exit 94; turn right
Roscoe
☎ 607-498-4422
Inexpensive

All rooms have private bath, TV, air conditioning, and a telephone on request. The Short Line bus stops 200 yards away.

Sullivan County

For an interesting glimpse at genealogy, check out Hendrix's long line of family portraits catalogued in the main hall.

Surely the best bet for reasonable accommodations. I saw the motel sign and was surprised to be given a choice of the motel or one of the eight guest rooms in the Victorian inn at the same low price: $43.60. Rates are the same regardless of day or season and haven't changed in the last seven years, according to the proprietor, Royal Felix Hendrix III. The inn has been in his family since "Uncle Billy" Reynolds built it in 1902. John D. Rockefeller was a regular guest in the 1920s, when B&Bs were called tourist homes. Hendrix, Reynolds' great-great-great nephew, says it's the only extant Sullivan County inn that started life as an inn.

My room in the inn was small, comfortable and charming, but the anglers next door started stirring before 5am. Hendrix later explained that he usually puts fishermen in the motel.

◎ TIP

For more area history, walk across the street to the church cemetery, which contains the grave of Rachel Williams, the first white woman settler in the vicinity in 1789. She was a descendant of Roger Williams, founder of the colony of Rhode Island and prominent proponent of religious freedom.

The inn provides muffins and coffee for guests in its antique-laden parlor. (Don't be fooled by the silvery sounds of jazz coming from the 1920 radio – it has 25-year-old tubes.)

For another eating option, the **"Famous" Roscoe Diner** is just down the road. Given that it's modern with modern prices, I asked the young hostess why it's famous. She thought it was because it was built in the 1960s, which is probably historic to her. I concluded that it owes its fame to its prime location, at both the entrance and exit off Route 17.

HICKORYHAVEN LODGE
Route 55
Barryville
☎ 888-557-8077
Inexpensive

A cross between a motel (low rates, breakfast not included) and an inn (nice touches in the room like hard candies and toiletries), this is the perfect place to bed down. Tall pines and hickory trees shade the 16-room red and white bungalows, located slightly past the intersection of Highway 97 and Route 55. The three owners bought the 40-year-old property three years ago and have installed an outdoor pool, among other improvements. My room ($60) had a TV, air conditioning, and was geared for a single or for couples who don't mind sharing a double bed. Doubles are $75 and can accommodate four. Open May-November.

Food is just down the driveway at the **Barryville Coffee Shop**. A popular spot with locals, it opens at 6:30 am with hearty breakfasts to start your day. It also has an ice cream concession for later on.

Directional Info: To get to the lodge from Route 17, at Exit 123 take Route 6 the five miles to 84W. Get off at Exit 1 (or you'll land in Pennsylvania) and go through Port Jervis to Route 97N (which parallels the river). It's curvy at first but extremely scenic. At the intersection of Routes 97 and 55 (52.9 miles), make a right at the flashing light in Barryville; you'll see the archway to the lodge on the left.

Sullivan County

FOSTERDALE MOTOR LODGE
Intersection of Routes 17B/52 at the blinking light
Fosterdale
☎ 914-932-8538
www.fmlodge.com
Inexpensive

Summer week-ends at Foster-dale fill early; advance plan-ning is ad-vised.

Both motel rooms and efficiency units have a TV and telephone, and the efficiencies have fully equipped kitchenettes with microwave. Video game room, 24-hour laundry room, picnic tables and gas barbeque grills. A hot breakfast is included during hunting season.

The 18 units are clean and comfortable and are a good value for singles and families. Summer evenings can be spent right on the property.

In late August 1999, Fosterdale sponsored Sullivan County's First Annual Stickball Contest, in addition to the annual Yo-Yo Competition, Foul-Shooting, and Kite Flying Contest. It also celebrated its 11th anniversary with a giant pig roast with vendors and entertainment.

TRAVEL INN
Broadway
Monticello
☎ 914-794-8660

Large, clean rooms with TV, telephone and air conditioning.

LANDER'S TEN MILE RIVER
MOTEL & RESTAURANT
Route 97
Narrowsburg
☎ 800-252-3925

Large rooms with TV, air conditioning and a fabulous shower. In addition to motel units and two efficiencies, Lander's has two dorms that sleep nine, and three cabins that sleep 10. (The Getaway Packages for four or more adults are quite reasonable.) The restaurant is open for three meals but dinner times are erratic, so call first.

Retreats

MY RETREAT
Lincoln Road
South Fallsburg
☎ 914-436-7455
Inexpensive

If you crave solitude in a rustic setting, My Retreat is for you. Four cottages tucked away in the woods are the perfect antidote to civilization. Mine had four bedrooms, 1½ baths, a kitchen, sitting room and living room. This cottage is ideal for several singles. Another has two private apartments, each with its own kitchen, bathroom and entrance. They aren't fancy, but comfortable and unpretentious like your own home. Even shampoo and lotions are provided. Books are everywhere for your enjoyment, and there is a stack of used books for sale in the basement.

Last-minute reservations are welcome at My Retreat.

⊙ TIP

The nearby Rivoli Movie House has been taken over by the Sullivan County Drama Group. For the theater schedule, ☎ 914-794-5034.

About half the guests at My Retreat are devotees of the ashram about two miles away. Choosing to stay at My Retreat for its comfort level, they attend intensives and workshops there during the day. Other guests may be involved in a workshop at the retreat, such as writing or nutrition. An outsider arranges the workshops and the kitchen is at their disposal.

Still others who stay at the retreat do not fall into either category. They are simply "tree-starved urbanites," as one NYC guest put it.

Directional Info: From Route 17 take Exit 107 to 42N and drive through the village of South Fallsburg. After passing the old Rivoli Theater, make the first right turn onto Lincoln Road and drive to the end. The cottages are the last driveway on your left.

Seasonal Rentals

Helen Morrell is well known for her fashionable boutique, "Helen Morrell, Contemporary Sportswear to Party Formals." She opened the shop next to her home on Masten Lake many years ago. With Helen now in her 80s, her daughter Patty helps out selling the elegant evening gowns, beaded bags, sportswear and jewelry.

Melissa Lanza, broker/owner of Lanza Realty, occasionally has rental listings in the Wurtsboro/Ellenville area. ☎ 914-888-5221, ext. 103.

The women also maintain six lovely **rental cottages** on the property, all decorated differently by Patty, a professional interior decorator. "It's utopia here," she says. The cottages are in the woods, across the road from the quiet lakefront. All have a screened-in sunroom and heat (no need for air conditioning – it's always cool here). The kitchens are fully equipped and have eight windows and a ceiling fan. Most of the cottages have new oak kitchens. Renters have access to the lake, its floating dock and boat. One- or two-bedroom cottages rent for the whole summer season at $3,500 and up. Most are rented to couples or small families. ☎ 914-888-2468.

Directional Info: From Route 17 take Exit 113 one mile to light in Wurtsboro. Turn left and follow for

3½ miles. At sign, turn right onto Sarine Road and continue .3 mile. You'll see a yellow and green sign, "Welcome to the Home of Fashion."

Best Places to Eat

The Catskills is a casual place, and so are the restaurants. This is no reflection on the quality of food, though. It's surprisingly good, with chefs taking advantage of local farm produce and the abundance of trout and game. What's more, prices are reasonable compared to the surrounding metropolitan areas.

Sullivan County

> ### ⊚ *TIP*
>
> For additional dining information (including menus) in Sullivan County, consult www.scsmag.com/dining. htm and www.heresmymenu.com.

With Sullivan County known for its all-inclusive Borscht Belt hotels, it's surprising there are so many excellent restaurants here. I especially give credit to those that survived through the height of the hotel era when restaurants were surely superfluous. Those still operating are usually family affairs, run by second and third generations. Italian, American and seafood restaurants are commonplace; Asian restaurants are practically nonexistent. Perhaps that's why **Bernie's** (see page 74) specializes in Oriental cuisine.

The biggest problem in Sullivan County is the distance from one restaurant to another and their irregular and seasonal hours. Planning ahead is vital.

I learned that lesson the hard way, searching for an open restaurant on a Tuesday night in the off-season. I finally found the **Rockland House** (see page 77) and was so grateful.

Casual Dining

The price scale for restaurants can be found on page 21.

ELDRED PRESERVE
Route 55
Eldred
☎ 800-557-FISH; 914-557-8316
Moderate

As you'd expect, the restaurant at Eldred Preserve specializes in trout, prepared in nine different ways ($15.25 to $16.95).

An old proverb states that if you give a man a fish, his hunger will be satisfied for a day. But if you teach him how to fish, his hunger will be satisfied for a lifetime. Well, not a lifetime exactly, and even fisherfolk like to be served occasionally. It's fortunate that this fine restaurant is right beside the ponds. The trout almondine is superb and the portions generous. I was there on a Tuesday night in late August and while the motel was not filled, the restaurant was crowded. Still, service was impeccable and I didn't have to ask for the basket of warm rolls. (On a subsequent Saturday night in mid-winter the restaurant was even busier and I had to ask, but the service was just as pleasant.)

GIOVANNI'S INN
Route 209
Wurtsboro
☎ 914-888-2099
Moderate

Giovanni's Inn is festooned with heads of elk, boar, bear, antelope and pheasant. Should that bother you, rest assured the family kills for food, not sport. As Anthony Mennella, whose dad's first name is Giovanni, told me, "Everything in here has been digested in the form of loins, steaks and chops." In addition, live lobsters are always available. Open daily June-October.

Directional Info: From Route 17 heading west take Exit 113 to Route 209, south of Wurtsboro business district.

COAL & STEAM
Wurtsboro Plaza
Wurtsboro
☎ 914-888-5080
Open all year for lunch and dinner; closed Monday
Moderate

Inside the Wurtsboro business district is this new kid on the block, which opened July 1999 in Wurtsboro Plaza, opposite Custer's Last Stand. The tables are all in one large, painted pink room. The owner's wife, JoAnn Bitjeman, is a gracious hostess and waitress. The menu is new American cuisine, and dishes – steaks, seafood, poultry – are made to order. Portions are generous. Children's menu items range from $5 to $9.

Across the street from Coal & Steam is **Danny's.** I never got to eat there, but one man recommended the mussels and another swore it has the best burgers in town.

Sullivan County

BERNIE'S HOLIDAY RESTAURANT
Route 17, Exit 109
Rock Hill
☎ 914-796-3333
Moderate

Jay Weinstein, the friendly chef/owner, took over for his dad, Bernie, who opened the restaurant about 34 years ago. The fine Continental cuisine and smooth service reflect their experience. The large portions begin with delicious raisin rolls. The menu emphasizes fresh seafood, duck, chops, and Oriental specialties. Bernie's is open daily for dinner, except Monday, year-round.

Directional Info: Turn right at Exit 109 (off Route 17) and continue for ⅛ mile.

OLD HOMESTEAD RESTAURANT
Bridgeville Road
Monticello
☎ 914-794-8973
Open daily, April-November
Moderate

Since I started my research, no restaurant has been touted to me more than the Old Homestead. After dining there, I can understand why. In an earlier incarnation, the restaurant was a hotel, and we felt like choice guests. The moment my husband and I entered, we were welcomed warmly by the co-owner, Mark Edelman, and his staff. A waitress escorted us to a table on the glass-enclosed terrace, where soft music played and images of harness horses surrounded us. I thought it was because Monticello Raceway is close by, but it turns out that Edelman's late mother, who worked in the restaurant from 1959 to 1977, owned trotters. Mark and his brother have operated the business since 1962, begun by their late father a decade before.

© TIP

Meat portions at Old Homestead are enormous, so consider sharing.

The specialties are steak and seafood. Try the pork chops smothered in red onion marmalade sauce and you'll be a patron for life. Of course, this will happen soon after you taste the homemade raisin bread and poppy seed rolls. Like many people, we saved the raisin bread for dessert. Take a look at the menu on the wall when you walk in because you won't see it again. Your waiter will recite it.

Directional Info: From Route 17 heading west take Exit 107. Make left at the stop sign. Follow Bridgeville Road for two miles.

MR. WILLY'S
3595 Route 42S (on way to Forestburgh)
Monticello
☎ 914-794-0888
Open year-round
Moderate

This casual restaurant and cocktail lounge are in separate rooms so diners can enjoy a quiet meal. The bar, a favorite of local politicos, has live entertainment on selected nights. The restaurant serves good American cuisine and has nice touches (a lollipop with the bill, for instance). In keeping with its slogan of "Mr. Willy's specializes in hospitality," Bill "Willy" Sipos makes it a point to greet every table. I wasn't sitting five minutes when he came over to say hello (before he knew I was writing this book). Each evening offers a different theme, such as bistro night, seafood night, or steak/chops night.

Mr. Willy's was voted #1 caterer in 1998 by the local paper.

ALBERT'S LIBERTY HOUSE
11 Old Route 17
Liberty
☎ 914-292-4510
Open for lunch and dinner, Tuesday-Sunday
Moderate

While in Liberty have lunch at this family-style eatery, bar and unofficial museum of Liberty history. Pork is its specialty but I enjoyed a generous chicken fillet sandwich, twister fries, lettuce and tomato, coffee and dessert ($4.50).

The walls are jammed with artifacts. I learned, for example, that there was another Liberty House, a resort built in 1895 that burned down in 1926. Apparently it was known as the grand dame of Liberty hotels – "a pinnacle of luxury with its steam heat and 'speaking tubes.'" Although the restaurant owner, Albert Bitjeman, was born and raised in Liberty, he says it was pure coincidence that his establishment has the same name.

Directional Info: From Route 17 heading west turn left at Exit 100, and left at light near Sports World.

DEAD END CAFE
12 Main Street
Parksville
☎ 914-292-0202
Open year-round, except January. Summer hours: Open at 4pm Monday, Wednesday-Saturday; open 2pm on Sunday; closed Tuesday.
Moderate

For a good Italian dinner and a fun time, try this lively and cozy restaurant. When we arrived one Friday night in August, pianist Angelo Babaria (who appeared in *Godfather I* and is at Villa Roma every June) was playing *When Irish Eyes are Smiling,* followed by Jewish and Italian songs. Everyone clapped and sang along. Shortly after, Tom Calta-bellotta, the owner and a bass baritone, launched into an operatic aria, as he does every night. Reservations suggested.

Directional Info: From Route 17 take left at Exit 98; continue one block to stop sign; turn right and go to end of street.

ROCKLAND HOUSE
Rockland Road
Roscoe
☎ 607-498-4240
Moderate

This converted rec room lacks intimacy but it has a varied menu of chops, steaks and seafood. Its specialties include Beaverkill brook trout, and the duck à l'orange is crisp-tender. Some months after eating here I overhead a patron at another restaurant across the county raving to his friends about Rockland House. "The place is really nice," he told them. "I had a prime rib. It was spectacular. I could have made a meal of the beef and barley soup."

Directional Info: From Route 17 heading west, travel 1.8 miles west of Exit 94 on Route 206.

SILVIO'S
Route 52
Jeffersonville
☎ 914-482-5100
Open year-round for dinner
Moderate

Unfortunately, this restaurant (owned by the superb 1906 Restaurant in Callicoon) falls short of expectations. A child-friendly eatery with paper tablecloths and crayons and candles on the tables, Silvio's has a varied wine selection and a separate bar. The food is fresh but service was slow on a Thursday night despite near-empty tables. The corn soup was thin and some of the string beans over-sautéed. I ordered linguine Sinatra with shrimp and scallops for $17.95 and got clams instead of scallops. Another in our party ordered penne à la vodka and was served marinara sauce instead. The substitutions were okay and our dishes tasty, but an explanation from either the chef or waitress would have been nice.

GAETANO'S CAFE
Route 17B
Mongaup Valley
☎ 914-796-4901
Dinner served Wednesday-Sunday
Moderate

My Sunday night dinner at Gaetano's did not begin favorably. It was a frigid February night and I was happy to be inside this lovely-looking restaurant that affords views of the Mongaup River. However, the manager, Rifo Murtovic, glanced right past me. He apologized after I stood in front of him, then whisked me to a table where I waited an inordinately long time for attention. The attractive room was crowded and noisy with diners having a good time. I finally caught the manager's attention, at which point he apologized again and became my devoted waiter. Thereafter, service was speedy (especially on the part of the busboys). My ravioli in meat sauce (lamb) was light and delicious. Along with Italian-American dishes, the menu features steaks, chops and seafood and portions are ample but not excessive.

Toward the end of the meal, a couple started smoking and I learned I was in the smoking room. Had I been asked I would have chosen the non-smoking room, which was empty. I asked Rifo why all the non-smokers chose this room and he said that people like to be near the bar and be seen by others.

Directional Info: Located four miles west of Monti-cello Raceway. Take Exit 104 off Route 17.

THE 1906 RESTAURANT
Main Street
Callicoon
☎ 914-887-1906
Moderate

Treat yourself to some of the best food in the county. Chef/owner Bob DeCristofaro and his wife, Rosie, purchased and restored this historic building on Main Street and opened the restaurant in 1988. It has since been honored for its food as well as the modern wood and brick décor.

The menu changes according to the season. Summer meat choices included ostrich steak with portobello mushrooms, buffalo steak, and venison Gruyère. Os-trich, which tastes similar to filet mignon, is low in calories, fat and cholesterol. Not an adventurous eater, I scanned the numerous fish, chicken and pasta offerings and chose blackened tuna – the best I've ever had. As for soup, I enjoyed the intensely-flavored German potato soup, followed by a mixed salad in a homemade dressing. The entrée was served with fresh steamed vegetables and a baked potato.

HOUSE OF LYONS
Jefferson Street
Monticello
☎ 914-794-0244
Open all year; closed Monday
Moderate

Make sure you call Lyons be-forehand – it's a popular spot for weddings and such.

The first thing you notice is the attractive glass-enclosed terrace, aptly called the Greenhouse Room. With its easy listening music, wood paneling, fire-

Sullivan County

place, and candles on each table, this intimate restaurant is a lovely spot for lunch or dinner.

Service is first-rate, the food is fine and fulfilling. Meals begin with a loaf of homemade white bread that melts in your mouth. The small menu is heavy on steaks and seafood, although listed favorites include chicken Kiev and fresh roasted duckling.

Directional Info: Take Exit 104 off Route 17.

INN BY THE FALLS
Exit 101, Swan Lake Road
Ferndale
☎ 914-292-2520
Open for dinner; closed Wednesday
Moderate

A new greenhouse window allows diners to look out at the Falls of the Middle Mongaup River. During our dinner, several people got up to enjoy the view from the window, but do step outside where the view is even better.

Sitting in our captain's chairs with a lantern on the table, a diamond-shaped porthole above my head, original wood walls around me, and a low ceiling, I felt I was on a ship. But the history of this restaurant has nothing to do with far away places. It was a blacksmith shop and tannery when Mae Townsend's grandfather converted it to a restaurant in 1944. (She's also the chef.) The original part of the house was built between 1850 and 1860, and if you're interested in construction, Mae's amiable husband, Nelson, will gladly take you down to the cellar for a look-see.

The food is a mixed bag. It would seem that the restaurant is on far firmer ground with seafood dishes. I'd suggest sticking with their specialty: trout almondine. Served with curly waffle fries, the fish is divine. Nelson ships it from out west, shunning local trout. In contrast, the veal Marsala is nothing to write home about.

The restaurant's twilight menu, its own version of the Early Bird Special, offers complete dinners from $8.95 to $13.95, from 5-6:30pm, and on Sunday from 5-5:30pm.

★ WHAT'S IN A NAME?

When Ferndale was called Liberty Falls, it was a thriving village with a hotel, schools, stores, groceries, post office, and the O&W depot. Three sawmills, a gristmill, a shoe factory, and two tanneries derived their power from the rapidly running water passing over the falls. In 1897, the O&W Railroad deemed the name Liberty Falls not sufficiently elegant for the growing resort industry and changed it to Ferndale.

FRANKIE & JOHNNY'S
Main Street
Hurleyville
☎ 914-434-8051
Open daily, year-round
Moderate

This family restaurant and bar is no better or worse than your local Italian restaurant. However, a man so much as warned me that if I failed to include this restaurant in my book, it wouldn't be worth a nickel. So I went. Did it warrant his rave review? No. Was it pleasant with pleasing cuisine? Yes. Did I leave hungry or dissatisfied as its ads claim you won't? No. But had this man eaten in as many fine restaurants in Sullivan County as I have, he might not have singled out this one.

My only complaint was with the waitress. I can't speak for the rest of the wait staff, but she was so speedy I was out in record time. I was halfway through my wine when she returned for the second time to ask if I'd decided on dinner. There was one shrimp left on my plate when she asked about dessert. Before I could blink, coffee was on the table. She'd be super in a city coffee shop, but who wants to be rushed during dinner?

LAKE VIEW FARM RESORT
149 Airport Road
Yulan
☎ 914-557-3550
Moderate

At the intersection of Highway 97 and Route 55, head north for a short distance before turning left onto Route 21 to Yulan. Lake View is open to the public for lunch and dinner (and breakfast on summer weekends) and has a smashing view of Washington Lake. Lunch offerings include salads and bountiful sandwiches like the Monte Cristo – French toast grilled with turkey, ham and Swiss – for $6.95.

CROSSROADS LOUNGE & COUNTRY KITCHEN
Four Corners
Yulan
☎ 914-557-6949
Open for dinner all year; closed Wednesday
Lunch served Saturday and Sunday
Moderate

Opposite the post office and at the intersection of Routes 21, 22 and 33, Crossroads is a "no credit card" kind of place to go to hell with yourself – gastronomically speaking. Dimly lit and wood-paneled, it's a seat-yourself restaurant with a children's menu at $2.95 and a pool table by the enclosed bar. The menu offerings range from hot platters and weekend dinner specials to burgers and sandwiches. A yummy open steak sandwich smothered in onions, twice-baked potato, coleslaw and salad cost $11.95.

BRIDGE RESTAURANT
Intersection of Highway 97 and Route 55
Barryville
☎ 914-557-6088
Inexpensive to Moderate

The food is not exceptional, but if you're lucky enough to score an outdoor table, you'll be rewarded with a knockout view of the Roebling Bridge. Select from one of the restaurant's many desserts, sit on the patio and be mesmerized by the swirling river below.

Lite Bites

LA CUCINA
Main Street
Livingston Manor
☎ 914-439-4161
Open year-round
Inexpensive

Hungry for pizza? La Cucina makes wonderful individual pies (four slices). They also serve pasta dishes, sandwiches and ice cream.

PIZZA THE ROCK
Corner of Glen Wild Road and Route 58
Rock Hill
☎ 914-796-3900
Open daily at 11 am, year-round
Inexpensive

Sullivan County

Serves pizza, hot and cold Italian sandwiches and ice cream.

THE POTAGER
180 Sullivan Street
Wurtsboro
☎ 914-888-4086
Open for lunch, daily except Tuesday
April-December
Inexpensive

A charming café for lunch or a homemade dessert. Also open for dinner during season on Friday and Saturday, 5-8:30pm. Has a beautiful garden, plus a quaint gift shop upstairs (see page 135).

PROVISIONS
37 River Road
Callicoon
☎ 914-887-6462
Open Thursday-Sunday, 9:30am-5pm
Mid-June through September or October
Inexpensive

On a stroll through the village, I discovered Patricia Von Beulow tending her flower and herb garden, just past the post office. A sink was parked on the lawn, surrounded by goodies for sale. Provisions had made its debut three weeks before and her outdoor shop was set up with a jar of pickles (from NYC), organic produce, and ice cream. She also sells painted cards and decoupage plates by local artists, explaining that the community has a wealth of talent.

The following morning I availed myself of her coffee and homemade banana bread on a log table facing the garden. The birds chirped, the chimes tinkled and, except for the sink and coffeepots, it felt like the Garden of Eden.

Sunup to Sundown

Sightseeing

*When I die, bury me in the woods, so my
husband will come hunting for me.*
– Sign in a general store

Bethel

Start your tour at the site of the infamous August
1969 **Woodstock Music Festival** on Max Yasgur's
Farm. At the moment, the site is nothing more than
a green field closed to the public. A memorial plaque
outside bears the names of the Grateful Dead, Sly
and the Family Stone, and all the other performers
from the historic concert.

I met two aging hippies at the site, brothers from
California who in 1969 had hitchhiked across the
nation to Woodstock. As we chatted, one videotaped
the field while the other listened to a song called
Woodstock On Your Mind. Nostalgia knows no bounds
even when the reality was not quite perfect. When
asked what they most remembered about the infamous concert, one replied, "I was stoned," and the
other simply said, "I remember the mud."

At this writing, Sullivan County's most recent and
biggest foray into promoting tourism occurred in
Bethel in summer 1998. Construction crews transformed the field into an arena for "A Day in the Garden," a three-day event in August that drew an
estimated 75,000 people. Performers included Richie
Havens and Joni Mitchell. The promoter, Liberty
millionaire Alan Gerry, plans to build a year-round,

world-class performing arts destination center at the original Woodstock site.

In the process of building an indoor and outdoor stage, Gerry's immediate plans are to hold eight shows a year. In July 1999, the first in a series of A Day in the Garden concerts was held with Britney Spears as the headliner, but the show drew an audience of only 6,500. The next show, in mid-July, featured the Beach Boys, Credence Clearwater, and Survivor. For information about the concert series, ☎ 914-295-2448 or check out www.dayinthegarden.com on the Internet.

Bethel has the largest area of flat land in the otherwise hilly county.

Directional Info: From Route 17, take Exit 104 to Highway 17B west to Hurd Road in Bethel. Turn right on West Shore Road and look for field on the right. If you follow West Shore Road to the left, you'll come upon an interesting wooden archway to a horse farm with carved figures of bears and other wild animals.

By the 1960s, Woodstock had become more mainstream and was adverse to the influx of rebels. Arrests were made for drug possession and skinny-dipping. In this atmosphere, mention of holding the 1969 concert in Woodstock was anathema to city fathers. It tried to stop Bethel from using its name, but the name "Woodstock" had the cachet.

For more Woodstock memorabilia, head back on Highway 17B east less than a mile to Dr. Duggan Road. Turn right. Immediately on the left and across from Hector's Inn you'll see a brightly decorated bus beside a concession. This is **Larry's Dog House** although the sign may be covered. The bus serves refreshments just as it did at Woodstock. For sale are inexpensive items like necklaces, beads and T-shirts. Pricier items are Max Yasgur's milk box for $500 and a special edition of *Life* magazine for $1,000.

The bus is also for sale – at the right price! Open July through Labor Day, 10am-6pm or by appointment. ☎ 914-583-5991/9740.

◎ TIP

Hungry? Heading west out of Bethel just before Perry Road, there's a country emporium on the right that sells sandwiches and has picnic tables outside. Note the lone shack across from Perry Road on the corner of Puckyhuddle Road. It used to be the tollhouse on the old Cochecton-Newburgh Turnpike, a toll road connecting the Hudson and the Delaware.

Ready to relax? Off Route 17B, turn down Dr. Duggan Road and travel roughly 1.6 miles. You'll come upon the scenic **Lake Superior State Park**, operated by the county. Admission is charged for the beach area. The well-maintained 1,409-acre park offers a swimming area with lifeguards, boating and fishing. It has a boat launch and dock and you can bring your own boat or rent a rowboat at $6 an hour in return for your license and $20 deposit. There's also a food concession, picnic tables, grills and a bathhouse.

★ WHAT'S IN A NAME?

Bethel means "House of God" in Hebrew. The town is the center of Sullivan County and is touched by nine of the county's 15 towns.

Sullivan County

Covered Bridges

The truth is, you don't need to spend gobs of money to have fun in the Catskills. If you keep your eyes open there are lots of lovely side roads that aren't advertised. For instance, had you not turned left for the fish hatchery but continued on DeBruce Road, in less than two miles you'd come upon the **Willowemoc Covered Bridge Campsite**. It's a private campground but the covered bridge and general store are open to the public.

In Livingston Manor you might want to check out some more of the famed covered bridges of Sullivan County. If you take Exit 96 off Route 17, one bridge is 1.4 miles from there. Make a right at the stop sign to Old Route 17 and follow the road until you see the bridge sign.

The **Livingston Manor Covered Bridge** spans the Willowemoc Creek. John Davidson built it in the late 19th century in a lattice design, as he did the **Beaverkill Covered Bridge**. Both are situated in lovely parks.

To reach the **Beaverkill Public Campground**, continue on Old Route 17 for a few yards to the sign and the campsite is roughly another four miles on Route 151. A sign along the creek notes that this stretch of the Beaverkill, where I saw families wading, was a favorite of Theodore Gordon (1854-1915), one of the creators of the first purely American dry flies. The entrance sign indicates a fee is $3, although when I drove in at 2pm on a Friday no one was in attendance.

Waneta Lake

Henry David Thoreau once wrote: "A lake is the landscape's most beautiful and expressive feature." He could have been referring to **Waneta Lake**, a spectacular spot five miles north of Exit 96 (off Route 17) and just .8 mile before the Beaverkill Inn. Day use is encouraged. You can fish or picnic, but there's no bathroom, so plan ahead.

Directional Info: Take Route 179 toward Lew Beach, which leads into Routes 151/152.

Stone Arch Bridge Park

One of the most photographed spots in Sullivan County is **Stone Arch Bridge Park**. Built around 1880 by two Swiss German immigrants, the bridge spans Callicoon Creek in Kenoza Lake. The beautiful setting has a playground, picnic tables and trails. One path runs along the stream, but it's marked "steep and rough."

Directional Info: Take Route 17B to Route 52N. If you want to park, the lot entrance is a few feet before the junction of Routes 52 and 52A.

☺ TIP

No one seems to heed all the "No Swimming" signs at the Stone Arch Bridge Park, and, as one boy remarked, "everybody swims here." The water is cold, but kids don't seem to mind – they love disappearing under the little falls.

Sullivan County

The Legend of the Hex Murder

One of the few murders on record in the Upper Delaware Valley occurred on the Stone Arch Bridge in 1892. A troubled 22-year-old, Joseph Heidt, shot and bludgeoned his uncle, George Markert, a middle-aged farmer, before throwing him from the bridge into the cold waters of the east branch of Callicoon Creek.

Like his father Adam, Joseph believed in witchcraft and thought that Adam had been bewitched by his brother-in-law George. The men had been friends from boyhood and were in business together until one transaction soured their relationship. Adam claimed that, about that time, his brother-in-law gave him three pats on the back, which caused him great physical pain. It was alleviated only when George moved away from the neighborhood, but Adam's misery returned when George did. No doctor could cure his ills and a practitioner of folk medicine diagnosed his problem as a hex placed on him. Six months later Joseph Heidt was found guilty of second-degree murder and his father was acquitted of all charges. Joseph was released from Dannemora after serving about 20 years and returned briefly to Sullivan County before marrying and moving out west.

Scenic Drives

Route 97

The portion of **Route 97** from Port Jervis to Barry-ville, between mountains and river, is quite dramatic. It's a winding road so drive carefully. The 74-mile stretch of the Delaware River in the Catskill region runs from its headwaters above Hancock (in Delaware County) to Sparrow Bush, near the borderline of Sullivan and Orange counties. When the highway was completed in 1934, it was christened the Delaware Trail. Most of the property on the river side is privately owned.

Starting from the east, stop at **Nolan's** in Pond Eddy for a fresh deli sandwich if you're hungry. It has an outdoor deck and a nice view of the Pond Eddy Bridge. The general store is part of a complex. The restaurant is open for dinner every night except Wednesday.

You'll next see the **National Park Service** South District ranger office on the left. The white building was once a lock-tender's cottage on the D&H Canal and is situated between the canal and the river. Although it's a field office for park personnel and not a visitor center, the building has some brochures and a restroom. (If no one is there, ring bell.) There are also picnic tables on the grounds for public use. ☎ 914-557-0222.

Another two miles down is Barryville, at the junction of Highway 97 and Route 55. **Books Unlimited**, which sells used, out-of-print, and hard-to-find books for adults and children, is next to Reber Realty. The bookstore was closed when I visited, but the sign said it's open Friday to Sunday or by ap-

Sullivan County

In Pond Eddy, Whitewater Willie's rents rafts, tubes & canoes (see pg. 105).

pointment. ☎ 914-557-0767. If you haven't eaten, the **Barryville Coffee Shop** is good bet.

The **Roebling Bridge**, 4.3 miles west of Barryville, was designed by John A. Roebling (1806-1869) before he became famous for the Brooklyn Bridge. For 50 years, the Roebling Bridge was one of four suspension aqueducts he designed for the D&H Canal. These aqueducts carried the canal boats over the river to avoid the continuing problem of boats and logging rafts crashing into one another. After the canal closed in 1898, all but the Roebling were abandoned, and it now remains the oldest existing wire suspension bridge in the US.

An interpretive center next to the Bridge Restaurant is housed in the only tollhouse left on the Upper Delaware. During the years when the bridge was privately owned, tolls were collected at this house. The displays contains wonderful photos and information on the canal.

    ◎ **TIP**

Need a restroom? Take the one-lane
bridge to the Pennsylvania side.

On the Pennsylvania side of the Roebling Bridge, you'll see the **Zane Grey Museum** (in Lackawaxen, PA), once home of the dentist-turned-novelist of the American west. His best-known work, *Riders of the Purple Sage*, is still considered one of the finest Western novels ever written. For those with a great interest in this prolific author, the museum sells an interesting pamphlet for $3 called *So You Want to Read Zane Grey.* ☎ 570-685-4871.

Back on the New York side, cross Route 97 to the entrance of the **Minisink Battleground Park**. This is more than a walk in the park – it's a history lesson every step of the way. Drive up the hill to the parking lot. Alongside the interpretive center is a trail leading to two others.

I picked the one-mile Battleground trail on the right, which has easy footing but is hilly in spots. I soon came to a clearing with a memorial to the men who died at the Upper Delaware's only major Revolutionary War skirmish. On July 22, 1779, Iroquois Indians and Tories faithful to the British and led by Chieftan Joseph Brant slaughtered nearly 50 American rebels that were part of a hastily assembled militia unit. Two days earlier, Brant's troops had burned the settlement of Minisink (in the Port Jervis area), killing at least four settlers, and the colonials retaliated. They were defeated, but both sides suffered losses in one of the bloodiest battles of the war. The area was so wild and inaccessible that the bones of the dead were not collected for burial until nearly a half-century later.

I followed the path to Hospital Rock and found it hard to fathom that this peaceful spot was where injured soldiers and their physician, Lt. Col. Benjamin Tusten, were set upon and massacred. Shortly after, I spotted a turkey and her young, which lent a bittersweet touch to the moment.

The park is 57 acres and really requires several visits to see all the markers and digest the history. Admission is free. Open dawn to dusk. ☎ 914-794-3000, ext. 5002.

Sullivan County

★ HIGHLAND HIGHLIGHTS

Information on the town of Highland, which includes Eldred, Yulan and Barryville, can be found online at http://town.highland.ny.us/interests. For river and weather information, ☎ 914-252-7100.

Continue northwest along Route 97 to Narrowsburg and **Fort Delaware** (about 45 minutes from Port Jervis). A reconstruction of the first stockaded settlement in the upper Delaware Valley, this complex of 10 colonial cabins from the mid-18th century should not be missed. Whether alone or with the kids (there are programs geared for ages eight to 12), you'll enjoy touring the meeting house, armory, trapper's cabin, loom shed and homes of the Connecticut pioneers who purchased the land in the Cushetunk (Cochecton) region from the Delaware Indians. Farmland had become scarce in eastern Connecticut and these energetic Yankees needed land to feed their large families. Descendants of these hardy frontiersmen are still living in Sullivan County.

Tours of Fort Delaware are self-guided, but county employees in period costumes are on hand to answer questions.

The Joseph Skinner and Moses Thomas families were the first of the 75 original settlers and their cabins are quite modest. An observer in 1761 reported that he saw only four houses and that in Thomas' he "observed that there were a great many families, the beds lying as thick on the floors as they commonly do in a hospital." The Tyler cabin, built in 1776, was the home of a wealthier man, Bezaleel Tyler, a Revolutionary War hero who died in the Battle of Minisink. It has a window of hand-blown glass and three bedrooms with mattresses of hay and straw.

Candle making, blacksmith and woodworking demonstrations, and a petting zoo are part of the fun. Start with the introductory film and then follow the numbered cabins.

The gift shop displays a model of the fort conceived by James W. Burbank, who was county historian and a resident of Narrowsburg. Fort Delaware was opened to the public in 1959 and has since been rebuilt. Director Eileen Bruetsch described Burbank as a multi-talented man and an artist with great foresight to build the fort. "There are really two histories told here," she said, "of the early colonists and Mr. Burbank."

Special activities are scheduled throughout the season, including Scouting Days, when all Girl and Boy Scouts in uniform are admitted free, and a Civil War re-enactment is held. (The fort is near the site of a stopover point for Confederate prisoners of war on their way by rail for internment in Elmira.)

Fort Delaware is open weekends, Memorial Day weekend through mid-June, then daily through Labor Day, from 10am-5:30pm. $4 adults, $2.25 children. ☎ 914-252-6660.

Animal Farms

> *Care, and not fine stables, make a good horse.*
>
> – Danish proverb

APPLE POND FARMING CENTER
Hahn Road
Callicoon Center
☎ 914-482-4764

Apple Pond is a family treat either for a brief visit (by appointment) or a stayover. Co-owner Richard

Riseling is a horse whisperer in his own right. The gentleness with which he bonds with his horses has obviously rubbed off on them, because they crave affection like golden retrievers. "Never put a horse in a box stall. A horse should be outside," is his credo.

Dick raises and sells horses, sheep and goats. Most of them, along with the cats, dogs and mule, were born at Apple Pond so "they know they belong here." His contention is that they are super gentle, and they truly are. The Scottish border collies greet you warmly and the goats love to be petted.

Be sure to see the collection of Dick's carriages, some made by the Amish.

Dick runs the 80-acre farm with assistance from his partner, Sonya Hedlund, agricultural apprentices from here and abroad, and overnight guests who are so inclined. When he bought the farm in 1973 he knew nothing about farming, except that he wanted to do things in the old-fashioned way – horse-powered and organic. Part American Indian and a former instructor of international economics and law in New York City, Dick explains it like this: "I get 14,000 pounds of manure and that's my garden." (He no longer sells produce.)

You can visit the farm or stay over in a one- or three-bedroom apartment with fully equipped kitchen, including microwave and toaster oven. There's no place to eat for miles around so come prepared.

Remember it's a working farm and not the Ritz. Guests are more or less left to their own devices. The rooms are not air-conditioned (there are ceiling fans) and there's no TV reception (only a VCR and some tapes). No food is provided but you'll have a chance to milk the goats and taste fresh goat's milk that, according to Dick, is naturally homogenized. "Then we pasteurize if we want to make cheese." Guests also learn about wool spinning and may even get to watch Dick train his horses for dressage.

The one-bedroom apartment is $250 for the week-end and sleeps four. The three-bedroom is $500 for a week and can accommodate two couples and several kids.

Dick says 6,000 people come for tours annually, "mainly little kids, up to [ages] 12 or 13." On the one-hour tours visitors learn why and how crops are organically grown, about cheese and yogurt making, and the farm's different breeds of horses (painted draft, Belgian draft, stallions and warmbloods). Children can feed the lambs and milk the goats. On the two-hour tour visitors also get to drive a team of Belgians – huge but gentle animals. "He's only seven," Dick told a 10-year-old girl, as he was harnessing Bill, a Belgian draft, for a wagon ride with Bill's half-brother Bart. "What?" she exclaimed. Bill is big. He weighs about 2,300 pounds and his rump nearly touches the top of his stall.

One-hour tours are $30 for one to five people. A sleigh ride in the winter is $75 for 10 people. Tours are by appointment only. Open 10-5 daily year-round.

Directional Info: From Route 17, get off at Exit 100 and take Route 52W to Youngsville. Turn right onto Shandelee Road and continue 1.2 miles; turn left on Stump Pond Road and proceed 2.4 miles; turn left on Hahn Road and go 1.1 miles.

★ WHAT'S IN A NAME?

The town was named Callicoon for good reason. In Dutch it means "turkey" (kalkoen) and Dick says he has seen as many as 10,000 of them on his field.

TAIVAIL FARM
Exit 105
Woodbourne
☎ 914-434-6475

Trained as an architect, Kalman also transcribes the Torah & other holy Jewish documents on commission.

Kalman Freidus and his wife, Gittel, have nine children and lots of animals on their 130-acre farm. The former Long Island couple loves animals and bought the Woodbourne farm 15 years ago. The afternoon I arrived all was quiet and a peacock graciously spread his feathers for my camera. I later learned that spring is mating season and he was trying to attract the two females. The peacocks are caged, but most of the animals roam free, including goats, roosters, donkeys, ducks, geese, cats and chickens.

Kalman makes beautiful lithographs that are on display and for sale on the porch in the summer. One of his daughters (three children are married but the rest still help out) showed off some of them in the dining room. Each depicts a Jewish tradition – songs sung on Friday night, blessing the Sabbath candles, and so on. A colorful Noah's Ark is painted on an ostrich egg that spins on a stand for effect.

Open Sunday through Friday, 10am-6pm. Admission: $3.50 adults, $3 children, $2 hay rides.

Directional Info: From Route 17, exit onto Route 42N to Woodbourne (eight miles). Right before Yum Yum Glatt Kosher Gourmet, turn left on Hasbrouck Drive and continue 1.4 miles to the farm.

◎ TIP

Although Taivail Farm is open year-round, summer is the best time to visit, when all the animals are out. Parents and kids are free to pet and feed the animals.

RIVER BROOK FARM

Route 97 and C. Meyer Road
Cochecton
☎ 914-932-7952

It's hard to believe that only 1¾ acres of this 15-acre property are devoted to growing vegetables. Corn, carrots, beans, beets, cucumbers, cantaloupe, asparagus, sandwich onions, watermelons, zucchini – you name it – grow row upon row as far as the eye can see.

In comparison, a whopping eight acres is given over to hay to feed the emus, goats and sheep, which in turn provide the fertilizer. There are also chickens and hens. The day I was there a hen was sitting on five or six eggs – some from other hens.

Proprietor Neil Fitzgerald has been gardening all his life. His father was a semi-organic gardener in the suburbs of Philadelphia, where Neil was raised, along with goats and sheep. Eight years ago, he and his wife were looking at property when the agent took them to this site, once an Indian cornfield where Indian stones and flints are occasionally found. Neil remembers standing on the property, at the confluence of Mitchells Pond Brook and the Delaware River, in late August. Yellow and pink flowers were everywhere and warblers and goldfinches were flying overhead. "I whispered to Alice, 'Don't look too excited.' The real estate agent was standing there smiling because he knew he had us."

The vegetables are sold at local health food stores, at the Liberty Farmer's Market on Fridays, and at the farm on Saturdays, 11am to dark.

Directional Info: The turnoff for the farm is .8 mile north of Skinners Falls on Route 97. Driving north, the sign for C. Meyer Road is obscured, so look for a red house and turn left. Follow signs to the farm.

Sullivan County

Fishing

*To fish opening day on the Beaverkill is
like celebrating Christmas in Bethlehem.*
– Red Smith, sportswriter (1905-1982)

*Willowemoc is
pronounced
WIL-lo-WEE-
mock.*

The Roscoe/Livingston Manor region in the western
end of Sullivan County is world-famous as Trout
Town USA because of the pure, trout-filled waters of
the Beaverkill, Willowemoc and Neversink rivers.
This is the birthplace of American dry fly-fishing,
and the tiny town of Roscoe (its high school gradu-
ated 11 students last year) caters to fishermen.
Signs all over town welcome anglers. For a daily report on fishing conditions of the Beaverkill and Willowemoc rivers from April 1-July 1, ☎ 607-498-5350.

★ WHAT'S IN A NAME?

The fabled Beaverkill derived its
name from the numerous beaver colonies settlers found along the headwaters. It was at Junction Pool, just
west of Roscoe where the Willowemoc and Beaverkill meet, that American fly-fishing was first developed.
Considered the northeast's leading
trout streams, they are often alluded
to as the BEAMOC System.

*For a complete
list of bait and
tackle shops,
see www.scva.
net. Click "The
Outdoor Life"
and then click
"Fishing."*

In Roscoe, visit these stores for fishing-related goods
and services: The **Beaverkill Angler** (☎ 607-498-
5194) is a privately-owned franchise of **Orvis**. **Done-
gal** (☎ 607-498-5911) sells fishing gear, gifts and
toys; **The Little Store** (☎ 607-498-5553), a variety
emporium, has a separate shop for fishing equipment, **Trout Town General Store** (☎ 607-498-

4670) has gifts for the angler. **Drehers Pro Country Store** (☎ 607-498-4333) is the only one selling worms.

Sullivan County

⑤ **DID YOU KNOW?**

Roscoe is so small that the main drag has a new name but no sign to that effect. When I asked a merchant if Broad Street was its name, she replied that it's been changed to Stewart Avenue. I protested that there's no sign and she quipped, "Well, this is Roscoe."

Narrowsburg overlooks the **Big Eddy**, a popular fishing spot and the deepest point in the Delaware River at 113 feet (there is often a whirlpool at the site). The Delaware River is stocked with trout, bass, shad and walleye. Both of these guide services charge the same for two people and supply the equipment at no extra charge: one driftboat with guide: $150 for half-day and $200 for full day, including lunch. Both are operated by licensed guides.

★ **FAMOUS FACES**

President Theodore Roosevelt, an avid trout fisherman, frequently vacationed in the Catskills at Peekamoose Lodge on the headwaters of Rondout Creek.

The Times Herald Record *publishes its annual **Online Fishing Guide** beginning the first week in April at www.threcord.com.*

Gone Fishing Guide Service in Narrowsburg begins operating in April. Anthony Ritter has an excellent Web site (www.gonefishing-gs.com) that covers everything about his business. ☎ 914-252-3657.

Sweetwater Guide Service, also in Narrowsburg and operated by Michael Padua, also does wade fishing. ☎ 914-252-3439.

◎ *TIP*

Michael Padua of Sweetwater Guide Service recommends that beginners as well as experts hire a guide – at least for the first time on the Delaware. He says there are limited access points known only to resident fishermen. In his brochure, Padua reminds you to bring fishing license, rain gear, sun screen, waders (felt soles) and polarized sunglasses.

Fishing-Related Attractions

The fish you release is your gift to another angler.
   – Lee Wulff, fly-fishing legend

CATSKILL FLY FISHING CENTER & MUSEUM
Old Route 17
Livingston Manor
☎ 914-439-4810

At the Catskill Fly Fishing Center there's a private video nook and a small library.

Between Roscoe and Livingston Manor on old Route 17 stands one of two museums in the nation devoted to fly-fishing (the other is the American Museum of Fly Fishing in Manchester, Vermont). It's a mecca for fisherfolk and artists alike. Flies are fashioned from thread, fur and feathers to imitate an aquatic insect and the colorful and exotic patterns are magnificent. Even more incredible is that 200-pound fish have been caught on fly rods that weigh little more than a candy bar! A nearly life-size bronze sculpture of Lee Wulff, the "Father of Catch and Release," has him enacting the very scene with a salmon. Another masterpiece is an operational line-braiding machine from the 1930s.

The 35-acre site has nature trails and a catch-and-release stretch on Willowemoc Creek in the heart of some of the nation's finest trout streams. The center opened in 1981 on former farmland. The museum was added in 1995.

The Angler's Summerfest, a flea market and festival, is typically held the last weekend in August, and the Environmental Weekends for children ages eight through 18 is during the month of July.

The center is open daily from 10am-4pm, April to October. On Saturdays, guest anglers teach basic fly-fishing skills from 1-4pm for a $3 donation; $1 seniors and children. Winter hours are Tuesday through Friday, 10am-1pm; Saturday, 10am-4pm.

Catskill Fly Fishing Center & Museum in Livingston Manor.
(Courtesy of Catskill Fly Fishing Center)

CATSKILL FISH HATCHERY
Fish Hatchery Road
DeBruce
☎ 914-439-4328

This amazing-looking operation specializes in raising more than a million brown trout and other species annually for distribution into public waterways and to other state hatcheries (there are 12). From October to May 1, most fish are in indoor tanks, and an appointment is required for a weekday visit. In the warmer months, they're in giant outdoor pools, swimming in water from streams, wells and springs.

I never went on the tour, but the outdoor tanks are awesome. If the gate is open you can walk in and take a peek – provided you obey the posted rules. You may be lucky enough, like one woman I met there, to catch a glimpse of the fish being transferred from the huge fish pump to the holding tanks on the trucks. The sideboard explains the whole process.

The fish hatchery is open 8:30am-4pm weekdays, and 8:30am-noon on summer weekends and holidays.

Directional Info: From Route 17, take Exit 96 (De-Bruce Road; Routes 82/83). Travel east past Trout & Bear Restaurant. About 5.4 miles from exit is Fish Hatchery Road. Turn left and go another 1.9 miles.

Canoeing & Rafting

If there is magic on this planet, it is contained in water.
– Loren Eisely, naturalist (1907-1977)

There are nearly two dozen tributaries to the Delaware River. One that's easily accessible and scenic is about 2½ miles east of Fort Delaware and 25 miles from the Roebling Bridge. **Ten Mile River Access** is maintained by the county; there are picnic tables, portable restrooms, a boat launch and Landers canoe rental.

There are several places to rent rafts, canoes, kayaks and tubes in or near Barryville. The rapids are mostly Class I and II meaning there are few riffles and small waves. Here, traffic on the Delaware is generally light or practically absent.

Landers has a strong presence on the New York portion of the Delaware, with a dozen substations or access bases no more than five-10 miles apart, ☎ 800-252-3925; www.landersrivertrips.com. Two other established outfits are **Kittatinny Canoes**, ☎ 800-356-2852, and **Indian Head**, ☎ 800-874-2628; www.indianheadcanoes.com.

For a complete list of Upper Delaware liveries & campgrounds, visit www.nps.gov/upde.

Kittatinny, a Pennsylvania-based company, has two outposts in New York, whereas Landers and Indian Head each have several. They all provide free one-way shuttle service. All charge $24 per person weekdays (and around $27 weekends) for canoes and rafts, based on two persons per canoe and four per raft (although Indian Head requires only two in a raft weekdays and three on weekends).

A third outfit, closer to the Thruway, is **Whitewater Willie's** at Pond Eddy. It operates in conjunction with Nolan's River Inn Restaurant & Motel, so your

Sullivan County

eating and sleeping needs are convenient. Fees are competitive with the others. ☎ 800-233-RAFT or 914-856-2229.

Works in Progress

A proposed $900,000 visitor center in the Mongaup watershed is, after 13 years, finally moving forward, according to a June 17, 1999 article in the Middletown *Record*. Originally recommended in the 1986 federal River Management Plan, the center has not materialized because the land designated for the site was suddenly bought by New York State when it acquired the Mongaup watershed in 1990.

The state is in favor of the center. In 1993, then-Governor Cuomo signed a 99-year lease to build a federal facility on state land, but it needed a final sign-off from Congress. The proposal is finally being addressed, but construction cannot begin until the act has gone through committee hearings and been passed by Congress.

The watershed is located in southern Sullivan County and western Orange County, near Port Jervis; the land designated for the visitor center is on the Orange County side. This federally-funded visitor center is considered vital because the vast majority of people coming into the river corridor enter at Mongaup. The annual report of the National Park Service reported that around 294,000 people visited the Upper Delaware River in 1998.

✗ WARNING

Weirs are placed at various places in the river to trap eels. Anyone using the river should avoid these structures, which resemble upside-down Vs with a wooden trap at the point. Ask park personnel how to locate and avoid them.

In the western part of Sullivan County on the Delaware River, **Skinners Falls** in Cochecton is the favorite watering hole. More like small rapids than falls, the river here is used for tubing, canoeing and swimming and can get crowded on weekends. In 1991 it was featured on NBC Today as "one of three best watering holes in the US." Tubers have two choices. **Lou's Tubes** is $5 a day. ☎ 914-252-3593. **Lander's** is $7 a day and tubes come with handles.

Directional Info: Skinners Falls is off Route 97, 4.7 miles north of Fort Delaware (you'll see a sign). Just past the railroad tracks is Lander's on the right, the parking lot on the left, and a bridge to Pennsylvania up ahead. To reach Lou's Tubes, look for the dirt road immediately before the parking lot and follow the right fork. To see the falls, follow the left fork and park in the other parking lot. Walk through the woods to the rocks.

Life jackets are provided at both Lou's Tubes & Lander's.

◎ TIP

Note that weather conditions have a great impact on the river. Lou Lothian, who has been renting tubes for 25 years, said she once told a caller the water was too low for tubing and was asked if she could do anything about it. "That's nature," she said.

Sullivan County

Tubing on the Delaware River.

Swimming

If it's hot and you need a swim, head to the lake at **Mongaup State Campsite**, a fun family experience. It's a scenic spot within the State Forest Preserve with a beach, picnic areas with barbeque pits, changing rooms, showers and lots of shade trees. When the lifeguard is on duty, the fee is $5 per car; otherwise it's $3. ☎ 914-439-4233.

Directional Info: From Catskill Fish Hatchery (see page 104) continue on Fish Hatchery Road for less than a mile and you'll come to a fork. Follow the sign to Mongaup State Campsite.

⊚ TIP

You can also walk or drive around the lake at Mongaup State Park. There are several confusing loops so be sure to request a map when you pay.

Lake Superior Park is another option for recreation and swimming (see page 87).

Hiking

A mountain and a river are good neighbors.
– George Herbert, English poet and clergyman (1593-1633)

Feel like taking the kids on a hike? **Walnut Mountain** in Liberty's **Pearson Park** is a fairly new-growth forest, rising to Sullivan County's highest point. It's little known, except among bikers (non-motorized). While it lacks the mystique of ancient woods, the mountain is ideal for family hikes. Elevation is 2,157, but keep in mind that the park entrance is about 1,750 feet.

Follow the easy, red shale trail from Upper Kennesaw Road and loop around to the mountain overlook. There's a nice grassy ledge for picnicking or you can eat at tables in the park below.

Near the summit, look for the foundation of the **Walnut Mountain House**, a first-class hotel opened in 1887. Liberty historian Delbert Van Etten wrote that the hotel boasted "beautiful groves, shady walks, tennis courts, croquet lawns and drives," but that by the fall of 1918 it was gone. No one knows if it was destroyed by fire or torn down for lumber.

Witch's Rock, a large outcrop resembling a witch's profile, is barely visible through the dense forest, although it's supposed to be cleared. In an old photo, two people standing at the rock's precipice are clearly visible from afar. The caption identifies the rock as "one of the natural attractions on our grounds. The view cannot be surpassed for weird magnificence." Farther along you'll see a segment of a stone wall, possibly the remains of a caretaker's cottage or stable. ☎ 914-292-7690 for directions.

Legend of Otto Hillig's Treasure

During World War II, saboteurs in this country aimed to blow up electrical plants, telephone switching facilities and railroads. One day they targeted Ferndale, a hamlet in Liberty, planning to destroy its railroad trestle to cripple the flow of arms from upstate New York to its ports of departure in New York City. German sympathizers had trouble finding the dynamite, however, and often had to purchase explosives from the black market.

One group schemed to force a local pilot to fly them to an airstrip on Long Island for this purpose. As they staked out a Liberty airstrip for a victim, a local photographer, Otto Hillig, and his pilot Holger Hoiriis prepared for a sunset flight. As they boarded, two men hijacked the plane and giddily displayed the huge sum of money for purchasing the dynamite. Once in the air, Holger rolled the plane and Otto grabbed his gun from the cockpit and killed both captors.

Afraid they'd be accused of robbery, Otto and Holger contacted the authorities but withheld information about the money. Instead they buried it in a box agreeing to use the funds only for a noble cause. As they grew old, Otto asked a young aide to recover the money and deposit it in a savings account. The assistant was directed to place a large coin engraved with Otto's initials, OH, to mark the spot. He was further instructed to place the story in the local newspapers and on radio and to assure that clues to the location be published periodically.

The money is presently in an unnamed account at the Fleet Bank on North Main Street in Liberty. The Sherlock who finds the coin, which is supposedly out in the open, can redeem it for the bounty. The assistant, who still lives in the community but remains anonymous, never claimed the money for himself.

A brochure provided by the Town of Liberty Parks & Recreation Department lists 25 clues to finding the coin. To obtain the brochure, write the department at 119 N. Main Street, Liberty, NY 12754, or ☎ 914-292-7690.

Here's another good hiking/walking area. In 1844 writer Washington Irving traveled the entire length of the D&H Canal reporting that "for upwards of ninety miles I went through a constant succession of scenery that would have been famous if it existed in any part of Europe."

You don't have to walk that far to experience the same exhilaration. An easy stroll in the park is less than three miles north of Wurtsboro Airport on Route

209 in the **D&H Canal Linear Park** on the left. (Look for brown sign on right.) It's in Summitville, so named because it's the highest point of the canal between the Hudson and the Delaware rivers. The town developed when it became a stop on the canal at Lock #50. The one-mile park has 10 locks and used to take 30 minutes for each boat to go through. For those five hours, the women and children aboard got off and went shopping.

You can still see the remains of the locks, waste weirs (which regulated the water level) and towpath. When completed, the towpath trails will access locks 42, 43, 44 and 45. The paths along the canal are wide, flat and grassy, making for easy footing. On a walk in August, there was a wondrous display of purple loosestrife.

Route 209 connects New England, upstate New York and Pennsylvania.

There's a different section of the canal recently opened off Route 209 between the village of Wurtsboro and the airport called Hornbeck's Basin Access. This is more like a hike in the woods on rocky and hillier terrain.

In addition to the hiking/biking trails, both Pearson Park and D&H Canal Linear Park have picnic tables and portable toilets. Open 8am to dark. Free admission.

Biking

Walnut Mountain Biking Center rents mountain bikes and organizes about a half-dozen annual races. Tim Quilty, a professional biker, and John VandeVelde, a former Olympian, operate the center. Walnut Mountain, off Route 55 on Walnut Mountain-Pearson Park Road, has 15 miles of mountain biking and hiking trails. ☎ 914-292-3588 for Liberty Parks and Recreation.

Bicycle Club of Sullivan County provides guided road tours every Saturday or Sunday from May through October at no charge. You bring your own bike and helmet (mandatory), and the club provides refreshments. According to Carl Silverstein, the club secretary, all ages participate but the Catskills are hilly so you must be in shape. He said the route starts out at 12 miles in May but gets longer, about 25 miles, as the season progresses. ☎ 914-794-3000, ext. 5010 for information on specific tours and guides.

Skiing

Sullivan County has one downhill ski area and it's ideal for the novice. **Holiday Mountain** in Monticello is known as a "training mountain," although it has more difficult slopes with 400-foot vertical drops. The Kinderski program for children four to six enables parents to ski solo while their youngsters are learning the ropes. Snowboarding is a growing attraction and the center is expanding its 90% snowmaking in order to open more terrain. Snowboarders and skiers are both welcome on the all-terrain park with its jumps and obstacles. Holiday Mountain has 15 trails and eight lifts, and there's night skiing every day except Sunday. It also features a cafeteria and lounge, rental shop and ski school. Daily weekend fees are $29 adults and $25 juniors (groups of 10 or more can ski for $8 each on weekdays). Snowshoe rentals are $10. ☎ 914-796-3161.

Directional Info: From Route 17, take Exit 107 and turn left toward Bridgeville. Make another left at stop sign. Follow Bridgeville Road for two miles; watch for ski area sign.

On the slopes at Holiday Mountain in Monticello.

Ski Fest

At the 26th annual ski festival at Holiday Mountain in late February, toddlers to teens seemed to be having a great time. The sun was shining brightly, events were planned all weekend and Saturday night featured fireworks for the first time in many years. Cookie Monster and other *Sesame Street* characters were out in full force to entertain the little ones. I spoke to a couple from nearby Middletown, who said they usually ski in Vermont but that Holiday Mountain is closer, more manageable and half the price. The pair gave high marks to Rich Conklin, director of the ski school and his instructor Gary Malman. Admission was free and daily attendance estimated at about 2,500.

⑨ TIP

Gather cross-country ski info online at www.scsmag.com/skiing.htm, or call the Department of Environmental Conservation (DEC). For Sullivan and Ulster counties, ☎ 914-256-3075; Delaware & Greene counties, ☎ 607-652-3722.

Golf

Golf is the most fun you can have without taking your clothes off.
        – Golfer Chi Chi Rodriguez

Sullivan County boasts several challenging courses, including the most renowned Monster course at the Concord. What they all share is scenic views. All are open to the public April through November unless otherwise noted. Sullivan County's golf Web site is www.scsmag.com (click "Golf").

What could be lovelier than a golf course atop a mountain? **Swan Lake Golf & Country Club** is only one mile up Mt. Hope Road, but the 18-hole course on 6,820 yards of softly rolling hills is private and undisturbed. Opened in 1965, the par 72 course has a PGA rating of 71.8 and a 132 slope. The Club features a driving range, pro shop, circular bar, 100-seat restaurant, snack bar and spa.

Soft spikes are advised at Swan Lake to prevent slipping on the mountainside.

The PGA golf pro at this course is Hyung Chin Park, nicknamed Central Park, who is also Vice President of the new Swan Lake Resort Hotel. Call 10 days in advance for tee times. Cart rentals are included in the price. Exit 101 and follow signs to Swan Lake. Pass the lake and make a right at Mt. Hope Road to the mountaintop. ☎ 914-292-0748 or 914-292-0323.

Concord, Kiamesha Lake. 18-hole, par 73 (7,471 yards) Monster course and 800-yard International course; 80-seat restaurant. ☎ 914-794-4000.

Forestburgh Country Club, 80 Tannery Road, Forestburgh. 18-hole, par 72 (6,700 yards); practice range. ☎ 914-794-6542.

Grossinger's Golf Resort, Liberty. 27 holes featuring the famous and formidable "Big G" 18-hole course, par 72 (6,839 yards). Driving range, practice sand traps, putting greens, pro shop, PGA staff, bar, a new 109-seat restaurant and club, carts, locker rooms, equipment rentals, lessons. Open April 15 through November 1. ☎ 914-292-9000.

Huff House, Roscoe. Nine-hole course, par 3. Open to the public. ☎ 607-498-9953 or 800-358-5012.

Island Glen Country Club, Route 17B, Bethel. Nine-hole, par 36 (3,009 yards) municipal course. Golf carts (not mandatory), practice green, clubhouse, bar. Plastic spikes preferred. Open daily at 7am, Memorial Day through October. Tends to get busy on weekends. ☎ 914-583-1010.

Kutsher's Country Club, Monticello. 18-hole, par 71, spikeless course. Clubhouse, lessons, chipping and putting green, driving range, riding carts, pool, housing, restaurant, pro shop. Carts mandatory. Open mid-April to mid-November. ☎ 914-794-6000.

Lake View Golf Course, Lakeview Drive, Highland Lake. Nine-hole, par 29. Carts not mandatory, rentals. Spikeless. Open mid-April through October, daily 8am-7pm. Executive course is narrow and challenging and rarely crowded. ☎ 914-557-6406.

Lochmor Golf Course, Loch Sheldrake. 18-hole, par 71 (6,500 yards). Practice greens, driving range, clubhouse, lockers, pro shop, restaurant, cart and club rentals, lessons. Spikeless. New cart paths and some redesigned holes. Public, championship course borders Morningside Lake and is tougher since its redesign four years ago. ☎ 914-434-9079.

Sullivan County Golf & Country Club, Route 52, Liberty. Par 72. Golf carts, practice green, clubhouse, restaurant, pro shop, lockers. Semi-private, challenging nine-hole course has alternate tees for 18 holes. Open May through November. ☎ 914-292-9584.

Tarry Brae Golf Course, Pleasant Valley Road, South Fallsburg. 18-hole, par 72 (6,900 yards). Spectacular course with practice greens, driving range, clubhouse, restaurant, pro shop, cart rentals (carts mandatory weekend mornings), lessons. Spikeless. Considered one of the best public courses in the state. Championship course has it all – rolling fairways, woods, water, doglegs, elevated tees. (Tarry Brae and Lochmor in Loch Sheldrake advertise together, offering golfers the chance to play both courses the same day for one greens fee. The two courses are about one mile apart). ☎ 914-434-2620.

Tennanah Lake Golf & Tennis Club, Hankins Road, Roscoe. 18-hole, par 72 (6,900 yards). PGA pro, driving range, golf shop, club rental, restaurant, coffee shop, Olympic-size pool. Spikeless. A semi-private championship course built in 1952 and designed by Sam Snead, Tennanah bills itself as the "Best Kept Secret in Sullivan County." Tough course with woods separating the holes. The John Jacobs Golf School opened here in 1997. Course open May through October. ☎ 607-498-5502 or 888-561-3935.

Inquire about special "Stay & Play" packages at the Inn at Tennanah Lake.

Villa Roma Resort Hotel, Callicoon. 18-hole, par 71 (5,416 yards). Driving range, putting green, restaurant, coffee shop, club pro, club repair, carts, pro shop, locker rooms, lessons, equipment rentals. Beautiful fairways. Considered the best-conditioned course

Sullivan County

in the Catskills besides Grossinger's. Open April through mid-October. ☎ 914-887-5097.

Driving Ranges

Amapro Golf Range, 6560 Route 52W, Liberty. 18-hole mini-golf; driving range; 25 matted tees; 25 grass tees; six practice sand traps. ☎ 914-292-9022.

Birdies of Mongaup Valley, four miles west of Monticello Raceway on 17B. Two new attractions added to its 300-yard driving range with covered tees. It now has an 18-hole miniature golf course, open-field batting cages for soft and hard ball, and a petting farm with llamas, emus, pigs and goats. The game room is wall-to-wall with futuristic and classic arcade games. Open daily April through October. ☎ 914-583-6652.

◎ TIP

The **Bagel Bakery** is in the Birdies complex and is one of the few places to get breakfast or lunch along 17B. Besides bagels, it has deli sandwiches and hot food. Open daily, year-round.

Horseback Riding

*The influence of fine scenery, the presence
of mountains, appeases our irritations
and elevates our friendships.*

— Emerson

Hadley Stables is a fixture in the Fallsburg/Monticello area. A former dairy farm, it was Circle M for 12 years, and 15 years ago was purchased by Hadley Kashan, an amiable chap. The picturesque 100-acre property has riding trails and a hilltop campsite for overnights. The overnight fee is $75 and includes four hours of riding. Says Hadley, "We provide tents and people bring their own food and sleeping gear." Horseback riding is $20 per person for one hour, $35 for two, and $50 for three hours. Riders range from beginners to advanced and the small fry can enjoy a pony ride and the small petting zoo. Open daily year-round. ☎ 914-434-9254 for reservations.

Directional Info: From Route 17, take Exit 105B (42N) and make an immediate left. At the intersection of 104 and 107, follow County Road 107 to Hadley Stables.

Arrowhead Stables is an 800-acre ranch a mile north of Best Western on Cooley Road. Owner Trish Blessington gives lessons to beginner and advanced riders. The stable also offers one- to three-hour guided trail rides ($15-$18), overnight trips ($85), and lunch ($25) and dinner ($30-$40) rides. Open daily in the summer and weekends year-round. Weekdays by appointment. ☎ 914-292-6267.

RR Stables at 2 Sullivan Street in Wurtsboro is located just beyond the village center. Morris C. Smith has a stable of 16 horses. Whether you're a novice or an advanced rider, all the rides are guided. Experi-

Sullivan County

enced riders might be allowed to go out alone, but only when Smith gets to know them. There are several places to ride including the railroad bed leading from his stable to Summitville, a two-hour round trip. The fee is $25 per hour. The stable is open all year, but in the winter rides are by appointment. In any season it's a good idea to call first, ☎ 914-888-0712.

Hunting

> *Dear Lord, Please give me hunter's luck*
> *To shoot a mighty eight-point buck*
> *When luck like this is in the bag*
> *I'll have a reason then to brag.*
>   – A hunter's prayer

The non-hunters among us may cringe at the thought of killing an animal for sport. Yet you get a less slanted picture after talking to Fernando Neves, a warmhearted, responsible hunter who loves animals and would never shoot a baby or endangered species. (The fawn in his workshop was hit by a car.)

A hunter and licensed taxidermist, Neves expresses it this way: "I love animals, I love hunting. I respect people's beliefs. But if you don't control [populations], they will feed and multiply." A native of Portugal, Neves relishes the quietness of the woods, studies its habitat, and meets up with his buddies around the campfire "to see which ones tell the biggest lie." He says he feels sad after shooting an animal. "I wish we could do like fishermen who catch and let go, but we can't." After sustaining an injury as a truck driver, Neves attended school for taxidermy and considers it "the best move I made in my life. I don't consider it work."

His studio is a testament to his skill at mounting deer, birds, raccoons, fish, squirrels and even lions and buffalo that look lifelike and bright-eyed. The eyes and teeth are fake, although you'd never know it. Man-made jaws and eyes in different sizes are kept in boxes and foam mannequins for every animal fill an entire room. To encourage visits, Neves plans to open a museum above his workshop.

★ **DID YOU KNOW?**

The word taxidermy comes from the Greek words meaning "arrangement" and "skin." It's the taxidermist's job to give each creature a natural expression and stance.

Neves uses his own dogs and cats as live models for wolves and lions and refers to a scrapbook of pictures of other wild animals. The largest animal he ever stuffed was a 1,000-pound elk. In 1998 he entered his first competition, sponsored by the United Taxidermists, and took second place out of hundreds of entries for his Corsican ram.

If he's gone hunting, his wife or 21-year-old son, Paulo, also a licensed taxidermist, will show you around. Neves smiles at the thought of the outdoors and comradery. "I enjoy meeting my friends from different states – we meet every year in Colorado. I would rather be out there than pay $50 to a shrink," he said.

Neves Studio of Taxidermy is on Route 17B in Bethel, nine miles from Monticello Raceway and directly across from Dr. Duggan Road. If you're headed that way, look for the sign on the right partially obscured by the sign for Superior Lake Park. Turn

Sullivan County

right on Donaldson Road to the entrance. ☎ 914-583-7814.

Flying

WURTSBORO AIRPORT
Off Route 209; Exit 113 from Route 17
Wurtsboro
☎ 914-888-2791
Open daily, 9am to dusk, year-round

The adventurous among you might want to take off here. The nation's oldest soaring site, this privately-owned airport was established in 1927. Any day of the year, weather permitting, you can take a 15-20 minute demonstration ride in a sailplane (glider). In the introductory lesson ($37), your sailplane is towed 2,500 feet in the air and then released. You'll soar along with air currents and then land. Introductory lessons in piloting a power plane ($30 for one hour; $50 for three hours) are also given.

Spectator Sports

Mountaindale is home to the **Catskill Cougars**, a minor league professional baseball team based at Baxter Stadium. Several sports writers and baseball professionals have described the 3,500-seat stadium as the most beautiful setting for baseball ever seen. The season runs from June to September with about half the games played at home starting at 7:05pm. General admission is $6; seniors $5; and children $4. Box seats are $7. ☎ 914-436-GAME.

Wildlife Watching

Screaming the night away
With his great wing feathers
Swooping the darkness up;
I hear the Eagle bird
Pulling the blanket back
Off from the eastern sky
              — Iroquois song

For 10 weeks out of the year, Sullivan County has an attraction few other places can boast about. More than 100 **bald eagles** migrate here every winter from New England and Canada, the largest winter population in the northeast. Twelve thousand state-owned acres have been set aside for their habitat. You can spot bald eagles along the Delaware River throughout the year, but chances of observing them increase dramatically in winter. About 10 breeding pairs stick around permanently, but eagle watching is discouraged during the breeding season from April to June.

★ DID YOU KNOW?

Native Americans out west called eagles "Thunderbirds" because of their great power. The bald eagle has a six- to eight-foot wing span and is the largest bird in the northeast.

From late December through February, look for eagles where major tributaries meet the river, especially where tall trees line the shore. They build their huge nests high up, generally on white pines and always near water. The inflow from the tributaries keeps the river free of ice, thus providing adequate areas for eagles to fish. Reservoirs are good viewing areas also because the hydropower plants discharge water.

A prime lookout is the **Bald Eagle Observation Hut** at **Mongaup Reservoir**. Inside you'll find information about the official symbol of the US since 1782, when 500,000 bald eagles filled our skies. Sadly, the eagle was made the symbol because it represented power and free spirit, yet it won't be removed from the endangered species list before July 2000.

Directional Info: From Route 17, take Exit 105 in Monticello and follow NY42 south to amber flashing light in Forestburgh. Turn right, and after passing Plank Road, go another 1½ miles. The blind is on the left side of the road just before the Mongaup Falls Reservoir Bridge.

Another place to spot eagles is at the **Rio Reservoir**. To reach it, follow the above directions, but instead of passing Plank Road, make a left. You'll see an Orange and Rockland Utility Company power plant before the Bald Eagle Observation sign on your right.

⊚ **TIP**

Eagle spotters must be patient and quiet since eagles are intolerant of human activity.

One of the prime areas for eagle watching is the **Basherkill Wildlife Management Area**, 2,175 acres of state-owned land in Sullivan and Orange counties. (The entrance, in Wurtsboro heading south on Route 209, is on the left [Haven Road] immediately before Giovanni's Restaurant.) The freshwater wetland, encompassing 1,333 acres, is the largest in southeastern New York. You can view the eagles from your car, electric-powered boat, canoe or along the D&H Canal towpath.

Although eagle watching is usually best in winter, you certainly don't have to wait until then to observe wetland wildlife. In the summer, the marsh provides premier viewing of herons, osprey, beaver, migratory ducks and white-tailed deer. The Basha Kill (also spelled Basherkill and Bashakill) is a tributary of the Neversink River that forms these wetlands south of Wurtsboro. Wildflowers, such as purple loosestrife, are abundant. A beautiful but invasive plant, loosestrife pushes out native plants to make room for itself. Fields of purple can be seen everywhere, especially in August when the color is most brilliant.

You can fish, bird watch or hike along Basherkill's 15 miles of trails. Hunting (with a special permit) and canoeing are also encouraged.

Directional Info: From Route 17, take Route 209S (Exit 113 in Wurtsboro) 1½ miles. Parking areas are all along the road on the left side.

If you prefer a one-hour guided nature hike with a delightful, informative and vigorous octogenarian, drive to **Tomsco Falls**, the "Niagara of Sullivan County" in Mountaindale. Park your car on the right side of the road and, as the sign says, honk. David and Sylvia Rashkin live in the red brick house across the street from the falls. One or the other will come out. If David is conducting a tour, his wife will summon him. David, who once owned the Rashkin Pharmacy in Woodridge, says he's been leading these tours "forever." Admission is $6 for adults, $4 for children. ☎ 914-434-6065.

Sullivan County

Directional Info: From Route 17, exit at 209N. When you come to the sign for Spring Glen, make a left and follow the road to the stop sign across from the grocery store. Turn right and follow County Highway 55 for five miles.

★ **WHAT'S IN A NAME?**

"Tomsco" is actually an acronym for the Iroquois Indian tribes who lived in New York State – the Tuscarora, Oneida, Mohawk, Seneca, Cayuga and Onondaga.

I picked up the Sullivan County **Rails-to-Trails** in South Fallsburg, but only with the help of a nice gentleman on the road (again no signs or easy access). Once on the trail, I walked toward Hurleyville but only made it slightly past Echo Lake. This trail is less groomed than the one in Greene County and the track marks are more visible. It's a lovely walk though going through, in part, a new-growth forest. The only sections officially open run from South Fallsburg to Hurleyville (about three miles) and for a small stretch in Mountaindale. Exit 107 and take 42N to the village of South Fallsburg. At the first light turn left and before reaching the stop sign, pull into the parking lot on the left. Walk past the stop sign and make an immediate left onto the basketball court. Walk through it to the trail.

Nature Walks

Bird watchers and others interested in nature in general will delight in the free walks conducted on weekends by the Sullivan County chapter of the **National Audubon Society**. A non-profit organization, it issues a newsletter every eight weeks announcing its upcoming walks that focus on bird watching, star gazing, trees, and butterfly counting. For a subscription to *Warblings* or to sign up for a walk, call Renee Davis, the chapter president, ☎ 914-482-5044, or Valerie Freer, ☎ 914-647-5496.

Always held around July 4, the butterfly count in 1999 was the largest since the count began in 1994 – 33 species.

If you don't know the difference between a sparrow and a crow, don't be intimidated about joining a walk. I showed up with a pair of opera glasses and little knowledge of birds. The group of about 15 women and men couldn't have been kinder. They enjoy sharing their enthusiasm, I realized. The leader of this expedition at the Bashakill, Valerie Freer, recognizes birds just from their calls. She had brought along a birding scope that magnifies objects several times and she encouraged everyone to use it. That's the way to bird watch!

The walks are generally two to three hours long, but ours was shortened by rain. In a dry hour we spotted kingfishers, swallows, a bittern, a blue heron, red-tailed hawks, and a gallinule (the red-billed mud hen of Florida). According to Valerie, this bird can be seen only at the Bashakill and nowhere else in the Catskills. "It requires this kind of environment," she says.

Sullivan County

⊚ **TIP**

Bird watching sites get crowded in the spring with bird watching clubs. Unlike my walk in August, in spring there's little foliage and birds are in full plumage and are more visible. A good reason to join Valerie's group: she knows where to go to avoid crowds.

The Eagle Institute

I recently joined the third and last eagle watch of the year sponsored by the **Eagle Institute**. About 80 people of all ages showed up in the rain from New Jersey, Philadelphia, Long Island and Binghamton. The Institute staff monitors the eagles all winter and believed the reservoirs would provide the best sightings. We piled into two school buses and stopped at the Rio and Mongaup Reservoirs, but the inclement weather tried our patience and we left disappointed. The picture changed radically at lunch at Eldred Preserve. An eagle's snowy white head was all that was visible through the picture windows but everyone was satisfied. And when he flew off his perch, diverting our attention from the slide show, the excitement in the room was akin to fans at a football game. We later learned that a pair of eagles comes to Eldred regularly to feed on the trout, much to the dismay of the Eldred staff. But we were rewarded and learned much about our magnificent national emblem.

The mission of the non-profit Eagle Institute, a year-old volunteer organization, is to educate the public so that the bald eagle, which has no natural enemies except man, will be protected. The Institute runs programs at schools in the Catskills and Hudson Valley.

Bill Streeter of the Delaware Valley Raptor Center in Milford, PA cares for birds of prey injured in accidents or shootings that can never be released back to the wild. In a presentation organized by the Eagle Institute at the Haviland Middle School in Hyde Park, Streeter showcased his red-tailed hawk, barred owl and American kestrel (a small falcon). To no one's surprise, the bald eagle, King Frederick, elicited the biggest swoon from the audience of adults and children. Streeter related how man-made poisons like DDT and water pollution practically wiped out the eagle population by 1970. (DDT disrupts eggshell calcification causing falcons, eagles and other raptors to lay eggs with paper-thin shells.) With the banning of the pesticide in 1972 and the passage of the Endangered Species Act a year later, the bald eagle began making a dramatic recovery. But it wasn't until 1997 that a Hudson River nesting pair produced the first eaglet in more than 100 years. No longer endangered, the bald eagle is still listed as threatened in New York State.

Streeter introduced one bird at a time, holding it on his arm and walking around the auditorium so everyone could get a closer look or take a photo (flash photography is okay). Holding a sweet-looking owl named JJ, Streeter explained how some thoughtless person shot the owl and left it to die. Fortunately JJ was saved and has been at the center for 18 years helping educate some 300,000 people.

The Eagle Institute has 15 trained volunteers who monitor viewing locations to report on eagle habits. State officials band and color-code eagle chicks in order to collect data about their survival, age, migratory routes, feeding, nesting and wintering areas. New York State, one of the leaders in helping the bald eagle's recovery, started the program in 1976. One has to wonder, though, if an eagle has seven or eight times the vision of a human, who's really watching whom?

These weekend programs are free and open to the public. The guided habitat field trips are $25 and include lunch. Contact the Eagle Institute at PO Box 182, Barryville, NY 12719, or call its personable president, Lori McKean, at ☎ 914-557-6162/6152 to get on the mailing list.

Sullivan County

Museums, Art & Theater

BLOOMINGBURG DUTCH REFORMED CHURCH
Main Street
Bloomingburg
☎ 914-733-1444; 914-733-1409

At the gateway to the Catskills off Exit 116 from Route 17, this church could easily be the gateway to the beyond. Built in 1820 on the highest hill in town to be closest to heaven, it's situated in an utterly peaceful setting. The church closed in the late 1960s and in 1975 the Bloomingburg Restoration Foundation began restoring it. Listed on the National Register of Historic Places, it now operates as a museum and cultural center, open by appointment. Elsie Hultslander, past president of the Foundation, told me that the curved white and brown pews originally "faced the door so everybody saw you coming in late." In the 1860s, the altar was moved from the front of the church to the rear and the pews were turned around.

The impressive number of events and theater listings for all seasons assures one that the arts are alive and well in the Catskills.

The Foundation sponsors cultural events from April to October and monthly coffeehouse entertainment year-round. A Civil War Encampment is held annually in late August with re-enactments, marches, music and informative lectures from dawn to dusk. There's no admission charge.

Directional Info: Make a right off the ramp past the diner and follow the sign to Bloomingburg. Make a right at the yield sign onto Main Street. Go past the traffic light and look for a sign on right that says, "Catholic Church–Our Lady of Assumption Church." Make a right onto High Street and go around the church. You'll see the white steepled church on the right.

SULLIVAN COUNTY MUSEUM, ART & CULTURAL CENTER
276 Main Street
Hurleyville
☎ 914-434-8044

Hurleyville is a sleepy hamlet with a few antique shops that's virtually shut down in the winter. The only year-round attraction is this three-story Federal-style house that was built in 1912 and served as an elementary school until the 1950s. It's actually in the heart of the Borscht Belt, but reflects the whole county – and beyond. There are permanent and changing exhibits on two floors. A permanent exhibit of the Catskill tanneries features interactive displays explaining the process.

The exhibits give you a real taste of early rural life from the kitchen to industry. I got a kick out of a life-size mom at the ironing board with her gasoline-fired iron. She and baby are surrounded by modern conveniences – a "Detroit jewel" stove, an oven big enough for one loaf of bread, a carpet sweeper called "Our Leader," and a wooden washing machine named "Divine."

The building also houses the **Catskill Arts Society**, which maintains the same hours as the historical society. I attended its first annual Wildlife Exhibit that included an art exhibit. Some of the photographs, paintings and mounted animal sculptures were exquisite. I wasn't alone in my enthusiasm – some guest book comments were "gorgeous," "wonderful," and "a real treat." Founded in 1970, the Society sponsors periodic exhibits of mainly regional artists in all mediums, as well as bus trips, classes, and studio and architectural tours. A monthly newsletter publicizes members' showings and accomplishments. Each summer, the two organizations hold an arts and crafts fair on the lawn and inside the museum. Open Wednesday through Saturday, 10am-4:30pm; Sunday, 1-4:30pm; and Tuesday by appointment. Suggested donation: $2. ☎ 914-436-4227.

Directional Info: From Route 17, take Exit 105B (Route 42N) and travel north to the intersection of Routes 104 and 107. Take 104 into Hurleyville. The museum building is at the edge of town and is easy to miss. It's directly across from Mobile Medic Ambulance Service. The museum is 5½ miles from the Route 17 exit.

DELAWARE VALLEY ART ALLIANCE
41 Main Street
Narrowsburg
☎ 914-252-7576

There are some three dozen cultural groups in Sullivan County.

This is the arts council and funding agency for Sullivan County's artists founded in 1976. It produces theatrical productions at the **Tusten Theatre** on Bridge Street, Narrowsburg, from April to December and also sponsors gallery exhibits year-round at the **Delaware Arts Center**. The exhibits change monthly and each show is juried. This assures high quality work by professional and emerging artists who live part-time or full time in the mid-Hudson, Catskill or Upper Delaware River regions. The gallery is open year-round, Monday through Saturday.

The Alliance sponsors **Jazzfest** on weekends in May and June at the Tusten Theatre and co-sponsors (with the Narrowsburg Chamber of Commerce) **Riverfest**, Narrowsburg's annual summer celebration in July. The **Delaware Valley Opera** performs at the Tusten Theatre and is a traveling musical-education program for children in grades three to eight (☎ 914-252-3136). In addition, the Alliance publishes a 12-page bimonthly *Artsletter* for members, which is available free at public libraries and cultural institutions.

In 1999, the Alliance published a new map and guide of cultural spots in the county for tourists. It also inaugurated the **Narrowsburg International Independent Film Festival**, a four-day event in August that featured seminars on acting and producing independent films, screenings, and panel discussions. Jocelyne and Richard Castellano, residents of Cochecton Center, organized this first-time event. She is an independent film producer; he starred in the *Godfather* movies and most recently appeared in *Analyze This*. Zachary Sklar, co-author with Oliver Stone of *JFK*, was on hand over the four days, along with more than a thousand other film-makers, scriptwriters, producers, directors and film lovers. The mid-week events were well attended and seminars and evening events were sold out each day.

FORESTBURGH PLAYHOUSE & TAVERN
55 Forestburgh Road
Forestburgh
☎ 914-794-1194
www.fbplayhouse.com

From late June to early September, equity actors perform Broadway musicals and comedies here. In 1999, *MASH*'s Loretta Swit returned for a special one-night performance in A.R. Gurney's *Love Letters*, with the income earmarked for upgrading the restrooms. Her sold-out benefit performance of *Shirley Valentine* in 1997 raised enough money to repair the leaking roof.

Tickets for the show are $25.95. The tavern is open every night before the show for cocktails, coffee and desserts. From Thursday to Saturday it has a post-show cabaret with talented young performers, once featured on *Sunday Morning* (on CBS) in a nine-minute segment.

The theater opened in 1947, and in 1998, it re-inaugurated a children's theater. Shows are held Thursday and Saturday at 1:30pm. Tickets are priced at $7 on a non-reserved basis.

SULLIVAN PERFORMING ARTS
Loch Sheldrake
☎ 914-436-9916
www.sullivanperformingarts.org

Sullivan Performing Arts celebrated its 25th anniversary in 1999. SPA is well known for its Summer Festival Series for adults and children, although it sponsors performances throughout the year. Whether you like big band sounds, chamber music, ballet, theater or comedians, there's something for you. Performances are at the Seelig Theater at Sullivan Community College. Tickets are $20 per show.

NUTSHELL ARTS CENTER
Lake Huntington
☎ 914-932-8527

Weekend chamber music concerts are held on the shores of Lake Huntington in July and August. Single ticket price is $18. The center's gallery is open Friday through Sunday. For a schedule, ☎ 914-932-8708.

Shopping

All these stores in Sullivan County are just off Route 17, and the exit numbers are listed in descending order for easier planning.

CANAL TOWNE EMPORIUM
Sullivan Street (Exit 113 off Route 17)
Wurtsboro
☎ 914-888-2100
Open daily, 10am-5pm

Sandwiched between all the antique shops is this old-fashioned country store bursting with gifts, collectibles and handcrafted furniture. Adjacent to it is a Christmas shop.

THE POTAGER
Sullivan Street (Exit 113 off Route 17)
Wurtsboro
☎ 914-888-4086

The mother/daughter team of Pat and Mickey Lanza, owners of the Lanza Country Inn in Shandelee for 17 years, purchased this century-old working church three years ago and converted it into a gift shop, garden center and café (see page 84). Both Pat and Mickey are friendly, lovely women who run the restaurant and have distinguished themselves in related fields. Pat does "creative catering" and Mickey is an award-winning garden writer. In 1999, the Garden Writers Association of America honored her with the Quill & Trowel award for her *Lasagna Gardening*, published by Rodale Press. Only her second book, it went into its second printing just four months after publication.

Be sure to visit the lovely gift shop upstairs, especially for the gardener in your life. Stop in the garden, Pat's pride and joy, to watch her at work. While outside, look up and you might just see an eagle soaring or a glider flying by from Wurtsboro Airport.

The Potager gift shop, café and garden.

The Potager is open for lunch daily, except Tuesday, April to December. The garden opens in May. Winter hours are erratic so call first.

O'TOOLE'S HARLEY DAVIDSON
Sullivan Street (Exit 113 off Route 17)
Wurtsboro
☎ 914-888-2426

Popular with the motorcycle set, O'Toole's sells cycle parts, accessories and clothing, and also customizes bikes.

GALLERY OF THE LAKES

Attention, Mickey Mouse fans! Check out Gallery of the Lakes.

63 Old Route 17
Rock Hill
☎ 914-796-3505; 800-692-3087
Open 11am-5pm; closed Monday

Gallery of the Lakes is a fun place for both kids and adults. It's a leading Disney franchise with several limited edition items, Swarovski crystal, Armani sculptures and a Pooh corner. Summer weekends feature music and Disney characters and two Disney events are scheduled in the fall. Prices range from $8 trinkets to $17,900 for the centerpiece mixed-media metal eagle with the five-foot wing span.

Directional Info: From Route 17, take Exit 110; turn right and proceed .7 mile.

★ **WHAT'S IN A NAME?**

Wurtsboro was named in honor of Maurice Wurts of the D&H Canal Co., who had a mercantile business here for a short period in 1828. He and his brother William came up with the idea of building a canal to run through a natural gap in the Shawangunk & Catskill Mountains.

APOLLO PLAZA
East Broadway
Monticello
☎ 914-794-2010
Opens daily at 10am

Though a bit dreary, this strip mall has 30 outlet stores offering discounts up to 70%. There are also some retailers, including Sears. The mall's food court is limited to two vendors selling sandwiches, soup, bagels and pizza. Mostly Books, Sullivan County's only bookstore, closed it doors in January 2000. Former employees hope to open a new bookstore in Monticello or Liberty.

Directional Info: From Route 17, take Exit 106 westbound, or Exit 107 eastbound.

Sullivan County

CHOO CHOO CHARLIE'S
199 S. Main Street
Liberty
☎ 914-292-4826

Fans of miniature trains will want to make an appointment with Charlie, a furniture dealer whose passion for antique, electric and toy trains turned into a side business. "I get to play with my toys and make it a business," he says. One section of Choo Choo Charlie's is reserved for his five "O" gauge electric trains and visitors of all ages enjoy watching them choo-chooing in unison. He says his hands-on layout is for everyone to play with. Charlie also has wind-up trains that go around the track, which he calls the poor kid's Lionel. "I've got more toys than some of the kids." A train set is $600-$800 but a starting set of Lionel less than $150. He also sells railroad hats and other hard-to-find memorabilia.

MEMORIES
Located between Exits 98 and 97 off Route 17
Parksville
☎ 914-292-4270; 800-222-8463
http://memories-antiques.com

By now you've seen numerous highway signs for this store, which surely wins the prize for billboard advertising. Imagine 25,000 objects under one roof! This Parksville emporium has five inviting showrooms packed with nostalgic items, from 25¢ baseball cards to a 1926 roadster for $17,500. You could easily spend hours here.

Napanoch

Near the intersection of Routes 55W and 209 is the turn-off for Napanoch, whose claim to fame is three prisons. (There's no sign for the village – look for

Church Street and turn right at the end.) **Victorian Country Store** is new and lives up to its name with bone china, lace sachets, Boyds Bears, soaps and the like. Holidays bring out the Christmas decorations and Valentine cards. Open Thursday through Sunday, year-round. ☎ 914-647-1492.

Napanoch Auction Service, which can seat 200, has been holding auctions every Saturday night since the early 1970s. "Trader Vic" Zolinsky is best described as a character with a quirky sense of humor. His motto is "we sell everything from chicken soup to bouillabaisse." "Three weeks ago we sold a coffin for $100," he says, but so far no one has bid on the cremated swans. Viewing is at 4:30pm with the auction at 6:30pm. Located around the corner from Ron's Sale on Huguenot Street. ☎ 914-647-6071.

Glen Wild

Glen Wild Auction Sales also holds auctions on Saturday nights. Located on Glen Wild Rd. ☎ 914-436-7221.

Stop at **Jan's Flower & Gift Shop**, across from the synagogue. Besides potted plants are small gift items such as candles and plaques. Open daily, 9am-6pm, April through August. ☎ 914-436-6455.

Livingston Manor

Worth a visit on Main Street in Livingston Manor is the **Wildlife Gift Shop** at Water Wheel Junction. Some of the items carried are field guides, fishing and home building guides, birdhouses, miniature lighthouses, clothing, chimes, prints and trout gifts. There's also a separate holiday shop. Owner Shirley

Fulton calls herself "the wacky blonde" and is the force behind the town's annual strawberry festival in early July. Open daily year-round. ☎ 914-439-3938.

Will Hardware is more than its name suggests due to the efforts of owner John Checchia. He claims it's the oldest continuously run hardware store in the state serving up old-fashioned service. He plays music, sells cat and dog food and encourages visitors from the city to relocate to the Catskills. ☎ 914-439-4480.

Fishermen should head for **Fur, Fin & Feather Sport Shop** on DeBruce Road. Open daily, it's the fly-fisher's source on the Willowemoc, and one of three gun dealers in town. ☎ 914-439-4476.

 # Festivals & Events

May through mid-October is a busy time in the Catskills. Annual events occupy every weekend giving tourists a wide choice depending on their interests. Always call to confirm the times and specifics. Here are some goings-on in Sullivan County.

May

Kite Festival, hosted by Loch Sheldrake at the Sullivan County Community College. Free admission, free kites to first 200 kids and free ice cream for as long as it lasts. ☎ 914-794-3000, ext. 5010; 800-882-2287.

Oldies Car Show, Apollo Plaza, Monticello. ☎ 914-794-7799 or 914-794-3000, ext. 5010.

June

Fishing Derby and Festival, Livingston Manor. ☎ 914-439-3938.

July

Fourth of July celebrations are held in Narrowsburg at Fireman's Field and in Liberty. ☎ 914-252-3306.

Strawberry Festival, Livingston Manor. Features a Teddy Bear Stroller Parade, chicken barbeque, strawberry shortcake and ice cream. ☎ 914-439-3938.

Outdoor Art Show, Barryville. ☎ 914-557-8856.

Walnut Mountain Classic Mountain Bike Race, Pearson Park on Walnut Mountain. ☎ 914-292-7690.

Riverfest (see story below), Narrowsburg. ☎ 914-252-7576.

Riverfest

One young man in Narrowsburg lamented that Sullivan County sometimes forgets the river town that's closer to Pennsylvania than any other place. Yet somehow visitors find this hidden gem with its picturesque views and cultural happenings.

The annual **Riverfest** brings folks out in droves despite the sometimes stifling hot temperatures. "It's always beastly hot," said a woman who's attended every festival. The stores lining Main Street are open for pedestrians and the one eatery on the street, **Chatterbox Café**, gets jammed. The **Na-**

Sullivan County

tional Park Service sells books on birds, insects, wildflowers and offers canoeing for adults and kids. The store is open Friday through Sunday, 9:30am-4:30pm, June through October.

Billed as a music, arts and environmental festival celebrating the wonders of the Delaware River, the event features the wares of local merchants and independent vendors, live music, displays and family fun. Nearby on Main Street is the bald eagle observation deck that overlooks the river and the Big Eddy – water moving against the current in a circular motion. I'm told the water is actually calmer in an eddy, which is why early settlers built and docked their rafts there for the night. One morning when I was here, a couple pointed to a formation of bald eagles. It was a bonus I never expected – in July no less!

◎ TIP

Parking for Riverfest is plentiful. If necessary, cross the Narrowsburg Bridge into Pennsylvania and walk the short distance back to Main Street. The bridge passes over the narrowest section of the Delaware, hence the name.

Directional Info to Riverfest: From the Thruway, take Exit 16 to Route 17W. Exit 121W to 84W (toward Port Jervis); take to Exit 1 and follow 6W through Port Jervis onto Route 97. At the blinker, bear left into Narrowsburg.

August

Jeffersonville Jamboree, Lion's Field, Jeffersonville. Features music, arts, food, exhibits, entertainment and a parade at noon. ☎ 800-461-5333.

For events in Wurtsboro, check online at www.wbot.org.

Little World's Fair, Grahamsville. Country fair with entertainment, arts, crafts and food. ☎ 914-985-2500/7666/2525.

Shandelee Music Festival, Livingston Manor. Features a series of seven concerts. ☎ 914-439-3277.

Catskills Conference (see page 47) offers a wonderful way to learn the history of the Catskills and recollect old memories from yesteryear. For information, contact The Catskills Institute, c/o Phil Brown, Dept. of Sociology, Brown University, Box 1916, Providence, RI 02912, ☎ 401-863-2367, www.brown.edu/Research/Catskills_ Institute.

September

Von Steuben Day Parade, Fireman's Field, Yulan. Features unique floats. ☎ 914-557-8600.

October

Dark Forest, Glen Spey. Held weekends throughout the month. Haunted walking trails and hayride. ☎ 800-881-FEAR.

Oktoberfest & Crafts Fair, Narrowsburg. German music festival featuring food, Oompah music, dancing, games, rides. $4 admission. ☎ 914-252-3345.

Fall Garden Harvest Market, Woodstock festival site off Route 17B, Bethel. Family fun fest. Farmers

Sullivan County

offer fall bounty; hayrides, petting zoo, entertainment, arts and crafts. Every Sunday, late September through mid-October, 11:30am-3pm. ☎ 800-882-CATS; 914-794-3000, ext. 5010.

Giant Pumpkin Party and Parade, Route 55, Grahamsville Fairgrounds. Children's games, pony rides, and hay- and horse-drawn rides, Old MacDonald Farm and Petting Zoo, obstacle course, haunted house, parade, carnival games, contests, live music. ☎ 914-985-7233/2429.

Sullivan County A to Z

Animal Hospitals

Jeffersonville Animal Hospital, ☎ 914-482-5500. **Animal Hospital of Sullivan County**, 1070 Old Route 17, Ferndale, ☎ 914-292-6711.

Banks

The First National Bank of Jeffersonville is well represented in the county. Besides the main office on Main Street in Jeffersonville (☎ 914-482-4000), it has branches in Eldred, Route 55 (☎ 914-557-8513); Liberty, Church Street and Darby Lane (☎ 914-292-6300); Loch Sheldrake, Route 52 (☎ 914-434-1180); Monticello, Route 42S and Forestburgh Road (☎ 914-791-4000); Livingston Manor (☎ 914-439-8123); Narrowsburg (☎ 914-252-6510); and Callicoon (☎ 914-887-4866). The latter three are located at Peck's Markets Banking Centers. All branches have 24-hour ATMs and drive-up hours Monday through Friday. www.jeffbank.com.

Community Bank of Sullivan County has locations on Route 42 in Monticello (☎ 914-794-BANK) and Route 52E in the Colonial Square Shopping Center in Liberty (☎ 914-292-CBSC); www.scsmag.com/cbsc.htm.

Fleet Bank is in Wurtsboro at 155 Sullivan Street (☎ 800-228-1281); and at 93 Main Street in Narrowsburg (☎ 800-228-1281).

Emergency Services

Catskill Emergency Services, daily at ☎ 914-794-5691.

Health Clubs

The Fitness Source, 132 Sullivan Street, Wurtsboro, has lots of workout equipment, including cardiovascular machines, aerobic classes, locker rooms and a tanning salon. Opened two years ago by the young couple Blair and Christine Wiseman, the modern wood-paneled club offers one-month to one-year memberships, as well as daily rates. ☎ 914-888-2564.

Liquor Stores

Having a party? Be aware that under New York state law liquor stores are prohibited from opening on Sunday. Most are open Monday through Saturday.

Sullivan County

Four Corners, Eldred, ☎ 914-557-8679. **Sports Bar & Liquor Store**, Yulan-Barryville Road, Barryville, ☎ 914-557-6158. **Main Street Liquors** (open Monday-Saturday), Narrowsburg, ☎ 914-252-3235. **Wurtsboro Liquor Store**, Wurtsboro ☎ 914-888-2712.

Medical Facilities

Community General Hospital is the only hospital in Sullivan County. It has divisions in Harris (☎ 914-794-3300) and Callicoon (☎ 914-887-5530). For a physician referral, ☎ 800-247-6414. For an appointment at one of the hospital's outreach centers in Mamakating, Rockland or Woodridge, ☎ 914-794-3300.

Movies

The following theaters play first-run movies: **Monticello Quad Cinema**, Jamesway Mall, Route 42, Monticello. Open daily, year-round. ☎ 914-794-2600.

Callicoon Theater, Callicoon. Open year-round. Shows both popular and art films in its 400-seat theater. ☎ 914-887-4460.

Hippodrome, Route 52, Loch Sheldrake. Open daily, May through September with two shows nightly; tickets are $2.50. ☎ 914-434-3888.

Liberty Tri-Cinema, 31 S. Main Street, Liberty. Open seasonally; tickets are $6. ☎ 914-292-3000.

Pharmacies

Gusar's Pharmacy, 290 Broadway, Monticello, ☎ 914-794-5757. **Peter's Pharmacy**, Route 97 and Kirk Road, Narrowsburg, ☎ 914-252-3003.

Medicine Shoppe, Route 52E, Colonial Square Mall, Liberty, ☎ 914-292-8200. **Thompson's Pharmacy**, 45 N. Main Street, Liberty, ☎ 914-292-4131.

Religious Services

CATHOLIC – **St. Anthony's Roman Catholic Church**, Yulan, ☎ 914-557-8512. **St. Volodymyr Ukranian Catholic Church**, Glen Spey.

CONGREGATIONAL – **Eldred Congregational Church**, Proctor Road, Eldred, ☎ 914-557-6216. The church was built in 1835. Adjoining cemetery includes graves of Confederate soldiers and some who fell in the Battle of Minisink.

JEWISH – Of the 20 Sullivan County synagogues built between the turn of the century and World War II, 15 remain. Some are closed for services while others are active.

Ahavath Israel, 39 Chestnut Street, Liberty, ☎ 914-292-8843. **Ohave Sholom**, Woodridge, open year-round, ☎ 914-434-7266. **Congregation Beth Sinai**, Kauneongo Lake, summer only, ☎ 914-583-7374. **Temple Sholom**, Port Jervis and Dillon Rd., Monticello, ☎ 914-794-8731. **Young Israel of Vacation Village**, Cty. Rd. 104, Loch Sheldrake, open July through September, ☎ 914-436-8359.

The following synagogues were recently listed on the National Register of Historic Places: **Agudas**

Sullivan County

Achim, Livingston Manor; **B'nai Israel**, Woodbourne; **Anshei Glen Wild**, Glen Wild; **Chevra Ahavath Zion**, Monticello; **Tifereth Israel Anshei** (a.k.a. Landfield Avenue Synagogue), 18 Landfield Ave., Monticello, ☎ 914-794-8470; **The Jewish Community Center of White Sulphur Springs**; and **Bikur Cholim B'nai Yisroel** in Swan Lake.

METHODIST – Pond Eddy Methodist Church, Berme-Church Road (off Route 97), Pond Eddy, ☎ 914-858-2607. **Barryville Methodist Church**, 28 River Road, Barryville, ☎ 914-557-6216. **Eldred Methodist Church**, Eldred Road, Yulan, ☎ 914-557-6216. **Liberty Free Methodist Church**, Route 52W, Liberty (sometimes holds concerts and interdenominational worship services), ☎ 914-439-5025.

Ulster County

Overview

The Hudson River is like old October and tawny Indians in their camping places long ago; it is like long pipes and old tobacco; it is like cool depths and opulence; it is like the shimmer of liquid green on summer days.
– Of Time and the River, Thomas Wolfe

Indians once occupied the Delaware River in Sullivan County and the Esopus Creek in Ulster County. Europeans did not arrive in Ulster County until the mid-1600s. Kingston, along with New York City and Albany, was one of the three Hudson River forts set up by the United New Netherland Company in 1614. Ulster was also among the 12 original counties of the province of New York. In 1683, the county was named for the younger brother of King Charles of England, who had the Irish title of the Duke of Ulster. The county's early settlers were mostly from Holland, who brought with them their wise laws of government.

Another important group was the Huguenots – so it's no surprise that county historians have found that the majority of names most prominent in Ulster's history are of Dutch and Huguenot origin.

One of the many books on local history pointed out that, of all the counties bordering the Hudson, Ulster had the most frontier hardships: Indian warfare at Wilwyck (1659-1663); the burning of New Dorp (Hurley) in 1663; and the British raid on Kingston in 1777, to name a few.

Happily that's all in the past. Ulster is a picturesque place with its Hudson River towns and shiny white Shawangunk ridges and glacial lakes. The "Gunks" stretch from the New York/New Jersey border northeastward to the Hudson River Valley below Kingston. The rocky cliffs of translucent quartz conglomerate are geologically intriguing to look at, climb or trail walk.

Furthermore, nearly half of Ulster County's 1,126 square miles lies within the Catskill Forest Preserve, which was created to protect the area's water resources, as well as provide the public with outdoor recreational opportunities.

Treasure Hunt

According to one writer, $100 million in gold is buried somewhere in the Catskills. During WWII, a professor in Germany, who was frightened of the Nazis, stole gold from The Medieval Museum in Dresden, with the help of its curator. To prevent capture, they melted the gold and recast it into auto parts destined for New York. These parts were shipped upstate, where the German professor hid them somewhere in the mountains near Kingston. He never revealed their location. Will you be the one to find the treasure?

★ DID YOU KNOW?

Ulster County has more artists per capita than anywhere else in the state, declares Jeffy Harrington of the Ulster Arts Alliance. "This abundance distinguishes our area from virtually any other area in the country," he said.

Kingston & Environs

 History

This chapter fittingly begins with Kingston, the county seat and birthplace of Ulster County about 130 years before Sullivan County. In 1652-53, the Dutch settled in the **Rondout Kill** (now part of the city of Kingston), the third-oldest settlement in the state after Albany and New York City. Governor Peter Stuyvesant called the fort Wiltwyck, meaning "savage refuge," or wild place. Could he have predicted that it would live up to its name?

In contrast with the peaceful settlement of New Paltz, Kingston began with a skirmish and a stockade. It occurred around the time the English wrestled control of New Netherlands (later New York) from the Dutch. When the colonists began expanding their territory war broke out in 1658 with the local Esopus Indians. Sixteen families appealed to Governor Stuyvesant for protection. As the Dutch governor of New York until ousted by the British in 1664, Stuyvesant promptly ordered a stockade built to shelter the settlers, and 70 of them moved homes and barns inside the 14-foot-high wooden wall. Later, English Governor Francis Lovelace renamed the city after Kingston L'Isle, his family seat in England.

⊚ TIP

For a virtual tour of historic Kingston, visit its joint Web site with the National Register of Historic Places at www.cr.nps.gov/nr/travel/kingston.

By 1700 the stockade was gone. During the Revolutionary War, Kingston was declared the state capital, where the Senate met for the first time. The English retaliated by burning the town in 1777. Fortunately, the old Dutch houses were so stoutly put together that there was relatively little damage. The Senate House (see page 157) roof was partially destroyed. The 21 Dutch-style stone buildings, several dating prior to 1700, are now used as private residences, offices, galleries, boutiques and restaurants.

Stockade District

Twenty-one of Kingston's most important buildings are within this eight-block area called the **Stockade District**. These include the Ulster County Courthouse, where George Clinton took his oath as first governor of New York State and John Jay as its first

Chief Justice. The courthouse is also where former slave Sojourner Truth won her son's freedom from slavery in Alabama. The only pre-Revolutionary stone house not burned in 1777 is the Van Steenburgh House. According to local legend, the British officer in charge was a friend of the owner's daughter, so the building was saved.

Hurley

During colonial days, Hurley was home to many industries. There was a woolen mill, distillery, brewery, tannery, brickyard, blacksmith shops, and Hurley cows. The cows supplied milk for pot cheese in such quantities that the cheese became synonymous with Hurley; it was even said to have "pot cheese mines." Kingston citizens called Hurleyites "pot-cheeses" and sang the jingle: "Some come from Hurley, some from the Rhine; Some pop fresh from a Pot Cheese Mine."

A century later the Township of Hurley was less fortunate. In 1907 eight of its villages were flooded to make way for the 12-mile-long Ashokan Reservoir.

Ulster County

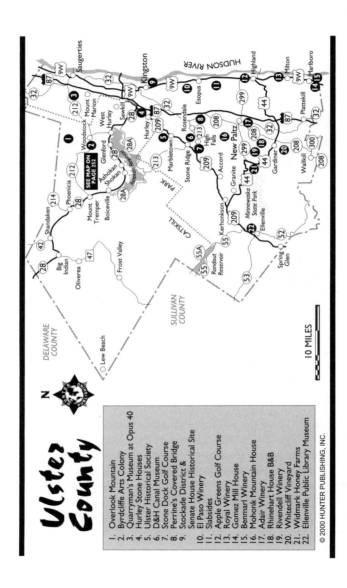

Ulster County

1. Overlook Mountain
2. Byrdcliffe Arts Colony
3. Quarryman's Museum at Opus 40
4. Hurley Stone Houses
5. Ulster Historical Society
6. D&H Canal Museum
7. Stone Dock Golf Course
8. Perrine's Covered Bridge
9. Stockade District &
   Senate House Historical Site
10. El Paso Winery
11. Slabsides
12. Apple Greens Golf Course
13. Royal Winery
14. Gomez Mill House
15. Benmarl Winery
16. Mohonk Mountain House
17. Adair Winery
18. Rhinehart House B&B
19. Rivendell Winery
20. Whitecliff Vineyard
21. Widmark Honey Farms
22. Ellenville Public Library Museum

© 2000 HUNTER PUBLISHING, INC.

10 MILES

Best Places to Stay

The price scale for lodging can be found on page 20.

Inns/B&Bs

All saints can do miracles, but few of them can keep a hotel.

— Mark Twain

BLACK LION MANSION
124 West Chestnut Street
Kingston
☎ 914-338-0410
Gourmet breakfasts
Moderate

Ulster County

This B&B had been condemned when Patricia Pillsworth and her husband Michael Waskew bought it in 1995, a century after it was built. The couple spent three years restoring it to elegance, adding all new furnishings. Shrubs that had obscured the view of the Hudson from the terrace were cleared. The exterior of the 10,000-square-foot mansion on Kingston's highest hill resembles a miniature Gothic castle. It has a slightly haunted feel – especially if you arrive at night as we did. Inside it's palatial yet comfortable. The eight opulent rooms are uniquely decorated and spacious, some with a fireplace or Jacuzzi. If you arrive late, look for the two black lions atop stone piers and ring the bell.

At the Black Lion Mansion, pets are welcome to join the hosts' six cats and two dogs.

Recommended Motels

The **Holiday Inn** at 503 Washington Avenue is AAA-approved; ☎ 914-338-0400.

Best Places to Eat

The price scale for restaurants can be found on page 21.

Casual Dining

HOFFMAN HOUSE TAVERN
94 N. Front Street (Stockade District)
Kingston
☎ 914-338-2626
Moderate

The building that houses the Hoffman House was constructed before 1679, and its original structure is largely intact. The walls are unusually thick (it was once a fort) and some of the floor planks are more than 15 inches wide. As far as the food goes, the onion soup served in a crock with half a sandwich and potato chips was a delicious and filling lunch ($8.35 with coffee).

CROSSROADS
38 Broadway (Rondout Section)
Kingston
☎ 914-340-0151
Moderate

You'll find this wonderful restaurant near the Hudson River in the Rondout section. The service and food are sublime, especially the key lime pie. Jazz piano is played on weekends.

Local Lore

On a grisly note, the Hoffman House was once the scene of a massacre. However, a livelier recollection was that during the Revolution a daughter of the Hoffman family was sitting on the stoop while Washington and his young officers rode past the house. Their glances were too much for the maiden who fled indoors, but not before displaying a well-turned ankle. "My God, what an ankle!" the commander-in-chief was said to exclaim.

Sunup to Sundown

Sightseeing

Senate House Tour

Begin your visit to Kingston with a guided tour of the **Senate House State Historic House**. Although the 1676 limestone building has been burned twice and has undergone massive renovation, it still contains many authentic pieces from our history. These include the wood floor (1778) of the room in which the state constitution was written. The writers were holed up here for one month when Kingston was the capital. It was here that these elected representatives of rebellious New Yorkers adopted a new state government comprising of a senate, assembly, governor and judiciary that still exists today. John Jay did most of his writing in the Senate House. No, George Washington didn't sleep here. But he did hold a Masonic Lodge meeting in this historic room.

★ DID YOU KNOW?

Built in 1676, the Senate House is the oldest public building in America. The intersection of Crown and John streets is the only one in the country where 18th-century stone houses stand on all four corners.

The Senate House was originally called the Abraham Van Gaasbeek House for the prosperous merchant-trader who lived there during that historic time in 1777. Augustus Schoonmaker was the last owner. Lisa our guide told us that two months before our visit, a 94-year-old visitor announced that she was Schoonmaker's granddaughter. "We were skeptical," says Lisa, "but sure enough she was. She had the deed to the house when her grandfather sold it to New York State for $8,000 in 1887."

Local Lore

Aaron Burr is said to have lived in or visited the Senate House on one or more occasions. Some profess to have heard his ghost on summer evenings playing the violin softly in one of the upper rooms.

Tours of the Senate House are every half-hour, mid-April through October, Wednesday-Sunday (and certain holidays) until 5pm, or by appointment. Admission is $3. The tour begins at the museum building, repository of the country's largest collection of John Vanderlyn paintings, drawings and papers. (Born in Kingston in 1775, Vanderlyn's enormous *Landing of Columbus* is in the Capitol Rotunda in Washington, DC, ☎ 914-338-2786.) To obtain a self-guided walking tour map of the area, ☎ 800-331-1518 or 914-339-0720.

Directional Info: From the Thruway, take Exit 19 and follow historic markers to the site.

Stone Houses & Tours

First, a word about stone houses. The largest number of intact stone houses in America – some built 300 years ago – is found in the Hudson Valley. Descendants of the original builders may still occupy some of them. There are more than 100 early stone houses in Ulster County, mainly in Kingston, Hurley and New Paltz.

Stone was the main building material used throughout the county even after the Revolution. What distinguishes Ulster County stone houses from those in other New York State counties is their uniformity in architectural design and material. The reason has been attributed to the topography of the region – settlers were isolated by mountain ranges so new ideas did not penetrate. Also, farms remained in one family for generations.

All the communities offer guided tours: Hurley has "Stone House Day" on the second Saturday of July, and New Paltz hosts their version everyday except Monday, May through October.

Ulster County

While in Kingston, be sure to visit the other historic district along the Rondout.

Hurley Stone Houses

Unlike New Paltz where the stone houses are vacant and unlike Kingston where the stone houses are mainly occupied by businesses, those in **Hurley**, a National Historic Landmark, are private residences. Many are inhabited by descendants of the original settlers. Ten of these 27 historic houses are open to the public only once a year – the second Saturday in July. ☎ 914-338-1661.

◎ TIP

History-minded *flâneurs* will find the brochure, *Walk or Drive Around Historic Hurley* a godsend.

Hurley is flecked with pretty houses. If you pass through on a weekend, spring through fall, stop in the museum and talk to Rebecca Wilson or other knowledgeable natives of the area manning the museum. Rebecca told us that the Van Deusen house (1723) two doors down and occupied, served as the temporary capital of New York State during the Revolution after the burning of Kingston. She also related the continuing debate between Hurley and New Paltz regarding which one has the oldest stone houses. To her knowledge, the houses in New Paltz are older, while Hurley was settled first.

Walking Tours

Self-guided walking tours are popular in Kingston's Stockade District (see page 152), where some of the 39 historic stone houses and official buildings date to the 1600s. (Ulster County is rich in old stone houses of thoroughly Dutch origin, especially here and in New Paltz.) The district is also home to several fine stores on Wall Street.

★ **FAMOUS FACES**

Although the Hurley Mountain Inn is not made of stone, its bar and a local farm were featured in the movie *Tootsie*. The tavern has been expanded and renovated since, but photos of Dustin Hoffman and other stars in front of the inn can still be seen on the wall near the restrooms.

Boat Rides

Three different boat rides leave from Kingston's waterfront. A 45-minute tour includes admission to the **Rondout Lighthouse** and the **Hudson River Maritime Museum**. Cost is $7 for adults, $5 for children and seniors, free under age five. ☎ 914-338-0071. The maritime museum also sponsors exhibits, lectures, workshops and festivals for adults and children, April through December. ☎ 914-338-0071. Also running cruises are **Rip Van Winkle**, ☎ 914-255-6515, and **Teal**, ☎ 914-679-8205.

Ulster County

 **Theater**

BROADWAY THEATER
AT ULSTER PERFORMING ARTS CENTER
601 Broadway
Kingston
☎ 914-339-6088; 914-331-1613

UPAC's semi-professional troupe presents dramas and musicals at prices ranging from $15 to $29 (winter holiday specials are less).

Theatergoers are reminded to visit the one-of-a-kind performing arts gift shop and Café Broadway for gourmet coffee, pastry or a light lunch before or after the theater.

NEW YORK CONSERVATORY FOR THE ARTS
120 Schildknecht Road
Hurley
☎ 914-339-4340

School for theater arts. On-going performances by students, both adults and children, are held on site. Tickets are $12.50. Reservations recommended.

 **Shopping**

ANYONE CAN WHISTLE
323 Wall Street
Kingston
☎ 914-331-7728

Stop in here and feel like a kid again. All ages are invited to make music. Drop 25¢ in the player piano or purchase a music-making item for yourself – CDs, jack-in-the-box, fun whistles, jingle bands, harmonicas, or Woodstock wind chimes. A table with music makers from around the world describes the store's philosophy: "Anyone Can Whistle tries to bring the world together through rhythm."

MARCUSE
319 Wall Street
Kingston
☎ 914-339-6468

This store is an award-winning craft gallery that carries handmade decorative items such as ceramics, scarves, blown glass, jewelry and cards. A transplant from lower Manhattan where she ran a photographic gallery, Marcuse Pfeifer calls her shop "a little bit of Soho moved up river." Items range from $5 to $4,000.

> ⊚ **TIP**
>
> A free antiques brochure lists 61 dealers, and a map pinpoints the location of each. To get the most out of your antiquing adventure, pick up a copy of *Ulster County Antiques* at any area antique store or write to Antiques Dealers Association of Ulster County, Box 246, Hurley, NY 12443.

CRAFTS PEOPLE
262 Spillway Road
West Hurley
☎ 914-331-3859
Open daily, year-round, 10:30am-6pm

This is a more commercial establishment of four buildings representing 500 craftspeople from all over the country. Among the thousands of items are pot-

Ulster County

tery, clothing, furniture, chimes, baskets, jewelry, handcrafted sterling silver tableware, picture frames, plants and Christmas ornaments. Prices range from $3 earrings to a $1,200 handmade table. Located in a woodsy setting between Woodstock and Kingston, it has outdoor chairs and tables for relaxing after shopping.

Directional Info: Ten minutes from Thruway Exit 19 (Kingston). Take Route 28W (toward Woodstock/ Pine Hill) for five miles. At West Hurley traffic light (BP station), turn left onto Basin Road. Proceed .7 mile. At Reservoir Inn, turn right and proceed one mile. Turn right onto Route 28A and go one mile. Turn left onto Spillway Road. Crafts People is just over a mile on the right.

In & Around New Paltz

New Paltz (www.newpaltz.org) is for the traveler who enjoys the convenience of an urban environment, a touch of the historical, and the challenge and beauty of the wilderness. It was founded by French Huguenots in 1678, and their surviving stone houses lie along one of the oldest streets in America. Incorporated in 1887, the village has a population of 5,257 and is located 97 miles due north of Manhattan at the base of the Shawangunk Mountains.

Best Places to Stay

The price scale for lodging can be found on page 20.

Hotels & Resorts

MOHONK MOUNTAIN HOUSE
Lake Mohonk
New Paltz
☎ 914-255-1000; 800-772-6646
www.mohonk.com
Open year-round
Inquire about "Children Stay Free" weekends
Expensive

Mohonk is the perfect choice for an elegant, Old World-style weekend getaway. Afternoon tea and cookies are a tradition. At dinner, jackets are required, although that's the only meal when formality reigns. The culinary staff has won several blue ribbons at the Food Show at the Javits Center in New York City, which is sponsored by the Societé Culinaire Philanthropique.

The décor in the 261 rooms is Victorian (all with fireplace and balcony) or traditional. If you can afford it, the $540 traditional suite for two has dual exposures – of Lake Mohonk and the distant Catskills. The bright and cheery suite features a private entrance, skylight, antique headboard and marble commode.

The resort also offers footpaths, trails, carriage roads, groomed ski trails, snowshoeing, greenhouse, nine-hole golf course, putting green, tennis, riding stables, barn museum (one of the largest barns in the Northeast, it houses century-old items, many still in

Ulster County

The majestic Mohonk Mountain House.
(Ruth Smiley, courtesy of Mohonk Mountain House)

working order), carriage rides, croquet, ice skating, exercise classes, children's activities, nightly entertainment. And yes, it has shampoo. Each weekend features a theme program, a tradition started at the turn of the century. House guests are invited to participate in the open sessions, which range from chocolate and conversation to birding.

Castle In the Sky

Perched imperiously on a mountaintop, Mohonk's mismatched, turreted buildings could be described as either an eyesore or a fairy-tale castle. An essayist writing in *Resorts of the Catskills* described it perfectly: "Wood meets stone, shingle shifts to tile, browns and grays give way to green and reds – creating either a disturbing eclecticism or an enchantingly varied romantic fantasy, depending on the eye of the beholder."

For sure, I couldn't stop gawking at this lumbering landmark surrounded by sensational scenery and 128 summerhouses (gazebos) only two hours from home. It was a reaction similar to that of naturalist John Burroughs, who wrote this diary notation following a visit in 1893: "Am impressed afresh each time I go to Mohonk with its unique beauty, nothing else like it in the whole country."

Four US presidents have visited Mohonk. More recently, The Road to Wellville, *starring Anthony Hopkins, was filmed here.*

I've never met anyone who didn't love Mohonk – the National Historic Landmark perched above 2,200 acres in the Shawangunks adjoining 63,000 acres of Mohonk Preserve. Fortunately, this magnificence is not restricted to the affluent. The hotel grounds are open to day-trippers (myself included) who have had some of the best times scrambling up its rocks, shimmying through crevices and hiking its paths. Those were the days when admission was only the parking fee of $11. But something this good had to catch on, and still, $9 per person (the current admission rate) is not extreme and is worth every cent.

In season a van transports visitors from the parking lot up the mountain to the hotel. Out of season you're on your own and you'd better be in good shape to climb more than two miles upward!

While the resort is geared to the outdoors – the modest gym and game room are buried in the basement – many people lounge on rockers on the vast veranda gazing out at the crystal-clear lake and majestic rock formations.

In the winter, guests cozy up to a roaring fire, and in summer swimmers and small boats float lazily along as in a Seurat painting. Albert Smiley, who, along with his twin brother, Alfred, founded Mo-

Ulster County

honk, planned it that way: "I have treated this property as a landscape artist does his canvas, only my canvas covers seven square miles." Mohonk's award-winning gardens are testament to his vision. The twins' half-brother Daniel was a naturalist, whose 13,000 natural history observation cards and research papers are the basis of Mohonk Preserve's Daniel Smiley Research Center. (For more on Mohonk Preserve, see page 200.)

Mohonk Mountain House History

Quakers Alfred and Albert Smiley, identical twin brothers, founded Mohonk. Alfred, a Poughkeepsie farmer, discovered the region on an outing with family and friends in 1869. The Smileys purchased 280 acres with an eye to creating an unspoiled wilderness retreat. The original 10-room inn and tavern on the lake was transformed into a rambling seven-story hotel. Except for the dining room extension, the last building was completed in 1902, a year before Alfred's death.

Sky Top Tower is Mohonk's "lighthouse" in the sense that it can be seen for miles. Perched at the topmost crest of the Shawangunk Mountains, it's reachable by foot or horse-drawn carriage. The stone tower was completed in 1923 as a memorial to Albert Smiley.

Mohonk is one of the great surviving Victorian resorts, and no visit to the Catskills is complete without at least a day trip. Day passes are available at the gatehouse. (Arrive early as only a limited number of passes are issued.) First-timers and others who want access to the hotel can make a reservation for lunch (a hot and cold buffet) in the large, airy dining room. The all-inclusive fee is then $26 weekdays and $29 weekends.

Directional Info: Take Route 299 west from New Paltz. After crossing the Wallkill Bridge, turn right onto Springtown Road and follow signs to Mohonk.

WILLIAMS LAKE
Off Binnewater Road
Rosendale
☎ 914-658-3101; 800-382-3818
www.willylake.com
Inexpensive

A lot of people in the Catskills – residents and guests alike – oppose change. A tranquil resort like Williams Lake (capacity 120) appeals to many because it successfully melds past and present. The old-fashioned sauna at the lake has been left untouched. It's not due to negligence but to the local "polar bears" who swim there all winter and to the summer beach club members who prefer it that way. An elderly guest told us that the sauna looks the same as it did 50 years ago when she stayed at Williams Lake. "A lot of people don't know this place is here," she said. "That's why it's not spoiled."

As to the new, the 700-acre resort abounds with water coolers for the newest generation. With no swimming pool, fitness club or shops (only a game room and cocktail lounge), it appeals to both outdoor types and couch potatoes. There are outdoor tennis courts and wide, marked hiking trails (for walking and cross-country skiing) that lead to man-made caves, kilns, smokestacks and railroad trestle ruins from the age of the Rosendale cement industry. The largest of the caves, which is along the Perfume trail, is accessible but creepy.

Ulster County

Mohonk Preserve, High Falls, Kingston and New Paltz are all nearby.

⚠ WARNING

Though the trails near Williams Lake Resort are suitable for every level hiker, children should be watched carefully as there are some dangerous drop-offs.

The lobby and dining room are charming and have sweeping views of the 24-acre lake used for swimming, boating and fishing. During our stay over the Thanksgiving weekend, the wood-paneled lobby was as cozy as the cat curled up in a rocker. The sunken sitting room was a Christmas card setting: a roaring fire, Christmas tree, fish tank, and large stuffed bear in the window.

Guests of Williams Lake who plan to be away for the day are offered a boxed lunch by the resort.

The property has been in the same family since Gustav Williams purchased it in 1929 when there were just a few cabins and a hot dog stand. Once geared to honeymooners, Williams Lake is now a family resort but also attracts young couples and seniors. (It's a regular stop on the Elderhostel circuit.) Anita Williams Peck, granddaughter of the founder, took over when her father Walter died in 1987. Several wall plaques attest to the family's involvement in business, education, health and deer management. The resort has many regulars and issues a quarterly newsletter to keep them abreast of upcoming theme weekends and reduced rates.

Our large motel room in the "Chalet" had a TV, telephone, two sinks and a lake view. It was a four-minute walk from the main house (other accommodations are closer and face the woods). In the dining room, Christmas music was a constant. So was the outstanding food – everything from the cream of tomato soup to the fish filet stuffed with crabmeat. The chef, Tim Rowell, 34, has worked there since age

14. He started as a dishwasher and attended the Culinary Institute before returning to the resort.

Cemented in Time

With the development of the canals the need for a water-resistant mortar became imperative. A mill built in 1828 in Rosendale became the center of the industry and the term "Rosendale cement" became synonymous with natural cement.

It all began when blasting for the canal bed in Rosendale uncovered a natural bed of limestone. With that discovery kilns were set up for the manufacture of cement. Jake Synder, a farmer, converted his water-powered flour mill into a cement-grinding mill. All the cement needed for the locks, dams, retaining walls and piers of the canal-bridge across the Delaware was made in Rosendale.

Soon everybody in the area was in the cement business. It became the biggest industry in Ulster County, employing 5,000 people in the early 1800s. In its heyday, 1825 to 1910, the industry made four million tons of cement a year, representing slightly less than 50% of the total production of natural cement in the US. The Statue of Liberty pedestal, the Brooklyn Bridge, the Treasury Building in Washington and other public structures were made with Rosendale cement. Eventually, quicker-setting Portland cement – discovered in England in 1890 – replaced Rosendale cement.

Ulster County

To insure that the remnants of this once thriving industry remain for generations to come, Williams Lake, in 1999, conveyed over 400 acres of woodlands and two lakes to the Rondout-Esopus Land Conservancy. The conservation easement insures that the kilns and caves will not be destroyed and that the land remains undeveloped. It does not affect the use of the property by guests. Ride around Rosendale and you'll see abandoned limestone quarries, kilns and caves all over.

Inns/B&Bs

WHISPERING PINES
60 Cedar Hill Road
High Falls
☎ 914-687-2419
Open May-November
Moderate

Two of Whispering Pines' four rooms have a Jacuzzi, and the carpeted Starlight Room has Jacuzzi under a skylight. There is no TV reception, but videos are available. Children over four years old are welcome.

Set deep in the woods, this four-year-old B&B is for anyone who enjoys a casual setting with a low-key and gracious couple. Horrified by the long list of "don'ts" that they discovered at another B&B, Celia and HD Seupel's first rule is to relax. Their philosophy behind their self-serve buffet breakfast is that guests shouldn't have to follow a strict schedule.

The farmhouse look belies a thoroughly modern interior in oak and pine with skylights and large windows to bring the outside in. A balcony overlooks the living room where guests are warmed by the fire.

H.D. Seupel is a woodworker (and musician) whose artistry is evident throughout the house and in a few local establishments. Celia is an educational writer with a first novel currently in the hands of four agents. She also teaches business writing at New York University.

It wasn't long ago when the Seupels lived in the city engulfed by throngs of people and buildings. Now surrounded by 50 acres of woods, their nearest neighbors are coyotes, owls, deer, foxes and pines that whisper in the wind.

EVELYN'S VIEW
12 River Knoll Road
Milton
☎ 914-795-2376
www.enjoyhv.com/evelynsview
Open year-round
Inexpensive to Moderate

Five spacious guestrooms are available at this plush and private B&B. A tennis court and swimming pool overlook the river and pond. Bring your own shampoo.

Want the intimacy of a B&B with the spaciousness of a resort? Siblings William Stiefel and Yvonne (Bonnie) Sherman, the congenial hosts, named their 14 acres on the Hudson for their late mother and the panoramic river view she enjoyed from there for roughly 60 years. The decor in the guestrooms is Victorian except for Captain's View in the main house. This neat "stateroom" in deep reds with antique cherry chests has its own deck on which to enjoy the finest view of them all.

Opened as a B&B in the summer of 1998, the stately house sits on rolling hills. The carriage house has two rooms with an adjoining bath and a kitchenette – ideal for families or close friends – and one room

Ulster County

You'll love having breakfast in the dining room that overlooks the water and the beautiful old sugar maple, where weddings are held.

has a small terrace. Two of the three guestrooms in the main house face the river. Brother and sister live elsewhere on the property, allowing guests more privacy.

Recommended Motels

Econolodge, ½-mile east of Thruway at Exit 18. ☎ 914-225-6200; 800-424-4777. Motel has some nice touches: cocktail lounge, complimentary continental breakfast, fresh flowers in the room and decent-size towels and bathrooms. Discount rates to AAA members. Another nice place to spend the night is at the **High Falls Motel** in High Falls; ☎ 914-687-2095.

 # Best Places to Eat

The price scale for restaurants can be found on page 21.

Casual Dining

LOCUST TREE INN RESTAURANT
215 Huguenot Street
New Paltz
☎ 914-255-7888
Lunch Tuesday-Friday; dinner Tuesday-Sunday.
Sunday brunch, 11am-2pm
Moderate

For those of you who remember the food at this restaurant as disappointing, it's now under new ownership with a wonderful chef. Before coming to Locust Tree in the fall of 1998, Genesee Ann Mallay ran her own 3½-star restaurant in Miami Beach's toney South Beach neighborhood. Proprietors Joseph and Karen Fitzgerald were married at the inn in 1997 – the same year as their purchase. Joe previously tended the stoves at the DePuy Canal House as sous chef to John Novi.

The stone and frame house was built in 1759 and was remodeled in 1847. The intimate and friendly restaurant has a true country inn ambience. In winter it's a perfect antidote to the frigid weather outside. In summer a terrace overlook affords a lovely view of the mountain countryside.

Meals always begin with crackers and cheese and something sweet in the breadbasket. I had a delicious melt-in-your-mouth spice bread. My entrée of pork in a ginger curry sauce served with carrots and mashed potatoes were all cooked to perfection. Service is lovely and the wine list is especially impressive. Menu selections include such delectables as veal sweetbreads au poivre, seared pork tenderloin roasted with a piquant mango and passion fruit glaze, and Hudson Valley mud pie.

Ulster County

TOSCANI & SONS RISTORANTE
119 Main Street
New Paltz
☎ 914-255-2272
Open daily for dinner; closed Monday
Moderate

New Paltz is a college town (SUNY New Paltz) so you'll find plenty of pizza joints, bookstores, cafés and restaurants along Main Street. My hunger met its match at Toscani's, where everything is oversize – portions, wineglasses and coffee cups. It was a Tuesday, pasta night, when every pasta dish normally $19.95 or less is only $9.95. Plus, other early bird specials are offered Wednesday through Friday.

Eat up! Hearty portions are served at Toscani & Sons.

Entrées are served with a nice house salad and crusty peasant bread and the wine selection is extensive. The rectangular room is made festive with Christmas lights, tapestries and ceiling fans. But overlooking a busy street and adjoining family grocery, the location is hardly pastoral.

Opened in 1966, 30 years before the restaurant, Toscani's Italian deli seems to be a hangout for family members so I'd suggest sitting farther back for a quieter meal. Otherwise, the four stars bestowed by the local papers are well deserved.

MOUNTAIN BRAUHAUS
Junction of Routes 44/55 & Route 299
Gardiner
☎ 914-255-9766
Open all year; closed Monday and Tuesday
Moderate

Along Route 55 are several eateries. Less than a mile east of Mohonk Preserve (see page 200) is this cheerful family-style restaurant serving hearty German standards. The large dinner/lunch menu is interchangeable with entrées from $9.95 to $15.95 and sandwiches and burgers for about $5. Dishes include Swabian Rostbraten and Kassler Rippchen.

⊚ TIP

Directly across the street from Mountain Brauhaus is a grocery and sandwich place with outdoor tables.

DEPUY CANAL HOUSE
High Falls
☎ 914-687-7700
www.depuycanalhouse.net
Open Thursday-Sunday
Moderate to Expensive

The four-star status is overrated but the historic (1797) intimate ambience and meal presentation more than compensate. Between courses be sure to roam around the landmark stone tavern. From the catwalk check out the open, sparkling clean kitchen below. Featured is an esoteric menu that changes frequently. A la carte dishes or meals with three to seven courses range from $30 to $55. Behind the restaurant is a 13-minute walk along the canal and locks 16-20 (too dangerous for children).

A "Gourmet" Road Rally

John Novi, proprietor of the DePuy Canal House for the last 30 years, sponsors an annual Epicurean Road Rally in May that combines touring with gourmet treats at several spots. $75 per person, with dinner.

CLOVE CAFE
Main Street
High Falls
☎ 914-687-7911
Dinner Wednesday-Sunday
Brunch Saturday and Sunday
Moderate

New owners Donna and David are also Culinary Institute graduates and live above their restaurant. At this writing, Donna and her short staff are struggling to keep customers happy. Yet Donna's sunny demeanor more than compensates for the wait. Be-

Ulster County

sides, everything is made to order so you must be patient. My meal began with mouth-watering garlic bread stuffed with capers and sun-dried tomatoes, followed by pan-roasted half chicken in a dark and delicious marinade of Jack Daniel's, shallots and herbs.

Samplings of à la carte selections at the Clove Café include coconut-crusted ahi (Hawaiian) tuna, baked penne pasta with sage cream and goat cheese, and Guinness-braised locally-farmed rabbit.

MILLIWAYS RESTAURANT (Hasbrouck House)
Route 209
Stone Ridge
☎ 914-687-0736
Moderate

On the first floor of the Inn at Stone Ridge, Milliways has a country ambience. For a memorable dinner, request the duck à l'orange; it's sliced thin and tender ($18).

THE WOULD RESTAURANT & BAR
North Road
Highland
☎ 914-691-9883
www.thewould.com
Dinner Monday-Saturday; lunch Tuesday-Friday
Moderate

I highly recommend this award-winning gourmet restaurant. You'd never believe that the nondescript apartment building set back from the street houses such a gem. Chef-owner Claire Winslow and her kitchen staff are all graduates of the Culinary Institute of America (located across the river in Hyde Park). Before Claire opened the restaurant 15 years ago, her mother had operated a bar and grill there.

Service is attentive and the wine list extensive. I had dinner in the back room where oil paintings in salmon and green done by the staff (for sale) complemented the like-colored décor of the walls and curtains. From the menu of beef and fish entrées at prices up to $25.95, I chose a winner at $16.95: black peppercorn-crusted pork loin with lingonberry and red onion marmalade served with side dishes of roasted eggplant, Asian slaw, snap beans and mashed potatoes.

You don't need to order a salad at The Would Restaurant. A house salad of curly leaf lettuce and julienne carrots comes with your entrée.

Wine lovers can have a field day here, sampling from the 295 wines priced from $18 to $200 per bottle. The quotation on the 11-page wine menu undoubtedly reflects the restaurant's philosophy and the reason why its wine selection has become renowned:

> *We thought of wine as something as healthy and normal as food and also a great giver of happiness and well being and delight.*
> – Ernest Hemingway, *A Moveable Feast*

Directional Info: From 9W North, turn left at the road just past Casa Mia, and then turn right.

Lite Bites

> *Eat, drink, and be merry, for tomorrow we may diet.*
>
> – Unknown

THE BAKERY
13A North Front Street
New Paltz
☎ 914-255-8840
Open daily for breakfast and lunch

When all the shopping makes you hungry, relax here with an espresso, soup or creative sandwich. Set in

Ulster County

from the road, The Bakery has a sizable outdoor café.

ROSENDALE CAFE
434 Main Street
Rosendale
☎ 914-658-9048
Open daily, year-round for lunch and dinner
Monday, dinner only
Inexpensive

Hosts live music every Friday and Saturday at 9pm ($6 cover charge) by local and national artists. No reservations taken. Music calendar: www.things-to-do.com. Lunch menu offers vegan and dairy foods along with creative sandwiches, salads and specials. Organic foods used whenever possible.

EGG'S NEST
Main Street
High Falls
☎ 914-687-7255
Open daily for lunch and dinner
Inexpensive

Quirky inside and out, this casual eatery moves from a bordello-like setting in the bar, to a "nudie" room, to a jungle-like porch, and to a children's room with mobiles, clowns and colored lights – all the work of Richard Murphy, owner and local artist. "This is his gallery. It's an ever evolving work of art," says the cheerful manager Linda.

★ **FAMOUS FACES**

Robert DeNiro owns a home in Gardiner.

LUNCH BOX
2356 Route 44/55
Gardiner
☎ 914-255-9394
Open daily, year-round
Inexpensive

This friendly place with bright yellow walls and blue trim has vintage lunch boxes dangling from the ceiling. Sit at either a table or at the counter for breakfast or lunch and enjoy a burger, sandwich or eggs. The owner-chef is a graduate of the Culinary Institute so you won't be disappointed. Situated in a small shopping plaza.

LYRIC CAFE
4 Main Street
Highland
☎ 914-691-7404
Open Thursday-Sunday
Inexpensive

This indoor/outdoor café adjacent to the Highland Antique and Art Center has a small menu of soup, salads, pastries and a daily special (such as crêpes filled with chicken or caramelized onions and cream). All prices are under $8. Take-out orders are welcome.

Ulster County

 Sunup to Sundown

Sightseeing

Stone Houses & Tours

For the background and history about stone houses, see page 159.

Huguenot Street, a National Historic Landmark, is the oldest street in America with its original homes intact. Descendants of the original 12 families that settled in New Paltz in 1678 lived in these houses until the 1960s and some still reside in the area. The descendants were largely responsible for forming the Huguenot Historical Society and a few are even volunteer guides.

Recognizing the diverse interests of tourists, the society is now offering theme packages so you can choose which of the six houses you wish to see. (You may want to see them all.) The houses were constructed between 1692 and 1890 and represent the Colonial, Federal and late-Victorian periods.

The **Jean Hasbrouck House**, the first to open to the public way back in 1899, is the largest and most authentic representation. Considered the "flagship" of Huguenot Street, it was originally one room but within 15 years had expanded to include a taproom for patrons, an attic that served as a sort of hotel with cots lined up next to the imposing chimney, and an intricately designed grate over the jamless fireplace. One bedroom contains a baby's cradle alongside a "senility cradle" for the old and infirm. The Jean Hasbrouck House is open weekends all year and tours are available daily on request. **Abraham Hasbrouck** was less affluent than his brother and his house is cruder, but touring both gives you a perspective on two different lifestyles in colonial America.

The stone-home sites on Huguenot Street include a French church, burial ground, library, museum, gift shop and picnic facilities. The simple church is the only reconstruction on Huguenot Street. It has no bell in the cupola; this was attributed to early frugality. Instead, a youngster was sent to the belfry to blow a conch shell, calling the settlers to worship. The pews face each other, suggesting a sharing of passages from the Bible.

Nowadays, a big annual event in New Paltz is Stone House Day featuring period food, traditional crafts, house tours, war re-enactments and entertainment. ☎ 914-255-1660/255-1889; www.hhs-newpaltz.org.

Ulster County

The annual Stone House Day in New Paltz features re-enactors in period costumes.
(© G. Steve Jordan)

Birth of New Paltz

The Huguenots came to America to escape religious persecution. They landed in Kingston – at that time a walled city. Forced to live outside the walls, they soon became targets of the marauding Indians who sought revenge on the Dutch for capturing Indians and shipping them to the Caribbean as slaves. The Huguenots protested that they were not Dutch and later purchased from the Indians 40,000 acres of land that stretched from the base of the Shawangunk cliffs to the Hudson River. They called their new city New Paltz after the Rheinland Pfalz in Germany where they first fled before emigrating to the US.

Pottery & Crafts

Crafts people are plentiful in Stone Ridge, Accord and High Falls, as well as West Hurley. While visiting any of the following spots ask for a **Hudson Valley Pottery Trail** brochure, which includes a map and suggestions for accommodations, restaurants and specialty shops in the area. Unless otherwise indicated, the potters are open only on weekends.

Directional Info: Take Thruway to Exit 18 and follow Route 299 into New Paltz. Go north on Route 32 to Rosendale. Turn left onto Route 213W. The first two galleries on the trail are 11 miles from New Paltz and are just before the DePuy Canal House.

★ DID YOU KNOW?

Red clay found in the hills around nearby Rosendale was the reason for High Falls' existence in the 19th century. Potters Smith and Cohen use that same rich red clay in their work.

CANAL CLAY COOPERATIVE
Second Street
High Falls
☎ 914-687-0630

What used to be called the Lanzrein Studio is now a cooperative of seven potters set beside two antique stores. Carolyn Leung and Lee Rubenstein are a husband and wife team working under the name of **Bittersweet Pottery Company**. Call for an appointment. He works in porcelain and she in stoneware. Rubenstein uses the glasswork method of millefiore to create colorful pointillist patterns and styles on the clay. Along with his candelabra and plates is a beautiful line of Judaica: goblets, challah trays and menorahs.

WESTCOTE BELL POTTERY
Main Street
High Falls
☎ 914-687-7256

Cat fans will love the stenciled and hand-painted whimsical pottery of Vaughan L. Smith and his Michigan-born wife, Jackie Cohen. Smith's vases, mugs, plates, bowls, teapots and lamp bases, sell from $10 to $1,000. They depict chickens, cows, elephants and sheep, reflecting his roots in Scotland. Smith says his stenciling and coloring technique, while commonly used on batik cloth and Easter eggs, is unique in working with clay. Cohen also does

Ulster County

paintings of High Falls, some reminiscent of Chagall. Watch artists at work in their open studios Wednesday through Sunday, 11am-6pm, year-round.

★ **DID YOU KNOW?**

Painter Marc Chagall lived in High Falls in a simple wooden house between 1945 and 1948, where he produced some of his important works.

KAETE BRITTIN SHAW
Route 213 (next to Bird Watcher's Country Store)
High Falls
☎ 914-687-7828
www.guild.com

Shaw's porcelain bowls, vases and teapots are both functional and sculptural. But it's her whimsical side that seems to sell best. Her unusual "rattles" are especially popular with musicians because they also serve as percussion instruments. Next time you attend a concert at the Accord train station, Rosendale Café or Anyone Can Whistle store in Kingston, you might hear Shaw's rattles contributing to the music.

TRIPLO STUDIOS
Route 209
Stone Ridge
☎ 914-687-4932
Open Tuesday-Sunday

Joseph Triplo also works in porcelain, which he fires to high temperature for lasting quality. His work, though functional, can best be described as elegant. Each item is lovingly crafted and decorated with an abstract design that takes much time and thought. Triplo, a painting and drawing major in art school, says he's become more selective about his work since then. "I've always wanted to stay connected to my work," he says. "Without that I don't think I would be successful."

Directional Info: From Route 213, turn left onto Route 209. Look for Triplo Studios on your right.

⭐ **FAMOUS FACES**

Actor Aiden Quinn has a home in High Falls.

CANAL FORGE
496 Towpath Road
High Falls
☎ 914-687-7130
Open year-round, 9am-5pm

Inside the crammed, tool-laden shop attached to his house you'll find Jonathan Nedbor, a working blacksmith who wouldn't be caught dead fixing horseshoes. As this amusing bearded man explained to a group of visiting Chinese students from Brooklyn, "I don't want to get under a horse. I like customers that don't kick!"

This blacksmith is an artist with a hammer, forging steel into functional pieces like nails and basketball hoops. Prices start at 75¢ for a nail, and every piece is engraved with his quatrefoil insignia.

It's fun watching Nedbor soften a solid piece of steel into the consistency of clay and then hammer it into shape. Nedbor is a photographer as well, and he'll gladly show you his photographs of metal door handles, keys and gates that he painstakingly reproduced for historic mansions in the Hudson Valley.

Ulster County

TUTHILLTOWN GRISTMILL
& COUNTRY STORE
20 Gristmill Lane
Gardiner
☎ 914-255-5695
Guided tours by appointment
Closed Monday and Tuesday

A mile east of Widmark Farm (see page 196) is the intersection of 55 and Route 9. To the right is the water-powered Tuthilltown Gristmill, which has been operating continuously since the year our Constitution went into effect. Operated by the Smith family since 1941, the mill produces 34 different types of natural stone ground flours and meals, including more than half a million pounds of kosher flour a year. The country store sells flour, grains, spices, homemade jams and organic cereals. It's a lovely setting for a picnic or for browsing.

⊚ **TIP**

Before stopping at the Tuthilltown Gristmill, be sure to find bathroom facilities as the gristmill has none.

Pit Stops

If you're feeling fatigued after making your way along Route 44/55, **Majestic Park** is about two miles east of Tuthilltown Gristmill. It has a playground and picnic tables. If you continue straight on 44/55, after the blue bridge, you'll find the village of Gardiner, where you can get pizza and sandwiches and browse the antique stores.

Wineries

Over the bottle many a friend is found.
— Yiddish proverb

New York State is the second-largest producer of wine in America, with 110 farm wineries. The Hudson River Region is one of its oldest wine-producing areas. Eighty percent of the grapes grown in New York State are for white wine, each vineyard in the Hudson Valley is distinctive, and vintners are generally supportive of one another.

Several years ago, seven wineries in Ulster and Orange counties began a cooperative venture called the "Shawangunk Wine Trail," covering 60 miles: Adair, Applewood, Baldwin, Brimstone, Brotherhood, Rivendell and Warwick Valley. In 1991 the first annual **Taste of New Paltz** was held in the fall to introduce visitors to local wineries and associate member restaurants. Several special trail events are held during the year as well. ☎ 914-744-8399 for a calendar.

In addition, the annual **International Wine Showcase and Auction** is held in September at the Culinary Institute of America in Hyde Park and at the Would Restaurant in Highland. ☎ 914-297-9127; www.mhv.net/~wineshow.

Route 9W is largely a one-lane commercial strip dotted with farm markets and wineries. To begin your wine tour in Ulster County start at Benmarl, one of the Hudson Valley's most famous wineries (see next page).

Ulster County

BENMARL WINERY
156 Highland Avenue
Marlboro
☎ 914-236-4265
www.benmarl.com
Open daily, noon-4pm, January through March; and
daily, noon-5pm, April through December

Even if you're not a wine drinker, Benmarl is unique.
Its 80-year-old owner, Mark Miller, realized a long-
ago burning passion to replant a historic vineyard in
Marlboro with premium European grapes and con-
tinues to experiment with his own grapes and those
Benmarl holds of other vineyards. He helped write the Farm Win-
winery License ery Act, which allows farmers to buy an inexpensive
No. 1. winery license.

A leading magazine illustrator who studied with
Norman Rockwell, Miller is busy turning his gallery
into a museum of his work and that of other illustrators from the 1940s and 1950s. He's also digitizing
his prints and paintings for posterity. As one of the
few surviving illustrators of that post-war period,
Miller is concerned that a slice of Americana will
otherwise be lost. So nine years ago he began orga-
nizing the artwork with help from his second wife,
Grace, widowed like Miller. "All those contemporar-
ies have, for the most part, disappeared," he says.
"Something in me wants to make sure their work is
not forgotten." He adds that these will be the "cave
drawings" of the future.

Open all year, the winery sits on a bluff overlooking
the Hudson River and the distant Berkshire Mountains. Harvest picnics and grape-stomping festivals
are held in the fall.

Directional Info: From the Thruway, take Exit 17 to
Route 84E and turn north on 9W. Less than a mile
north on 9W, or 7.8 miles from the Thruway exit, is

the entrance sign to Benmarl. Follow the road for about a mile to the sign on the right.

ROYAL WINERY
Route 9W
Milton
☎ 914-236-4281
www.kedemwines.com
Open all year, 10am-4:30pm, for tastings, tour and film. Closed Friday, Saturday and Jewish holidays.

Three miles north on Route 9W is this well-known producer of kosher wines, several under such familiar labels as Kedem and Baron Herzog. Now operated by the third generation of Herzogs, the winery buys its grapes, mainly the deep purple Concord variety, from local farmers and sells wine to liquor stores and restaurants.

Six thousand tons a year are crushed and processed under the supervision of a rabbi. His purpose, explains Michael Herzog, is not simply to bless the wine, but to ensure that it remains pure (no additives, preservatives, corn syrup, yeast or artificial coloring added). People often think all kosher wine is sweet. "Nobody knew how to make a good dry kosher wine," Herzog states, until his father Ernest produced the first in the market in 1976. Then, "everybody started to copy it." Royal's 144 line of semi-sweet wine is a big seller, along with its non-alcoholic grape juice. Annually the winery attracts 8,000 people of all backgrounds.

To order by mail or to receive a free kosher wine newsletter, contact Royal Wine Corporation, 418A Kent Avenue, Brooklyn, NY 11211.

Ulster County

EL PASO WINERY
Route 9W (look for old gray barn on left)
Ulster Park
☎ 914-331-8642
Open year-round; closed Tuesdays

About 16 miles north of Royal on Route 9W is El
Paso, the smallest wine operation of them all. Felipe
Beltra, a native of Uruguay, has been operating his
winery for 21 years. He buys grapes and produces
and bottles 3,000 gallons a year. He carries dry,
sweet and dessert wines. Best sellers include Cream
Niagara (fruity white) and Lambrusco (fruity red).
Tastings begin at noon.

When you visit El Paso Winery, tell Felipe what wine you like; he'll give you a taste.

ADAIR
75 Allhusen Road
New Paltz
☎ 914-255-1377
Open daily for tastings and informal tours, 11am-
6pm, May through October, and weekends, 11am-
6pm in the winter. Closed January and February.

This relatively new entry on the wine scene is five
miles south of the village of New Paltz. In 1984 Jim
Adair, a New York City art director, and his wife,
Gloria, bought the 139-acre former dairy farm and
set up the wine cellar in a 200-year-old Dutch-style
barn with an entrance plaque reading "Thaddeus
Hait-Farm, National Register, c. 1800." Two years
ago, Marc and Lori Stopkie bought the winery and
vineyard from them. The majority of Adair's wines
are sold right on the premises.

The vineyard currently grows five grape varieties on
10 acres, producing 2,000 cases annually, but Marc
hopes to plant two new varieties on another five
acres next spring. His dry wines are unfiltered, he
says, to avoid over processing the grapes and stripping them of flavor. He also believes he's the only

winemaker on the west side of the river growing 100% of the grapes used in his wines. Visitors are welcome to sample dry and semi-dry whites and red and dessert wines.

Directional Info: From the Thruway, take Exit 18 (New Paltz) and follow Route 299 to village. Turn left at Route 32S. After passing SUNY New Paltz and Mountainview Stables, follow the green Wine Trail sign to the left. Adair is less than a mile on the right.

★ WHAT'S IN A NAME?

Adair means "oak by the ford" in ancient Gaelic and an old oak at the head of the vineyard is the winery symbol. The wine label is a reproduction of an 1840 painting, "The Solitary Oak," by Hudson River School artist Asher Durand.

RIVENDELL VINEYARDS & WINERY
714 Albany Post Road
New Paltz
☎ 914-255-2494
www.rivendellwine.com
Open daily, year-round, 10am-6pm

Rivendell is a larger and better-known winery with an output of 10,000 cases a year. Few grapes are grown here – they're purchased from other growers for processing. Visitors can taste, shop, eat and take an informal tour of the modern cellar. The on-site Vintage New York Store sells its own labels – Rivendell and Libertyville Cellars – and those of eight other New York state wineries (none from the immediate area). "This is the place to buy the best of New York wines and learn about them too," says Bob Ransom, who took over in 1996 after his father re-

Ulster County

tired. "We're not afraid to talk about other people's wineries." A small gourmet shop sells locally made spices, salsa, vinegars, teas and handpainted glassware.

Bob proudly shares that he's planning to open a store in New York City, that Rivendell has received 500 medals in the last 10 years, and that *Wines and Spirits Magazine* has cited it among the top 26 Chardonnay producers in the nation. Other popular sellers are Rivendell Seyval Blanc (1996) and Rivendell Interlude, a fruity blend. Summer favorites are Libertyville Cellars Cranboise, a blend of cranberry juice and white wine, and Libertyville's Northern Lights, a cornucopia of tropical flavors.

An enclosed terrace with tables and couches overlooks a grand view. You can either bring your own food or purchase cheese and crackers, wine and non-alcoholic beverages. Rivendell is also the site of many festivals and art exhibits.

Directional Info: At the intersection of Route 44/55 and Route 9, go north 1.3 miles. At stop sign, bear right and continue a half-mile; turn left at Rivendell.

WHITECLIFF VINEYARD
331 McKinstry Road
Gardiner
☎ 914-255-4613
www.whitecliffwine.com
Open May through December 20, Thursday-Sunday and by appointment

This brand new winery was built from scratch. Michael Migliore and Yancey Stanforth-Migliore own the 70-acre farm located at the base of the Shawangunk cliffs.

The Migliores married in 1983, and by 1986 had built a house, planted vines and erected a barn (now the winery and tasting room). "Our first seven years or so of planting were small experimental plots to work out what would perform in our soil and micro-climate," explains Yancey. "We've taken this approach since our mission is to produce great wines from vinifera grapes, which are cold-sensitive and challenging to grow around here. We want to push the envelope on the traditional Hudson Valley wine – generally considered to be white and hybrid-based – by focusing on vinifera, including reds."

Visitors to Whitecliff are welcome to explore the tasting room and gift shop, or to picnic on the grounds.

Michael grew up in the Bronx where his Italian grandparents made wine in the basement. An engineer at IBM, Michael's the winemaker and vineyard manager. His wife's background is in fundraising, mostly as director of development for several NYC and Hudson Valley-based organizations. "I'm still a little surprised to be farming," says Yancey. "But as I tell visitors, my [NYC-based] childhood image of a farmer as a straw-chewing innocent in overalls couldn't be more wrong."

The Migliores opened the tasting room as members of the Shawangunk Wine Trail and value the efforts of fellow members to improve the quality of grapes and to build a reputation for the region. "It's a vibrant wine trail with lots of traffic," says Yancey.

Opening season, Whitecliff had much success, with the Pinot Noir and Merlot both selling out in three weeks. Yancey also expected to sell out the 125 Chardonnay and had just released a pleasant Gewurtztraminer. In addition, five of the 22 acres are reserved for Gamay Noir, the Beaujolais grape, which Yancey believes to be unique to the area.

Directional Info: From Route 299 in New Paltz, cross the Wallkill River and bear left at Libertyville Road just past Wallkill View Farm. Follow it six miles to the junction with Routes 44/55, where it becomes

Ulster County

Bruynswick Road. Continue another 1.9 miles, then turn left onto McKinstry Road. The vineyard is .8 mile on the right.

Animal Farms

WIDMARK HONEY FARMS
Route 44/55
Gardiner
☎ 914-255-6400
Open 10am-6pm
Admission $3.50, free for children under age five

A beehive of treats for kids and their parents, Widmark has been producing pure, untreated honey for over 100 years (and by four generations) on its 122-acre farm. Along with the bees, Widmark is best known for its trained American black bears, Objectionable (Objee) and Bodette (Bo), who help promote the sale of honey products. Visitors are invited to taste and learn about the different kinds that sell at $7-$9.75. But there's another reason for the bears. "My husband had a hangup for them," explains feisty Mary Widmark with a twinkle in her eye. "It's better than another woman." (Mr. Widmark has since died, but the bears are still there.)

Honey is on sale every November. Bring your own jar and you'll pay even less. Children can feed the farm animals – lambs, goats, sheep and roosters. Self-guided tours are on weekends only and weekdays are by appointment. During the season, there's a 3pm Sunday presentation that varies weekly.

Directional Info: Take 299W from New Paltz and turn left onto Route 44/55. Widmark is 2.7 miles on the left.

☉ TIP

Do not refrigerate honey, as this accelerates granulation. If it becomes granulated, simply heat a pan of water to 150°, remove it from heat and place the honey container into the heated water until the honey is liquid again.

Hiking, Biking & Skiing

Climb every mountain, ford every stream
Follow every rainbow, till you find your
dream!
— Oscar Hammerstein II (1895-1960),
The Sound of Music

Minnewaska State Park Preserve

Take Route 299 from Exit 18 (New Paltz) and continue west for six miles until the road merges with Route 44/55. Bear right and continue west another three miles. **Minnewaska State Park Preserve** (☎ 914-255-0752), designated by the Nature Conservancy as "one of the 75 great places in the Western Hemisphere," is situated on the Shawangunk Mountain ridge, rising more than 2,000 feet above sea level. Among the 12,000 acres are 28 miles of footpaths for hikers, 27 carriage paths for hiking, biking, cross-country skiing and horseback riding, and several waterfalls and streams. The footing on the carriage paths is easy so hiking boots are usually not necessary.

Because the geology, climate, flora and fauna are markedly different from the valleys on either side of

Ulster County

it, the largely undeveloped **Shawangunk Ridge** can be considered a "sky island." The lakes are thus called "sky lakes". These lakes are unique in that they are deep, oligotrophic lakes (deficient in plant nutrients, i.e., no algae) and are at high elevation with no water sources other than rain. Their great depths and hard quartz bottoms turn the water cerulean blue.

Two of the five sky lakes, **Minnewaska** and **Awosting**, are used for swimming, boating and scuba diving. At the upper parking lot walk the few feet over to Lake Minnewaska where the view of the rocky mountain ridge with a house built into the rock is just jaw-dropping. Evergreen trees and shrubs in the park make it a wonderland even in winter.

Minnewaska is Indian for "floating waters."

Sky Island Family

The Phillips family lives on this sky island as part of a life tenancy agreement signed when the state bought the land from the Smileys. In 1955 they sold the Minnewaska Mountain Houses and land surrounding them to Ken and Lucille Phillips: Minnewaska Mountain House, a sister resort to Mohonk Mountain House, built in 1879, and Wildmere, opened in 1887. The Phillipses had managed the declining properties (later destroyed by fire) for some time.

After building a golf course and a ski slope that failed, the Phillips family was heavily in debt. A foreclosure auction in 1977 was diverted by the state's offer to purchase 1,379 acres of the 2,600 remaining for $1.8 million. In 1987 the state purchased the rest of the land from the Phillips family.

It's scary to think that this treasure was close to being sold to private hands. In 1980 the Marriott Corporation wanted to buy the Minnewaska property and build a hotel and golf course there, which triggered a bitter battle between developers and environmentalists. Thankfully, the Friends of the Shawangunks persevered for six years, and in 1987 the state bought the land designating it a state park.

I hiked the ridge with a group led by Don Pachner. To reach our destination of Gertrude's Nose (a rock protrusion that resembles a nose), we hiked five miles (seemed like 10) along rocky paths to the Trapps ridgeline. It was late April and mountain laurel was abundant, though it hadn't yet bloomed. This was before the short season of those horrid black flies. We lunched at an overlook on Millbrook Mountain where pitch pine proliferates. According to Pachner, pitch pine is as characteristic of the park as its deep clefts and is the only Pine Barrens existing on a ridge. Subject to wind and little soil, these dwarfed trees may be a lot older than they appear.

The parking fee at Minnewaska is now only $5, but is soon expected to rise.

Ulster County

Minnewaska sponsors year-round guided walks, ski clinics and lectures. ☎ 914-255-0752 for schedule.

☺ TIP

During autumn, in order not to be closed out of the Minnewaska State Park Preserve, be sure to arrive by 10:30am.

Mohonk Preserve

Another option, a few miles past the world-famous Trapps, is **Mohonk Preserve**. Its brand new $2.8 million interpretive center is now the gateway to its 6,400 protected acres for hikers, cross-country skiers, mountain bikers and rock climbers. Called Trapps Gateway, the building was made from trees cleared from the site. The centerpiece is a topographical model of the preserve. The preserve manages over 25 miles of carriage roads and 31 miles of foot trails for the enjoyment of the public.

> ### ◎ TIP
>
> A sensory trail for the physically disabled that leads from Trapps Gateway is under construction.

Within 10 years of their purchase, the brothers Smiley were running two hotels – Mohonk Lake and Lake Minnewaska. In 1963, 6,250 acres were carved out to establish the non-profit Mohonk Trust, later named the Mohonk Preserve.

Mohonk Preserve is open all year; $7 weekends and holidays, $5 weekdays, children free with adult. ☎ 914-255-0919; www.mohonkpreserve.org.

Harcourt

Birders will love the **Harcourt Trail Wildlife Sanctuary**. At this writing, the bridge had "Keep Off" signs because it was shaky, but hopefully it's been repaired by now. Follow Huguenot Street around the bend and look for the entrance just beyond Mulberry

Street. If the dirt pull-off across from the trail head is full, other parking is available nearby.

You can also pick up the **Wallkill Valley Rail Trail** on Mulberry Street. The wide, graveled path runs for 12.2 miles from the New Paltz/Rosendale town line to the Gardiner/Shawangunk town line. The trail is designed for hiking, biking, jogging, bird watching, horseback riding and cross-country skiing.

The scenic and historical site of **Perrine's Bridge** in Rifton runs over the Wallkill River. The lovely covered bridge, now closed to traffic, was erected 1850 and restored in 1970. It's next to the Thruway and is accessible only from Route 213. Take North Ohioville Road and make sharp left at Dubois Road.

Perrine's covered bridge in Ulster County
is a scenic and restful stop.

Slabsides

Should you find yourself on Route 9W, be sure to visit **Slabsides**, John Burroughs' retreat in West

Park (☎ 914-255-5077; 626-5128). The rustic two-story cabin of bark-covered slabs is open for tours only twice a year (third Saturday in May and first Saturday in October), but the grounds are always open. This national historic landmark was built in 1895. Burroughs lived at his "Blessed Slabsides" off and on until 1920, a year before he died.

Park your car and walk the path toward the cabin. You can peek inside. It's a very quiet sanctuary. On the walk, realize that you're traveling the same path as Edison, Ford and Roosevelt when they came to visit their naturalist friend. Burroughs reported, after President Theodore Roosevelt visited one very hot day in July: "We walked from the river up to Slabsides, and Roosevelt sweat his white linen coat right through at the back."

Directional Info: From Route 9W, turn at Floyd Ackert Road (at Marcel's Restaurant) and continue over the railroad tracks until you come to Burroughs Drive (on left). Drive .3 mile until you see the wooden "Slabsides" sign.

High Falls

While in High Falls don't forget to see the falls for which it's named and where *Splendor in the Grass* was filmed. Behind the Locktender's Cottage (across from the DePuy Canal House) are two paths. To the left is a trail leading to the falls. When you come to the wire fence, notice that you can walk through it to the falls. Back at the entrance, take the path to the right to the ruins of the aqueduct that was removed in 1953 by Central Hudson Electric. Presumably it was dangerous, but as it stands now it's even more so since kids jumping into the water could now hit rocks. However, you can swim, fish or kayak here.

Golf

> *Visitor: So your son is planning to run the farm when he gets out of college?*
>
> *Farmer: Well, at least he's beginning to take an interest in it. He just showed me where we could have a golf course and how easy it would be to turn the barn into a clubhouse!*

Apple Greens Golf Course, Highland, ☎ 914-883-5500; www.applegreens.com. Public. Open March through December. Championship 18-hole, par 71 (6,510 yards). Seven-day advance reservations required; lessons, restaurant/snack bar, driving range, pro shop; carts mandatory on weekends; spikeless.

Apple Greens has come by its name honestly. Built on a working apple orchard, the apple trees dotting the course are the golfers' biggest obstacles. It's a scenic spot with the Shawangunks looming in the distance. *Golf Digest* gave this four-year-old public course a three-star rating for 1998-99. Nine more holes are being constructed across the way, scheduled to open summer 2000.

Directional Info: Conveniently located off Route 299. From Exit 18 (New Paltz) drive 1½ miles east and turn right at Route 9W; continue 3.9 miles and turn left at County Route 22; continue another 1½ miles.

Mohonk Golf Course, New Paltz, near the gatehouse at Mohonk Mountain House, ☎ 914-256-2154. Public. Nine-hole, par 35; pro shop; golf carts not mandatory. Call a week ahead for tee times. Open April through November.

Established in 1897, this course of Scottish design is not long but it's quite hilly, surrounded on all sides by the Mohonk Preserve and the Catskills and Berk-

Ulster County

Hungry hitters at Apple Greens may pick an apple for a snack, but bagging them is not permitted.

shires in the distance. The golf course belongs to Mohonk Mountain House, and green fees are waived for guests during the week and after 3pm on weekends. (About 35% of the golfers are guests of the hotel.) The old pro shop on the grounds was built in 1903 and is now a guest cottage with six rooms.

In 1994, Mohonk was designated a conservation course by the International Audubon Society, an honor bestowed on few golf courses in the state. What this means is that the caretakers are environmentally sensitive to the wildlife habitats on the 60-acre grounds.

Twenty-four birdhouses were installed on the course in 1996 and at last count three nesting pairs of bluebirds have taken up residence. Several areas especially around trees are left unmowed and are roped off to carts. As greenskeeper Tom Wright explains, carts are harmful to grass especially on the fragile areas under cover of trees.

★ DID YOU KNOW?

The Eastern bluebird, New York's state bird, has dropped from the endangered species list, largely due to private efforts to build bluebird houses over the past decade.

New Paltz Golf Course, ☎ 914-255-8282. This nine-hole, 36 par public course is more challenging than it looks. It's set against the backdrop of the Shawangunk Mountains and the fifth fairway borders the Wallkill River. Located next to the Locust Tree Inn on Huguenot Street. Open April through November.

Stone Dock Golf Course, Stone Dock Road, High Falls, ☎ 914-687-7107. Nine holes, par 36. Bar, restaurant, clubhouse, pro shop, putting green, club rental. Carts not mandatory.

This public course is fairly flat and in superb shape thanks to a new greenskeeper. Water is all about, but it's said to be one of the best courses after a rain because it's irrigated and well-drained. Not overly crowded. Fourth hole is a "nightmare." New: Tee times now available on weekends and holidays. Call one week in advance for reservations. Open April through November.

Skydiving

If jumping from a plane turns you on, the **Ranch Skydiving Club** operates from the privately-owned Gardiner Airport and touts itself as one of the biggest skydiving centers in the world. First-timers go with an instructor ($175). ☎ 914-255-9538; www.sky divetheranch.com.

Ulster County

Museums, Art & Theater

Once thousands o'er my towpath strode
While mules and horses pulled their load,
From early spring until late fall
The lumber boats did slowly crawl
From mines near Honesdale coal was sent
And after High Falls came cement
   – Memories of the D&H

D&H CANAL MUSEUM
Mohonk Road
High Falls
☎ 914-687-9311
Open Thursday-Monday in summer; fall weekends

This small museum is a fun way to learn canal history. It has a working model of canal lock, trail maps, photos and artifacts.

GOMEZ MILL HOUSE
11 Mill House Road
Marlboro
☎ 914-236-3126
Open mid-April through October
Wednesday-Sunday, 10am-4pm; other times by appointment. A small donation is requested.

At the Ulster/Orange County border before hitting the wineries along the Hudson River, you might want to stop at Gomez Mill House off 9W near Marlboro. The 1714 stone and brick blockhouse is a testament to five prominent families, each of whom built upon the fine workmanship of the previous owner.

Pioneer, patriot, gentleman farmer, craftsman and preservationist – each put a stamp on the house, adding furniture and artifacts ranging from a menorah and Stickley chandeliers to a printing press.

Luis Moses Gomez, a refugee from the Spanish Inquisition, built the house as a trading post with immensely thick walls. For more than 30 years he and his son, Daniel, conducted a thriving fur trade with the Indians. In the early 1900s, Dard Hunter, a renowned papermaker, refashioned the old gristmill into a millhouse in which to experiment with handmade paper. The cottage is now being restored along with the icehouse.

The Gomez Mill House in Marlboro has quite a history.

Gomez was the first president of the first Jewish congregation Shearith Israel in New York City. Near the Marlboro house is a stream that became known as "Jew's Creek."

The house is the oldest extant Jewish residence in North America. Several Gomez descendants are members of the board, although succeeding families were largely Presbyterians, Episcopalians and Christian Scientists. (Gomez's descendants included the poetess Emma Lazarus and Supreme Court Justice Benjamin Cardozo.) The Starin family purchased the home in 1947 and raised four children there. Mildred Starin, now 76, placed the site on the National Register, and after moving out three years ago, opened it to visitors.

The tour includes a 20-minute film on the five families. Tours are ongoing; feel free to join one in progress.

Directional Info: Off Hwy. 9W at Exit 17, follow 84E to Exit 10 (9W North). The sign for Gomez Mill House is 8.5 miles from the Thruway exit.

ULSTER HISTORICAL SOCIETY
AT BEVIER HOUSE
Route 209
Marbletown
☎ 914-338-5614
Open June through September, Wednesday- Sunday, 1-5pm. Free.

Stepping into this stone house is like reading a saga of one family over several generations. Seven generations of Beviers lived here and rooms were added through the mid-1900s. The first section was built around 1681, one room housing the entire family. It hasn't changed structurally and still retains the original Dutch doors. The scullery holds some original and unusual artifacts, such as swamp shoes for horses (to keep them from sinking in the mud) and farm tools and equipment. "The men love this room," says Phyllis Crawford, a tour guide here for 11 years.

All but one of the Bevier descendants were named Louis.

You'll go from the Colonial era into the Victorian when you reach the elegant dining room. Portraits of 19th-century notables in Ulster County adorn the walls: a self-portrait of Lionel DeLisser, author and historian; John Vanderlyn, a native of Kingston whose paintings adorn its Senate House and Museum; and Thomas Cornell, a Hudson River steamboat magnate from Rondout. There's a nice collection of blurry Flow Blue china in the corner and framed woodcock skulls designed by Mrs. Clarence Elting. (Clarence Elting, 1860-1942, donated his collection of Victoriana when the Bevier family presented the house to the society in 1938.)

The Civil War room on the second floor displays the collection of Will Plank of Marlboro, who scavenged the battlefields for objects. It's a war buff's dream. The Bevier House also maintains a library, family histories and documents of local interest.

★ WHAT'S IN A NAME?

Marbletown is named for the eight-mile ledge of limestone from which much of the stone for the old houses was quarried. The miners originally thought it was marble.

HIGHLAND CULTURAL CENTER
54 Vineyard Avenue
Highland
☎ 914-691-6008
www.hcc-arts.org

Several activities are sponsored by this non-profit multi-arts organization. Because it serves the mid-Hudson region, its Hudson Valley Summer Music Festival in Highland is held on both sides of the Hudson River. The nine free concerts alternate one week in Ulster and the other in Dutchess County, at 6:30pm in July and August. The Highland Concert is held in Peace Park, the same venue as the International Peace Festival, held every Columbus Day weekend.

The center also maintains a gallery with new shows every five to six weeks. Hours are Thursday and Fri-

Ulster County

day, 11am-6pm and Saturday, 10am-2pm, year-round except January.

The Story of Sojourner Truth

Ulster County had a long history of slavery reaching back to its early Dutch farmers. Sojourner Truth, one of the best known American abolitionists of her day, was a slave for 30 years before she became free in 1828 under a New York law that banned slavery. Born Isabella Baumfree in the late 1700s, she was the property of six slave owners in Hurley, Kingston and New Paltz until 1829.

The library at SUNY New Paltz now carries the Sojourner Truth name.

Her parents were slaves of the wealthy Dutch-speaking Hardenburgh family, owners of seven slaves. When Col. Hardenburgh died, Isabella became the slave of his son, Charles, who housed his slaves together in one room in a damp cellar. Isabella's father later auctioned her and her brother along with many sheep for $100 to John Neely, who operated a store outside of Kingston. Because she couldn't understand orders in English, Neely whipped her, scarring her for life. She later displayed her scars to still the hisses at one of her anti-slavery speeches.

In 1810, Sojourner was sold to her longtime master John Dumont of New Paltz. During that period she married an older slave named Thomas, who also belonged to Dumont, with whom she bore five children. When the youngest, Peter, was sold and imported illegally to Alabama, she enlisted some Ulster County Quakers who helped her successfully bring suit in the Ulster County Courthouse to secure his return.

After her emancipation in 1826, Isabella underwent a conversion experience in which she experienced Jesus, joined the Methodist Church in Kingston and changed her name to Sojourner Truth.

Information here was largely gleaned from a book on Sojourner Truth by Carleton Mabee (New York University, 1993), a Pulitzer Prize-winning author and retired professor at SUNY New Paltz.

HIGHLAND ANTIQUE & ART CENTER
71-79 Vineyard Avenue
Highland
☎ 914-691-5577
Open Thursday-Saturday, 10am-5pm; Sunday, 1-5pm

Housed in a recently restored neo-classical bank building, this business is comprised of a multi-dealer antique store, art gallery and café.

The art gallery is used for exhibits, concerts and special events. For a few weeks in April and May it becomes a museum of local history and an appraisal center. Matt Smith, the curator and president of the Downtown Business Association, says that in their own version of the popular TV show *Antique Road Show*, over 200 people lined up with all their little treasures the first weekend last year. One woman was surprised to learn that something she purchased at a yard sale was a Tiffany worth at least $15,000.

The Lyric Café (see page 181), inside the art center, is open for lunch and has a lovely courtyard where people can enjoy a bowl of soup, salad or pastry.

Directional Info: Located just beyond the intersection of Routes 9W and 44/55. Traveling north on 9W, turn left.

Ulster County

VILLA BAGLIERI
200 Fosler Road
Highland
☎ 914-883-7395
www.villabaglieri.com

More than 20 shows are scheduled annually at this matinee (and occasional dinner) theater, which is operated by the third generation of Baglieris. Their bread and butter are bus tours, since the theater can seat seven full coaches. Individuals, of course, are equally welcome.

The headliners are a mix of local and celebrity talent – I saw singer Julius LaRosa there. Remember him? Diners of a certain age and ethnicity certainly did, delighting in his sentimental songs and Italian-language jokes. When La Rosa began his performance, I moved in closer to snap his picture. He stopped singing and demanded I give him my camera. Hesitant to part with it, I refused. He insisted again and I refused. Then he revealed that all he wanted was for someone to take our picture. Someone did; it's on the next page.

Performances are held during the week and run the gamut from parodies (The Godfather's Meshuggener Wedding) to impersonations (The Sinatra & Elvis Experience).

The food is what you'd expect from a former resort (1946-87) – a cut above typical dinner fare and plentiful. In fact, the property feels more like a resort given the bocce courts and heated pool, and entertainment and dancing through lunch (at some shows). A woman at my table summed it up perfectly. "This is a nice day trip." Tickets are under $30, except for the annual all-day clambake in the summer.

Directional Info: From Route 9W, take Milton Turn-pike (opposite Stewarts) for four miles to the turn for Villa Baglieri. Follow the signs.

Author Francine Silverman with performer Julius LaRosa at Villa Baglieri.

Shopping

New Paltz

Both Main Street and North Front Street (opposite Plattekill Avenue) in New Paltz are filled with stores and eateries. It's a true shopper's paradise. Take your pick; you can't go wrong.

ECLECTIBLES II
Main Street
New Paltz
☎ 914-256-3803
Open Thursday-Monday at 11:30am

Ulster County

214   In & Around New Paltz

Sells vintage clothing (some never worn), jewelry and collectibles at reasonable prices. Owner Barbara Brensley looks for the eclectic. "I didn't want to be just another antique store," she says. Describing her military garments as military/vintage/retro, she stresses that they go beyond camouflage to vests worn by soldiers and sweaters worn by postal workers.

BARNER BOOKS
69 Main Street
New Paltz
☎ 914-255-2635
Open daily

Specializes in used, rare and out of print editions.

PAINTED WORD
36 Main Street
New Paltz
☎ 914-256-0825

An alternative bookstore featuring a coffee bar, it has a nice selection of books on local interest, mysteries, fiction, cooking and works of special interest to gays and lesbians.

ARIEL BOOKSELLERS

Ariel was selected as Best Book Store by Hudson Valley *magazine's readers' poll.*

3 Plattekill Avenue
New Paltz
☎ 914-255-8041
www.arielbooksellers.com
Open daily

Here's a general bookstore with large sections on local history and travel, and spiritual books. Located at the corner of Main Street and Plattekill Avenue.

ESOTERICA
81 Main Street
New Paltz
☎ 914-255-5777
Open daily

Woodstock isn't the only place to find books and gifts for seekers – Esoterica has it all: books on spirituality and holistic health, Christianity, dreams, Eastern religions, and an array of New Age gifts.

HANDMADE & MORE
6 N. Front Street
New Paltz
☎ 914-255-6277
www.handmadeandmore.com
Open daily, 10am-7pm

This is a popular shop for gift and holiday items, books, cards, chimes, clothing, jewelry, trinket boxes, glassware, bird feeders and pottery.

The store originally sold all handmade merchandise, but changed its name when other items were added. They provide free gift-wrap for any size package and has a restroom for visitors. The store was voted Best Gift Shop in the Hudson Valley in a 1998 Readers Choice poll by *Hudson Valley* magazine.

FOREIGN WIDE
3 North Front Street
New Paltz
☎ 914-255-8822

A unique gift shop that specializes in African and Indonesian masks and toys, futons and futon frames, wall hangings, jewelry, holiday ornaments and mobiles.

Ulster County

THE GALLERY FRAME & GIFT SHOP
5 North Front Street
New Paltz
☎ 914-256-0323
Closed Monday

Doubles as an art gallery exhibiting works by local artists.

NORTH FRONT ANTIQUES
15½ North Front Street
New Paltz
☎ 914-255-5144

Unlike the atmosphere in many antique shops with dusty troves of expensive heirlooms, North Front Antiques has light streaming in through several windows. It has two floors of very affordable antiques and also sells vintage linens, tablecloths, bedspreads, decorative accessories and furniture. The shop has a garden out back.

◎ TIP

North Front Antiques owner Julie McKelvey is a fount of information on Ulster County.

WATER STREET MARKET
10 Main Street
New Paltz
☎ 914-256-1870

This new $2.5 million, 18,000-square-foot pedestrian mall recently opened across from the Gilded Otter Restaurant. The mall houses 34 small shops and galleries, including gift shops, a candle shop, candy store and café, plus a renovated pole barn for a cooperative of more than a dozen antique dealers.

Additionally, look for the opening of **Spirit of the Woodlands** (☎ 914-883-6317) in the mall. This non-profit center's aim is to educate, preserve and promote the culture and artistic skills of Northeast Woodland regional tribes.

High Falls & Stone Ridge

BIRD WATCHER'S COUNTRY STORE
High Falls
☎ 914-687-9410
Open daily, 10am-6pm

Cross the bridge after the DePuy Canal House in High Falls and you'll come to this store filled with images of our feathered friends. According to the chirpy proprietor Bill VanHunter, bird watching is this nation's second-biggest hobby after gardening. The store's biggest seller, he says, is the in-house birdfeeder that fits in the window. Birds and other small creatures such as butterflies and squirrels figure on items like weathervanes, clog dancers, decoys and prints. The store also carries toys, field guides, cards, jewelry and birdseed. Items range in price from 39¢ trinkets to $2,000 furniture items.

GREEN COTTAGE
Main Street
High Falls
☎ 914-687-4810
Open daily except Tuesday

Open now two years, this attractive gift, flower and garden shop is operated by both Dennis Nutley, who was once the house florist at Mohonk, and by David Urso, who uses natural herbs and colored resins to create stunning brass and sterling silver jewelry.

Figuring that local artists have plenty of venues to display their wares, the partners decided to sell pottery and other gift items by non-resident artists. The store's biggest sellers, at $9 a pair, are scented Danish tapers that burn for 11 hours and are self-extinguishing. "They're very addictive," says Urso. "People get somewhat annoyed once they discover these unique candles, because then they don't want to use anything else." The garden shop also sells exotic perennials and garden furniture.

The quaint Green Cottage gift, flower and garden shop in High Falls.

HARMONY GIFTS
Route 209 (alongside Stone Ridge Towne Center)
Stone Ridge
☎ 914-687-4049
Open daily, year-round

This newly opened store has gifts for adults and kids, many made by locals. A big seller is Kripplebush Kids, collectible dolls wearing 1950-style clothes, made in Kingston by Kripplebush resident

Robert Tonner. The store also features wedding and anniversary items, Beanie Babies and Old World Christmas ornaments. Special orders are taken.

Ellenville to Accord

Best Places to Stay

The price scale for lodging can be found on page 20.

Resorts

HUDSON VALLEY RESORT & SPA
Route 44/55
Kerhonkson
☎ 914-626-8888
Moderate

The resort has 315 rooms, TV, telephone, 18-hole golf course, heated outdoor pool, indoor pool, cigar bar, tennis courts, basketball courts, boating, horseback riding, snow tubing, game room, two restaurants, scheduled activities and a European-style spa. It offers European or American meal plans.

A group of investors bought the old Granit Hotel in 1998, hired a top resort management company and poured $25 million into its remodeling (imagine carpeting 500,000 square feet!)

Lobby of the Hudson Valley Resort & Spa. (Courtesy of the resort)

Since most of the hotel has been fully renovated, no ugly stains or scratches mar its beauty. Joseph Ku, one of the four major investors and the interior decorator, visits the property weekly to insure all is shipshape. "When you care, it shows," he says. "When you don't care, it also shows."

The resort's new spa glimmers and promises to be the premier health spa in Ulster County. Guests pay $8 for use of the steam room, sauna and two areas of brand new Cybex equipment. Massages, facials and body wraps are being offered and there are plans to add a beauty salon and beverage stand. (Outside memberships are being limited to a few hundred.)

The hotel is also fanning the flames of businesspeople. With eight meeting rooms and a completely modern, multi-purpose 200-seat amphitheater, Hudson Valley has already hosted corporate meetings and hopes to attract more. Other improvements include a par-72 reconfigured golf course with direct access from the ninth hole to the hotel entrance.

Situated on 400 acres between the Catskill and Shawangunk Mountains, the modernized Hudson Valley Resort & Spa has such a large lobby it feels like the Metropolitan Museum of Art. Huge pillars and chandeliers dominate the furniture and voices echo off the walls. The zigzagging hallways and public rooms leading from the lobby keep guests from falling over one another. This is true even in inclement weather when everyone is inside. One August weekend it rained on and off so people socialized in the lobby. Others went to play pool or bingo. Two teenage boys retreated to the empty cigar bar to play poker.

The guestrooms are also spacious, with blonde-wood furniture, mirrors, comfortable beds and all the modern conveniences: shampoo, hair dryer, iron, ironing board, and coffee maker.

A *New York Times* article from Nov. 6, 1998 described poor management, dinner service and food at Hudson Valley, but it's all changed. The old management is gone, the staff is friendly and cooperative, and a new chef has come aboard – Scott Morosky from Windows on the World in Manhattan. Bentley's American Grill serves three meals and Sansui Restaurant (open to outsiders) serves sushi and teriyaki dishes (its menu will expand in time).

Directional Info: The turnoff for the resort, located on Route 44/55, is 1½ miles east of Route 209.

NEVELE GRANDE RESORT & COUNTRY CLUB
Nevele Road
Ellenville
☎ 914-647-6000
www.nevele.com
Inexpensive to Moderate

Ulster County

The Nevele and Fallsview hotels – just steps apart – are now under one umbrella in terms of name and ownership. All the facilities (except meals) are available to guests at either hotel.

With the closing of the Concord, these two hotels, totaling 680 rooms, now comprise the largest hotel property in the Catskills.

In its heyday the Nevele was one of the premier honeymoon destinations on the East Coast. Although it still has a riding stable, it once had racehorses and a championship trotter named Nevele Pride. (Benjamin Slutsky and Milton Kutsher were among the hotelmen who served as directors of Monticello Raceway when it opened in 1958.)

The Fallsview (Nevele Grande East) is smaller and is strictly kosher. After 70 years with a kosher kitchen, the Nevele (Nevele Grande West) converted to non-kosher in 1988, although it has a separate kosher dining room open in the summer and during Jewish holidays. Since the menu change, the Nevele has attracted a mix of races and religions and is by no means just a Jewish resort.

A below ground passageway connects all the buildings with guest rooms to the main building. It's rather spooky, so take a partner.

In 1999, both hotels were sold to Liberty Travel, which owns GoGo World Wide Vacations. Based in Ramsey, NJ, Liberty is the biggest privately owned travel chain in the US. Sadly, on October 6, 1998, its co-founder and driving force, Fred Kassner, died of cancer at age 71. A pioneer in bringing many of the world's exotic vacation spots within reach of people of modest means, his death affected the pace of renovations and operations at the Nevele.

In March of 2000, the hotels were sold to two former guests, Joe Hoffman and Mitchell Wolff. The two entrepreneurs currently own 11 properties throughout the US. They plan to continue the extensive renovations at the Fallsview and Nevele, and to keep general manager (and former owner) Charles Slutsky on board as a consultant.

We stayed at the Nevele during the renovation period on a supposed "off" weekend in November. It was packed with couples, families, singles and several groups – the largest a group of 800 attending the International Polka Festival Weekend. You can bet it was lively! All 120 tables were filled at some meals. Although some claim the food is better at Kutsher's, the meals at the Nevele are fine. Some dishes – like prime rib and baked ziti – are superb.

The best way to appreciate the resort is to walk around its well-tended 1,000 acres. In a valley sheltered by the Shawangunk Mountains, it offers its guests warmer and less windy weather in an idyllic setting. Dominated by the golf courses designed by Robert Trent Jones and Tom Fazio, it's tailor-made for golfers. A world-renowned designer, Fazio created Wild Dunes in South Carolina and the Nevele's 6,600-yard, par 70 golf course. The resort recently made the transition from nine holes to 36 and opened a Ken Venturi Golf Academy. Guest fees on weekends for 18 holes are $45, including cart.

Inquire about golf packages at the Nevele.

In the winter the courses are used for cross-country skiing. The Nevele also has downhill slopes, a chairlift and an ice-skating rink.

The day camp for ages three to 10 ($9 per child) operates weekends all year and every day in summer. Children ages two through 10 stay free in parents' room.

Directional Info: Take Route 209N out of Ellenville to hotel sign.

Ulster County

★ WHAT'S IN A NAME?

The Nevele derived its name from the falls behind the present-day Fallsview hotel. In 1884, 11 schoolteachers out for a picnic discovered the falls and named it for the number in their party, spelled backwards.

Dude Ranches

PINEGROVE DUDE RANCH
Lower Cherrytown Road
Kerhonkson
☎ 914-626-7345; 800-346-4626
www.pinegrove-ranch.com
Inexpensive

The ranch has 136 sizable guestrooms with TV, telephone, fireplace and air conditioning.

Pinegrove was voted Ranch of the Year by Family Circle *magazine.*

Looking for a place to keep your little cowpokes happy? (Read happy kids, happy parents.) Owned and operated by the Tarantino/O'Halloran families since 1971, this 600-acre resort in the Shawangunk Mountains is child-oriented in every respect. The activity list is endless – pony rides, petting farm, skiing lessons and snow tubing on a beginner slope, parlor games with prizes (and free bingo cards), fishing, boating, paint ball, hayrides, horseshoes, ice-skating, game room, indoor/outdoor pool (no lockers) and free snack bar (burgers, franks, fries, ice cream cones and coffee served morning until midnight). Also, something you wouldn't expect in the east – a daily cattle drive. The whole family is invited to watch and, for $25, advanced riders may participate in the roundup.

Besides all this, the Li'l Maverick Day Camp operates daily with activities in the wooden playground and on the field. There are also arts and crafts and swimming. The nursery cares for infants and toddlers.

With all this catering to children, parents are not forgotten. Second-timers are welcomed with a bottle of wine in their room and there are two cocktail parties a day, with the evening party featuring hot hors d'oeuvres. The food is basic and wholesome; meal service speedy. Dinner is over by 7:30pm; great for kids who can't sit still for long.

With roughly 75 horses available to ride, every guest is entitled to at least one guided ride a day through the pine groves. All levels of riders are welcome and each receives instruction. The wranglers are experienced and carefully watch riders, especially beginners, along the trail.

I never observed such a busy place or such a diverse ethnic crowd in the Catskills. The staff is friendly and the Old West decor is a nice mix of kitsch, antique and hunting lodge. In the evening there's music, magic, square dancing, campfires, snowtubing and karaoke. Open all year.

Directional Info: Take 209N and make a left at the light in Kerhonkson. Take the road to its end.

★ FAMOUS FACES

Peg-Leg Bates, the world-renowned one-legged tap dancer and vaudevillian who died recently at age 91, ran a resort in Kerhonkson for African-Americans for more than four decades. Cab Calloway, Sarah Vaughn, Lena Horne and Harry Belafonte were among the performers at Peg-Leg Bates Country Club (a.k.a. Mountain Valley Resort and Country Club).

Ulster County

Family Camps

FROST VALLEY
2000 Frost Valley Road
Claryville
☎ 914-985-2291
www.frostvalley.com
Weekend rate includes five meals
Inexpensive

In 2001, Frost Valley will celebrate its 100th anniversary.

A YMCA camp, Frost Valley in Claryville has three faces. In July and August it's a resident summer camp. Otherwise this YMCA of the Catskills is open to schools and youth groups on weekdays and to families on weekends, serving more than 30,000 children and adults each year.

Efficient and clean, Frost Valley stresses non-competitive activities, the environment, science and cultural diversity. It's got 6,000 acres, so expect lots of walking. In the winter the acres are used for cross-country skiing, tobogganing, tubing, snowshoeing and ice fishing.

The food is decent, the 650 rooms rustic, spacious and spare. There are no locks on the doors so leave your valuables at home. Frost Valley also hosts free musical concerts during the summer that are open to the public. Call for a schedule.

Directional Info: From Route 28, take County Highway 47 south at Big Indian for about 14 miles.

Best Places to Eat

*The price scale for restaurants can
be found on page 21.*

Lite Bites

VIVISPHERE
Accord Train Station
Accord
☎ 914-626-2105
Open all year
Inexpensive

If you love books and coffee, this recently opened
bookstore/café with its overstuffed couches and mel-
low music will please you to no end. Lodged inside
an erstwhile train station with the caboose right
outside, Vivisphere, a publisher as well, sells its own
books along with used hardcovers and paperbacks –
fiction, romance, science fiction, history and memoirs. Patrons are welcome to page through books
while enjoying an espresso, dessert or a bowl of soup.
On Friday nights, the café holds concerts ($6 cover
charge). Other regular events include poetry readings, writer's workshops, Sunday brunches and scrab-
ble tournaments.

★ WHAT'S IN A NAME?

Long ago, residents squabbled in this
Shawangunk community over what
to name their post office. The citizens voted on "Discord," but a wise
postal official wrote back that the
postmark would be "Accord."

Ulster County

Sunup to Sundown

Golf

Nevele Country Club, Ellenville, ☎ 800-647-6000, ext. 7373; www.nevele.com/nev. Three public nine-hole courses. Pro shop, lockers, practice area, chipping greens, club rentals, coffee shop, restaurant, lessons. Spikeless. Open April through November.

Built in the 1950s and designed by Robert Trent Jones, this championship course was redesigned by Tom Fazio in 1984. It's the summer home of the Ken Venturi Golf Academy.

Walker Valley Golf Club, Route 52, Walker Valley (eight miles from the Nevele). ☎ 914-744-3105/2714. Restaurant, bar, pro shop, club rental, pull carts. The flat layout of this executive nine-hole, par 32 course will suit you to a tee – especially if you're a novice. Open to the public daily, April through November.

Paragliding & Hang Gliding

Ellenville is a premier area for gliding through air. Mountains and wind conditions are near-perfect.

Two places that specialize in paragliding and hang gliding are Ellenville Flight Park and East Coast Paragliding Center & Mountain Wings Hang Gliding Center.

Tony Covelli has operated **Ellenville Flight Park** for 11 years. He owns "Ellenville Mountain" and the landing field where gliders take off. His flight school is for pilots and for others who want to learn paragliding or hang gliding. No experience is necessary for tandem rides. ☎ 914-647-1008.

East Coast Paragliding Center, in business since 1981, claims to be the largest paragliding company in the country. Gliders are either towed from the town's small Resnick (Ellenville) Airport or from Ellenville Mountain. A full-day introductory lesson is $125. The school also gives instruction in ultralight flying.

Judy Black, co-owner of **Mountain Wings**, said: "People often describe hang gliding as a very relaxing escape from the everyday grind. It's free flight – very quiet, no motor, no noise. You're soaring like a bird up there." Open year-round. Closed Tuesday and Wednesday. Located in town at 150 Canal St., across from Shadowland Theatre. ☎ 914-647-3377; www.flightschool.net/mtnwings.

Flying without an engine was recommended by Metrosports New York *as one of "30 Things To Do This Summer."*

Ulster County

Museums, Art & Theater

ELLENVILLE PUBLIC LIBRARY MUSEUM
40 Center Street
Ellenville
☎ 914-647-5530
Museum is open April-December on Wednesday, Friday and Saturday, noon-3pm.
Library and gallery open Monday-Saturday at 9am.

This museum is situated in the 1895 Terwilliger House adjoining the library. The permanent collection is of glassware and pottery from Ellenville's most important 19th-century industry. The centerpiece of the museum and most interesting display is the huge diorama of the Rondout Reservoir and the numbered buildings in the three lost hamlets, Eureka, Montela and Lackawack. In addition to private homes, the buildings included a tannery, lumber mill, gristmill, churches, cemeteries, post offices and tourist accommodations.

Monthly art exhibits and historical showcases line the walls of the gallery linking the library and the museum. An 1888 DeDion steam-powered automobile, reputed to be the oldest production-made auto in existence, dominates the gallery.

Library Lecture Series

The Ellenville Library has an interesting lecture series. In 1999, for example, a food historian spoke on the food of the Dutch and Iroquois, and the librarian from the Sojourner Truth Library at SUNY New Paltz spoke on the activist slave's formative years in Ulster County. Call for a calendar of events.

SHADOWLAND
157 Canal Street
Ellenville
☎ 914-647-5511

Completely remodeled, this is Ulster County's only professional non-profit theater, and most of the actors are Equity members. Performances are held July through September.

Woodstock to Saugerties

In 1845 a bunch of Woodstockers disguised themselves as Indians and tarred and feathered the local rent collector. So you see, our spirit of rebellion goes back a long, long time.

— Alf Evers,
Catskill historian and author

Woodstock is in a time warp. There are no empty storefronts; four independent bookstores have managed to survive; and heavy traffic sometimes clogs the village streets. Some folks believe the use of its name for the famed festival has had a lasting effect on its economy. Whatever the reason, Woodstock is a fine example of artistic expression and diverse lifestyles. A frequent visitor termed it "a very tolerant community reminiscent of Amsterdam."

Directions to Woodstock: From the Thruway, take Exit 19 (Kingston). Take 28W toward Pine Hill. Turn right onto Route 375 and turn left at Route 212W. Route 212 runs through the village, first as Mill Hill Road and then as Tinker Street.

Best Places to Stay

*The price scale for lodging can be
found on page 20.*

These following two establishments are in the thick
of town, but are removed from the hurly-burly.

WOODSTOCK INN ON THE MILLSTREAM
38 Tannery Brook Road
Woodstock
☎ 914-679-8211; 800-697-8211
Open all year
Inexpensive to Moderate

The inn has 18 rooms, seven of them efficiencies. TV,
buffet breakfast.

When Tom Bullard took over this motel in 1991, it
was "a mess occupied by druggies," in the words of
one frequent guest. That's hard to believe today. The
gardens are beautiful, the grounds well maintained
with lawn chairs for lounging, and the accommodations are comfortable and squeaky clean. Good
thing, too. A state health inspector showed up unex-
pectedly during my stay. The swimming hole behind
the inn is perfect for cooling off on a hot day.

The efficiency units are much larger than the standard rooms and are well worth the extra $25. Mine
had antique side chairs, an oak dining table with a
vase of fresh flowers, a fully-stocked skylit kitchenette, and king-size bed with a thick mattress. Singles, couples and families are attracted to this cozy
oasis just .2 mile from the main drag.

TWIN GABLES
73 Tinker Street
Woodstock
☎ 914-679-9479
Open all year
Inexpensive

This motel/guesthouse has very reasonable rates. Nine bedrooms are available and a large living room has a TV and reading materials. Robes are provided for guests sharing a bath. Adirondack Trailways stops one block away at the Village Green. Look for the yellow and green clapboard house with the twin gables across from Town Hall.

Best Places to Eat

The price scale for restaurants can be found on page 21.

Casual Dining

BLUE MOUNTAIN BISTRO
Route 212, between Woodstock and Saugerties
☎ 914-679-8519
www.bluemountainbistro.com
Open year-round for dinner Tuesday-Sunday; reservations recommended. Jazz on Saturday nights.
Moderate

A well-deserved four-star rating from the *Poughkeepsie Journal* is somewhat ironic, given that in the 1960s the 18th-century barn was taken apart and moved from Poughkeepsie to its present site where it was reconstructed with local wood. The raw wood is lightened with string lights and candles.

Three separate dining rooms offer top-notch service. Chef-owner Richard Erickson and wife, Mary Anne, took over a few years ago and specialize in French-Mediterranean cuisine. Members of the Chef's Collaborative, a network of chefs and farmers involved in promoting sustainable agriculture, these health-conscious owners grow their own vegetables and work closely with Cody Creek Farm in Saugerties. Rather than using oil or butter, Richard flavored my delectable spinach linguini, mussels and shrimp with fish stock, tomatoes, garlic and basil.

After studying the foods of the world for six years, Richard was a chef in New York City before becoming a chef instructor at the French Culinary Institute. In 1988 he opened Bistro du Nord, chosen by *New York Magazine* food critic Gael Greene as her favorite bistro in NYC. An April 1997 article in *Gourmet* magazine featured Erickson's recipe for shrimp with assorted grilled vegetables and orzo tossed with olive oil.

At Blue Mountain, only one roll is served with dinner. If you'd like another, just ask.

Main dishes at Blue Mountain offer multiple variations and reflect the chef's fondness for the foods of Spain, France, Greece and Morocco: rack of baby lamb with a roasted garlic, feta and olive crust; gnocchi with Italian gorgonzola, roasted walnuts, broccoli and tomato. And let's not forget the nightly Spanish tapas bar, offering more than 20 vegetarian dishes, including Tuscan white bean salad, Swiss chard, tzatziki (Greek cucumber salad) and tortilla Española.

Directional Info: Blue Mountain Bistro is two miles from the village of Woodstock. It's on the left across from the turn for Opus 40 on Glasco Turnpike.

★ **WHAT'S IN A NAME?**

Glasco Turnpike, once a toll road, is named for a sign on a glass company warehouse located along that road. Between 1809 and 1855 the company transferred its products to a shipping point on the Hudson.

NEW WORLD HOME COOKING

Route 212, between Woodstock and Saugerties (relocated from Zena Road)
☎ 914-246-0900
Open year-round
Inexpensive

I'd advise not ordering mild (0-3) – it's too bland.

Committed to healthy cooking, this casual restaurant serves creative entrées and small meals (priced at $6-$10) spiced to your favorite heat level. Dishes include big pot black-eyed pea gumbo and Iowa double-thick pork chops.

THE BEAR CAFE

295 Tinker Street, Route 212
Bearsville
☎ 914-679-5555; 914-679-8990 for Sunday brunch
www.bearcafe.com
Closed Tuesday
Moderate

If you can "bear" the noise from the busy bar, this popular restaurant has good food and service. My only quarrel is that the noise and smoke spills over into the dining room. If this also bothers you, request a table in the back.

Albert Glassman, personal manager to Bob Dylan, Janis Joplin, Peter, Paul and Mary and other musical greats, created this restaurant in 1971. Peter Cantine is the current owner, and paintings by his grandmother, an accomplished artist, decorate the walls.

Directional Info: Look for the red barn next to a theater and catering house.

Lite Bites

BREAD ALONE
22 Mill Road
Woodstock
☎ 914-679-2108
Open daily, 7am-5pm, year-round

Located in the village, this is a great place for breakfast. The crowd is an interesting mix of hippies and yuppies and everything in-between. There are lots of photos of Bob Dylan on the walls. Its breads are renowned for good reason. Have a slice or two of the organic farm bread with cream cheese and jelly – you won't be sorry.

★ FAMOUS FACES

Bob Dylan moved to Woodstock in 1965, but left in 1969 when the invasion of his privacy became intolerable.

TACO JUAN'S MEXICAN FOOD
31 Tinker Street
Woodstock
☎ 914-679-9673
Open daily, 10:30am-8pm, year-round

Don't let the name fool you. Next to the Golden Notebook, Taco Juan's sells everything from enchiladas to Hebrew National franks, bagels and ice cream. I tried Jane's homemade ice cream. It's good but does not come cheap – $2.25 for a cup of hazelnut fudge.

Sunup to Sundown

Hiking, Biking & Skiing

The mountains are calling me and I must go.

— John Muir

Fire Tower Hike

One recent spring day, I registered for a five-miler on **Overlook Mountain**. The hike, on National Trails Day in June, was to raise funds for five fire towers that are in disrepair. It was described as moderately strenuous and I'm grateful to my husband and a willing ranger for accompanying me on practice hikes.

Clear blue skies welcomed us on this fine summer day. After assembling and introducing ourselves, our group of 10 followed the **Overlook Spur Trail** 2.5 miles. To my surprise the hike upward was easy. Though rocky, the red-blazed trail was wide and the rise gradual. Our guides were George, a lanky forester with the New York State Department of Environmental Conservation (NYSDEC), and Ray, a wizened woodsman who champions hiking for health. Retired from the NYSDEC and now a volunteer, George told us tales about shooting snakes and fleeing forest fires.

The hiker with the heaviest backpack was a paunchy father toting his baby girl. The most dissatisfied had to be the seasoned hiker who found the unbroken stretch of hardwoods and softwoods boring. He would have preferred bushwhacking through the woods, but did concede that the view from the top was pretty good. Indeed it was. I'd lost track of time and we were soon off the path looking out at the Hudson to the east and the town of Woodstock below.

George then led us to the skeletal ruins of the **Overlook Mountain House**. Built during the Depression, the hotel was never completed, then was vandalized and burned.

⚡ WARNING

> Kids were climbing all over the ruins, but I'd be careful. Cracks are starting to erode the strong Rosendale cement, which had been produced right there in Ulster County.

We lunched on the 3,140-foot summit where one of five remaining steel fire towers presides. The youngest and most widely visited of the towers, it overlooks the Devil's Path, so called because of the substantial drops between the mountains in the chain.

The fire tower hikes are free and are led by experienced guides. Remember to bring lunch and water. ☎ 914-586-2611 for more information.

Directional Info: The entrance to Overlook Mountain is opposite the Tibetan monastery. Access is via Meads Mountain Road from the Village of Woodstock.

Fire Tower History

The state's first fire towers were built in the early 1900s so that fire observers could perch high in a tent with field glasses and a map and communicate through a cantankerous phone line to fire patrolmen below. It's hard to fathom that fire towers were last manned as recently as 1989.

A goal of the fire tower committee is to restore the observer's cabins as interpretive museums staffed with volunteers during the summer. If enough money is raised, these metal stilts will afford climbers an even greater view of the surrounding landscape. **Overlook Tower**, recently named to the National Historic Lookout Register, is the only one of the five awaiting an engineering study from the NYSDEC. When it's finally made safe for public use, the next challenge will be to climb those precarious steps another 58 feet upward.

From the project's inception in 1997 to the spring of 1999, $40,000 was raised through events, benefits, donations and the sale of merchandise. This represents one-half the amount needed to reopen all five towers by the year 2000. It is hoped that four towers (Balsam, Red Hill, Hunter, and Overlook) will be open by then; Tremper Mountain Fire Tower poses the biggest problem because it's been neglected for 20 years.

Ulster County

Shawangunk Mountains

The Gunks' high cliffs are world famous among rock climbers, who refer to them as the Trapps.

The Shawangunks (or Gunks) are a smaller mountain range than the Catskills and are considerably older. Formed about 450 million years ago, they are primarily composed of limestone and white conglomerate (fragments of rocks stuck together) not found in the Catskill chain. The Gunks are a northward extension of the Blue Ridge of Pennsylvania and the Kittatinny Ridge of New Jersey, all part of the Appalachian belt.

For a panoramic view of five states, follow Route 209 to Ellenville (Exit 113, Wurtsboro) and take Route 52E up the Northern Shawangunks to **Sam's Point**, a national landmark and the Gunks' highest point.

Local Lore

Legend has it that Sam Gonsales jumped off the 2,255-foot cliff here to escape the Indians and landed on a clump of hemlocks with only a few scratches. (Lucky for him, tanneries didn't start destroying hemlock trees to a great extent until the next century.)

The path is lined with blueberry bushes and is a favorite route of pickers. The shortest climb is .6 mile to the top. The footing is easy, the path slightly hilly, and it's worthwhile for the view. The site is open all year. From Memorial Day through October there's a $5 parking fee and the gift shop is open weekends. Only hiking and hunting are allowed, so if you go in the fall, wear bright colors. (Orange safety vests are available for a $1 donation.)

Ice caves created here 330 million years ago have now been closed and the site has been re-named

from Ice Caves Mountain to **Sam's Point Preserve**.
☎ 914-647-7989.

*Directional Info to Overlook Mountain: The trip past
the Nevele sign on Route 209 to the Sam's Point parking lot is less than 10 miles. Take 209N to 52E for 4.7
miles and turn left at Cragsmoor Road. In 1½ miles
you'll come to Sam's Point Road; turn here and continue another 1¼ miles and park in the lot. Should
you feel vigorous after walking the trail and enjoying
the splendid view, continue on to Verkeerkill Falls,
which is 2.8 miles from the start.*

★ **WHAT'S IN A NAME?**

The spelling of Gonsales was often
interchanged with Gonsalus. Could
Sam Gonsales have been a descendant of Sullivan County's first white
settler in about 1730 – a Spaniard
named Emanuel Gonsalus – whose
grave is near Wurtsboro?

Outdoor Tours & Workshops

John and Jackie Mallery have 20 years of experience
in leading bicycle, canoeing and ski trips. The couple
operates **True Wheel Tours** in Long Lake in the
Adirondacks. The Mallerys also serve as workshop
coordinators for the Appalachian Mountain Club.

Although they teach all over the East Coast, several
trips they offer are centered around the Catskills.
Also, many of the hiking and biking workshops are
combinations such as music and biking, hiking and
storytelling, and hiking and drumming. The weekend fee (Friday to Monday afternoon) includes lodging at Valley View Lodge in Oliveria (Ulster County)

Ulster County

and two meals a day. Non-member fees for these workshops and ski weekends range from $180 to $310. ☎ 518-624-2056.

Golf

Katzbaan Golf Club, 1754 Old Kings Highway, Saugerties. ☎ 914-246-8182/7604. Nine holes, par 35; lessons, snack bar, club rental; spikeless; carts not mandatory. During holidays, call two days in advance for tee times. Hal Purdy built this semi-private course in 1990. Gently rolling hills with Catskills as backdrop. Open all year, weather permitting.

Museums, Art & Theater

In Eighteen Hundred and Forty One
They put their long red flannels on,
They put their long red flannels on
To work in the bluestone quarries.
We left old Ireland far behind
To search for work of a different kind;
To work was hard, but we didn't mind
To work in the bluestone quarries.
  – "The Bluestone Quarries" from *Folk*
      Songs of the Catskills

QUARRYMAN'S MUSEUM AT OPUS 40
High Woods
Saugerties
☎ 914-246-3400
Open Memorial Day weekend through October, Friday-Sunday, noon-5pm.

Sculptor Harvey Fite bought an abandoned bluestone quarry in 1938, paying $300 for 12 acres. He built his house on the edge of the quarry and spent the next 37 years creating an astonishing series of sweeping terraces, fountains, statues and pools. He fit each stone without using mortar or cement, a technique he'd learned on a fellowship to restore Maya ruins in Honduras in the mid-1930s. A professor at Bard College until 1969, Fite's reasoning behind this 6½-acre outdoor gallery was that "Ancient cultures have left enduring monuments of their times and there's no reason why an American can't have the same idea." Fite's death in 1976 occurred three years short of his planned 40-year Opus.

Bluestone quarrying was an important industry from 1870 to about 1900, when it was replaced by Portland cement.

The museum showcases the primitive tools he used, and a seven-minute video gives a brief history of the project. Rubber-soled shoes are advised for walking on the stones. Sunset concerts are held on the grounds during the summer. $5 admission.

WOODSTOCK GUILD
34 Tinker Street
Woodstock
☎ 914-679-2079
Open Friday-Sunday, noon-6pm

This multi-arts organization sponsors concerts, exhibits, classes, and a retail craft shop that celebrated its 60th anniversary in 1999. The shop features work by local artisans and is open to the public. The guild was founded in 1939 by the town artists.

BYRDCLIFFE
Woodstock
☎ 914-679-2079
www.woodstockguild.org

In 1976, Peter Whitehead bequeathed Byrdcliffe Arts Colony, later listed on the National Register of Historic Places, to the guild. Peter's father, Ralph Rad-

Ulster County

cliffe Whitehead, built this complex of wood chalets in 1902. An Englishman and heir to a Yorkshire textile fortune, he was influenced by the aesthetic and utopian principles of his professor, John Ruskin, at Oxford University. Whitehead purchased about 1,200 acres of farmland below Mead's Mountain in Woodstock and set up workshops and accommodations. More than 20 of the original 30 wooden cottages are still rented to artists and writers (for a minimum of five months).

★ WHAT'S IN A NAME?

The name, Byrdcliffe, was taken from the middle name of Ralph Radcliffe Whitehead and combined with his wife's name, Jane Byrd McCall.

"In 1902 artists started coming to Ulster County," says Carla Smith, executive director of the guild. "It was going to be the best art school around." But Whitehead (1854-1929) was an autocrat, dubbed the Dictator of Byrdcliffe. Students left after the first summer and he fired one of the two men he started with. The other, Hervey White, left to found his own colony, called Maverick, on a farm in nearby Hurley. His open-air Maverick Festivals, begun in 1916, became the prototype for the Woodstock gatherings in 1969 and 1994. Concerts are still held at the **Maverick Concert Hall** (see page 246) a mile from the village. Yet history has it that it was the Art Students League Summer School, started shortly after Byrdcliffe, that brought Woodstock's first hippies.

Today says Smith, Byrdcliffe is "a pretty big dark secret." To counter this, the guild has drawn up a self-guided walking tour encircling the grounds, and every house is numbered. In 1995 it purchased the home of Mr. Whitehead, a 15-room mansion that will eventually be open to the public. The two-story house called White Pines was the centerpiece of the colony, says Smith and hopefully with the help of grants will be restored to its former grandeur by 2002, its 100th anniversary. Currently 2,000 items are being inventoried, including shelves of unglazed ceramic pots.

Whitehead popularized the arts and crafts movement and hired the finest craftsmen to build his stand-alone cabinets and built-ins. Many of the pieces are at top museums, but the guild hopes to locate more. Most of the woodwork is characterized by a fleur-de-lis design.

★ FAMOUS FACES

Painters such as Georgia O'Keeffe taught at Byrdcliffe, and John Burroughs came there for meals. Poet Wallace Stevens, author Thomas Mann and dancer Isadora Duncan were some of the other notables regularly entertained at Byrdcliffe.

Smith points out that other utopian colonies no longer exist or have been changed, whereas Byrdcliffe has 30 buildings still standing and devoted to the arts. Byrdcliffe "changed the face of Woodstock forever," she says. "We have more artists per capita than anywhere except Manhattan. It may not be the dream Mr. Whitehead had of a utopian society, but we certainly have tried to make Byrdcliffe a haven for artists and will continue to do so."

Directional Info: To reach Byrdcliffe, follow Rock City Road in the village of Woodstock for a quarter-mile to Glasco Turnpike. Turn left and continue a

Ulster County

*quarter-mile to Upper Byrdcliffe Road. Turn right
and proceed ¼ mile until you see the Byrdcliffe sign
on the theater. Parking is left of the theater.*

MAVERICK CONCERT HALL
Maverick Road off Route 375
Woodstock
☎ 914-679-2079

Summer chamber music concerts with top performers are held every Sunday at 3pm at this historic
concert hall. Founded in 1916, this is the oldest
chamber music series in the US. Concerts are listed
in *The New York Times* during the summer, mid-
June through early September.

CENTER FOR PHOTOGRAPHY
AT WOODSTOCK
59 Tinker Street
Woodstock
☎ 914-679-9957
Open year-round, noon-5pm
Closed Monday and Tuesday

This multi-faceted center caters to photographers,
students and the public through six-week exhibits,
June through October lectures and photography
workshops, and the use of its library and print collection. It also offers spring fellowships to emerging
photographic artists who live in eligible upstate New
York counties. The center also provides four college-
age interns one-year training opportunities along
with a $6,000 tuition remuneration. Most exhibits
are group shows; the photography is for sale.

According to program director Kathleen Kenyon,
the center is celebrating its 22nd year of workshops
and lectures. The average age of the attendees is 40.
She adds that in contrast to the International Center of Photography in Manhattan, which focuses on

creative photography, Woodstock concentrates on rural life.

At this writing, two rooms were being readied for galleries and the entrance changed from the back stairs to the street front. "We want to open doors to the public on the main street," says Kenyon. This goes along with its operating philosophy to create access to professional workspace, support living artists and their audience, and provide a bridge in the journey of recognition and presentation between artists and audiences.

PERFORMING ARTS OF WOODSTOCK
Woodstock
☎ 914-679-7900

The Performing Arts of Woodstock, which celebrated its 35th anniversary in 1999, presents three major shows with local actors during the autumn, winter and spring. Productions are held at the Woodstock Town Hall on Tinker Street, next to the fire station. Tickets are $10.

Shopping

Woodstock

In Woodstock anything goes. Mainstream stores like **Ben & Jerry's** compete harmoniously with **Jane's Homemade Ice Cream**, and **Birkenstock** caters to the barefoot generation. New Age emporiums sell tie-dyed T-shirts and crystals right next door to upscale art galleries and boutiques. Oddly enough, four bookstores, listed below, coexist in this quaint village.

GOLDEN NOTEBOOK
25-29 Tinker Street
Woodstock
☎ 914-679-8000
www.goldennotebook.com

This general bookstore offers a children's section and has a gift and card shop, **Golden Bough**, separate from the bookstore. The bookstore specializes in current literature, has a large section on Eastern philosophy, and takes special orders for books in and out of print. Proprietor Ellen Shapiro commented about her long-standing staff and strong customer base when a young couple from Canada interjected, "It's the only bookstore we come to when we visit Woodstock."

BOOKMART
40 Mill Hill Road
Woodstock
☎ 914-679-4646
Open daily at 11am; closed Monday

A smaller version of Golden Notebook, Bookmart carries children's books, books on tape, CDs, writing journals, games and stationery, and offers complimentary giftwrap. They will also order for you any book, whether it be in or out of print. "We get lots of special orders," says the cordial owner, Roz Chumsky.

MIRABAI
23 Mill Hill Road
Woodstock
☎ 914-679-7819
Open daily year-round

New and used books for the spiritual reader are sold here. Mirabai (with the accent on "Mir") is named for a 15th-century Indian poetess. The store has a Sacred Space Gallery in the back with statues of deities that's used for meditation classes. If the room is open and the tamboura, an Indian string instrument, hasn't been sold, take a peek. It's an exquisite work of art made from a gourd. It sells for $1,150.

A fourth bookstore, **Yesterday's Books**, is closed on Tuesday and has shorter hours.

DHARMAWARE GIFT SHOP & CAFE
54E Tinker Street
Woodstock
☎ 914-679-3270

A strong smell of incense pervades this shop, which sells New Age gifts, books and clothing. Visit the garden out back.

Saugerties

KRAUSE'S HOMEMADE CANDY
41 South Partition Street (off Route 9W)
Saugerties
☎ 914-246-8377
Open daily

Just try to walk out of this place without buying something. The aroma of chocolate will break the will of even the most diet-conscious visitor. Krause's makes chocolates, fudge and peanut brittle daily. It also sells a variety of non-chocolate candies. This store, as well as a branch in Albany, is being enlarged. There's yet another branch in Paramus, New Jersey.

Ulster County

BEACHVIEW CENTER CAROUSEL
61 S. Partition Street (across from Krause's)
Saugerties
☎ 914-246-5388
Open Friday-Sunday, May through October

"Cool! A merry-go-round," a little girl with a contingent of youngsters exclaimed with glee as they entered a red brick building for a birthday party. Beachview Center Carousel now occupies this turn-of-century building. Owner Bob Imbierowic tracked down and restored discarded horses, chariots and scenery panels. All the horses are authentic wood-carved Allan Herschell's, the last of the six major manufacturers from the glory days of wooden carousels. A ride on the carousel is $1, "the best bargain in town," says Bob.

SIMPLY COUNTRY
148 Main Street, Route 9W
Saugerties
☎ 914-247-8149
Open daily, Wednesday-Sunday

This zany country store (next to the diner and across from Stewart's) has too many items to name. Dolls seem to dominate, however – cloth, rag, rubber, vinyl, porcelain – they even line the stairs. The 16 rooms of the shop include fall and Christmas rooms. Sharon Benschoten bought the former B&B built in 1870 (Jackson's Tourist Home) three years ago and worked for seven weeks to convert it into her shop. When she opened, she says, "the lines were all the way down Main Street and it's been wonderful ever since."

HOPE FARM PRESS & BOOKSHOP
252 Main Street (between the two traffic lights)
Saugerties
☎ 914-246-3522
Open daily, year-round

Another must-see establishment. Founded in 1959 by a retired NYC librarian, this publisher and distributor carries general books along with 2,100 books on New York State – new, used, in or out of print. More than 1,500 of those titles can be found online at www.hopefarm.com. A 1996 article in *National Geographic* had this to say about owner Richard Frisbie: "In Saugerties, there is a book publisher who offers you a worn leather chair and pours out an encyclopedic knowledge of his town."

Along Route 28

Route 28 takes you 35 miles from Kingston on the Hudson River to Pine Hill near Delaware County's eastern border. From Kingston, Thruway Exit 19, the road is somewhat commercial, but as you reach the Shandaken area the mountains rise in all their magnificence. During the winter this is ski country, so there are many open eateries and B&Bs scattered along most of the stretch. You'll also pass picturesque villages, boutiques, lakes, an amusement center, and a campsite for picnickers, hikers and campers.

Phoenicia has recently been likened to the Woodstock of the '60s.

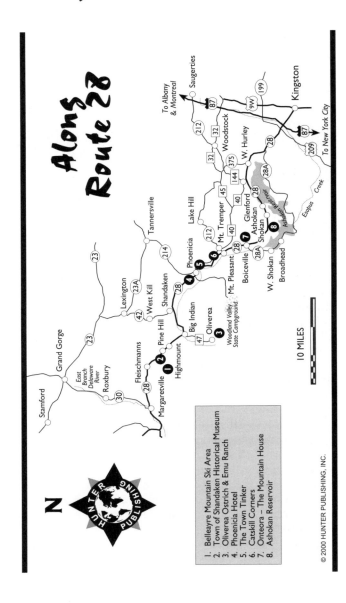

Along Route 28

N

1. Belleayre Mountain Ski Area
2. Town of Shandaken Historical Museum
3. Oliverea Ostrich & Emu Ranch
4. Phoenicia Hotel
5. The Town Tinker
6. Catskill Corners
7. Onteora – The Mountain House
8. Ashokan Reservoir

10 MILES

Best Places to Stay 🛏️

The price scale for lodging can be found on page 20.

Inns/B&Bs

ONTEORA – THE MOUNTAIN HOUSE
96 Piney Point Road
Boiceville
☎ 914-657-6233
Inexpensive to Moderate

If you're the romantic type who enjoys solitude and a stunning panorama of five mountain chains, check out Onteora. Innkeepers Bob McBroom and Joe Che bought this isolated mountaintop estate from mayonnaise king Richard Hellman in 1991. Hellman built it in the 1930s when told he'd die in six months if he didn't retire to the country. One guidebook calls the location one of the most beautiful of any B&B in the world. Each of the five rooms is named for one of the mountains. Only one guestroom has a private bath, so bring your own shampoo.

Hotels

PHOENICIA HOTEL
Main Street
Phoenicia
☎ 914-688-7500
Inexpensive

The hotel has twenty rooms, all with TV and air conditioning. The upstairs is completely restored.

Ulster County

The Trailways bus stops right in front of the Phoenicia Hotel.

Built in 1853, the Phoenicia Hotel certainly captures the imagination. It has a checkered history, postage stamp-sized lobby mixes the old (gumball machine) and new (video game), and a raucous bar that's the #1 local hangout. Carlito's, a Spanish-American restaurant separated from the bar by a half partition, is open for lunch and dinner. The large, mainly meat dishes are filling and tasty at bargain prices. What's more, the Phoenicia's rooms are less expensive than some motels.

"Weekends are crazy here," declares co-owner Richard Stokes, who hitchhiked to the Catskills from his home in Yonkers a decade ago and never returned. "We treat everybody like family," he added.

★ FAMOUS FACES

The cast of *Good Morning America* stayed at the Phoenicia Hotel. So did the *Seventeen* magazine crew. And even members of the United Nations stayed here.

Perhaps that's why Dutch Schultz, the notorious bootlegger and subject of E.L. Doctorow's novel *Billy Bathgate*, found the hotel to his liking. (He later bought a house in Phoenicia.) The mountains surrounding the village provided good cover for his bootlegging operation and undoubtedly appealed to his miserly side. Legend has it that he hoarded millions of dollars in gold coins and diamonds in two steel suitcases and buried them near a stand of big pine trees near Esopus Creek. Treasure hunters have visited Phoenicia, but none has found the stash.

Hostels

BELLEAYRE HOSTEL

Main Street
Pine Hill
☎ 914-254-4200
www.belleayre-hostel.com
Open all year
Inexpensive

Amenities include a rec building, full commercial kitchen for customers' use, gas fireplace, pool table, ping pong table, computer games, air hockey, TV with VCR, stereo system, two children's play corners, yard with outdoor fireplace for barbecuing or bonfire, picnic tables, lounge chairs, volleyball net, basketball hoop and sleds. (A slide and swing set, sandbox, and small pool are coming.) Linens, towels and sleep sacks for bunkers are supplied. Bunks have shared bathrooms. Cabins can accommodate four and each has private bath, small fully-equipped kitchen, TV and enclosed porch.

This is the only hostel in the Catskills. No longer affiliated with American Youth Hostels, it is private and independent so all are welcome. According to manager Tom, whose parents own the hostel, it's not restricted to youth. "In fact," he says, "most of our customers are adults aged 19 to 35, but we get a varied crowd here."

Located at the base of Belleayre Ski Mountain, the hostel naturally attracts skiers in the winter – youth groups and families. Other guests prefer hiking the trails in the immediate area or visiting Woodstock 40 minutes away. Summertime draws hikers, bikers, fishermen, hunters, environmentalists, swimmers (a man-made lake is within walking distance),

Ask at the hostel about discounts and ski packages.

Ulster County

tubers (riding an inner tube down Esopus Creek) and horseback riders (several stables are nearby).

The hostel runs two annual events, at New Year's and on Halloween. (Its haunted driveway is well known in the area.)

Best Places to Eat

The price scale for restaurants can be found on page 21.

Casual Dining

LES COPAINS D'ABORD
Route 28
Big Indian
☎ 914-245-4646
Open year-round, Wednesday-Saturday, 5-10pm;
Sunday, noon-9pm
Moderate

Loosely translated, Les Copains D'Abord is French for "friends."

This lovely French restaurant is about 13 miles west of Phoenicia in the Val D'Isere Hotel. The décor (flowers and lace curtains) and menu (frogs legs, free-range rabbit in port wine) are typically French, but true to its name the staff is friendly, not snobby, and the portions generous. My dish of roast loin of pork with roasted apples and strawberries and au gratin potatoes ($14.95) was deliciously tender and attractively presented.

★ **DID YOU KNOW?**

T. Morris Longstreth wrote that the town Big Indian was named for a strapping redskin (Big Injin) who got into trouble because he murdered people.

SWEET SUE'S
Main Street
Phoenicia
☎ 914-688-7852
Open daily, year-round, for breakfast and lunch

Word is that weekends are crazy at Sweet Sue's, *the* place for pancakes and French toast. And although several varieties are available, the blueberry pancakes are the biggest sellers. A summer offering sounds outrageous: a pancake sandwich layered with yogurt and fresh fruit.

Sunup to Sundown

Animal Farms

OLIVEREA OSTRICH & EMU RANCH
9917 Oliverea Road (Route 47)
Oliverea
☎ 914-985-7374
Open year-round on Friday, Saturday and Sunday. Call first during the week.

It's a fallacy that ostriches stick their heads in the sand to avoid predators; ostriches may actually be among the most curious creatures. Go near them and they stretch their long necks over the fence

Ulster County

watching your every move. The ranch also has ducks, chickens and rabbits for the little ones to enjoy.

⚠ WARNING

Ostriches lack teeth but can painfully clamp down on your hand. Children should be warned to look and not touch.

George and Helen Johnston and their son, Bob, raise and sell ostriches for breeding, meat, leather and yes, as pets. The emus they keep are also sold for meat (it's extremely lean), but they are mostly valued for their oils, which are sold in the shop as lotions. Also for sale is jewelry made from ostrich shells, full quill wallets, and cuts of ostrich meat (the red meat is lower in fat, calories and cholesterol than turkey or chicken). I settled on a pair of ostrich shell earrings with hand-painted ostriches. Also interesting is the ranch's computerized incubator – ostriches hatch in 42 days and emus in 40.

Ostrich & Emu Facts

There were about 100 ostriches and a handful of emus the day I visited. Ostriches have two toes and the larger one could rip you apart, according to Johnston. They are the biggest of all birds, standing as tall as 10 feet. Teams of ostriches were sometimes used in ancient Rome to pull chariots in races. Emus have three toes and are half the size of ostriches.

Family Fun

CATSKILL CORNERS
Route 28 at Mt. Pleasant Road
Mt. Tremper
☎ 914-688-5300; 914-688-7700 for calendar of events
www.catskillcorners.com
Open daily, 10am-7pm; closed Tuesday in winter.
$10 for three attractions, $8 children, $9 for a family
of four or more.

Both parent and child will love Catskill Corners, a
family entertainment complex that's the closest thing
to Disneyland you'll see in the Catskills. The big dif-
ferences are the lack of hard-sell commercialism and
the reasonable prices. According to a USA survey,
the cost for a family of four to spend just one day at
an amusement park has jumped 23% from $115.97
in 1993 to $142.90.

Opened in 1996, Catskill Corners includes restaurants, shops, a lodge, and the world's largest kaleidoscope. Since you stand in a silo and have to look up
to view it, there are cushioned neck supports. If it's
not crowded you can lie down on the floor for a more
comfortable experience. The converted 19th-century
barn also houses a smaller version and 18 interactive Rube Goldberg-like contraptions, each with its
own kaleidoscope.

Browse the six attractive shops at Catskill Corners –
prices seem surprisingly reasonable. The candy shop
has a cook's corner; **Scentsation** has scents to com-
bat stress. Aside from all the lotions, heart-shaped
bath fizzers promise to melt your worries away, and
happy heart massagers are designed to take away
those muscular aches and pains. Another store focuses on romance, selling music, hammocks, golf
gifts and scented candles. **Wild Things** sells every-

Ulster County

thing from Maurice Sendak's scary wild things to wooden kazoos and cuddly stuffed ducklings. For regional, gardening and nature books, visit the **Nature Adventure Store**.

⊚ TIP

Catskill Corners is also a tourist information center with the largest number of brochures I've seen anywhere in the Catskills.

The Spotted Dog is a tribute to the bravery of all firefighters.

Though you'd never know from outside, the **Spotted Dog Restaurant** in Catskill Corners is not just for kids. A room is set aside just for adults. The menu offers burgers, hot dogs, pastas, sandwiches and salads, at a top price of $8.95. It pleased my palate and my pocketbook.

Also try the **Catamount Café** nearby. It's open for dinner, Thursday through Sunday. ☎ 914-688-7900.

The Lodge motel is a bit hokey in keeping with the playland atmosphere. The 27 rooms are oversized and some have vaulted ceilings, whirlpool tubs, fireplace, decks, duplexes, and mountain views. A standard room is $95-$125; superior is $110-$140, deluxe is $135-$195, and suites are $175-$250. continental breakfast is included. ☎ 877-688-2828.

Dean Gitter, the founder of Catskill Corners and the controversial leader of the Route 28 revitalization effort, has plans to build an inn and spa across the street from The Lodge.

Fishing

Hank Rope of **Big Indian Guide Service** (☎ 914-254-5904, www.flyfishing.com) is a friendly fishing guide and an authority on fly-fishing, who gives lessons along the Esopus Creek between Boiceville and Big Indian. He prefers taking two people at a time, either experienced or beginners. The season is April 1 through November 30. His all-day fee is $125 for the first person and $65 for the second.

The Esopus Creek also runs through the small village of Phoenicia, which caters to fishermen as well as canoers. **Morne Imports** (☎ 914-688-7738) is part tackle store with a full-scale department of fishing equipment. The other section sells clothing, gifts, notions, greeting cards, camping equipment and jewelry. The second floor of the **Phoenicia Library** (☎ 914-688-7811) has an "Anglers Corner," a bonanza of books for fishermen. The good news is that non-residents may borrow books and/or a fishing pole for an $18 annual fee. The library also holds fly-tying workshops in the early spring.

Tubing

THE TOWN TINKER
Main Street
Phoenicia
☎ 914-688-5553

Phoenicia is headquarters of this popular tube-rental concern. (It also has an outpost at Catskill Corners.) Conveniently located on Esopus Creek and surrounded by mountains, this is an ideal spot to begin your journey down the river. Follow the sign into town and you'll see the red barn. Some tubes have wooden seats to prevent scraping your fanny on the rocks. The friendly staff accommodates both beginners and advanced tubers, but children must be at least 12 years old. Day rates are $7; $10 with seats; $2 for life jackets; and $3 for helmets. The season is May 15 through September 15, 9am-6pm daily, but you can call for information any time.

Another tubing outfitter, **F-S Tube & Raft Rental**, is located behind the Phoenicia Hotel, which is on Main Street. ☎ 914-688-7633.

Hiking, Biking & Skiing

Ashokan Reservoir

Between Boiceville & Belleayre, active families will find plenty to do. Depending on the season there's hiking, tubing, camping, swimming and skiing.

The Ashokan Reservoir is one of the largest of the Catskill reservoirs, 2¼ miles wide with a maximum depth of 171 feet. There's a 1¼-mile concrete walk along the water, the only one of the Catskills reservoirs offering the public a chance to enjoy a full view while walking, jogging or skateboarding. The path is generally quiet.

Directional Info: From Route 28 in Shokan, turn onto Reservoir Road and go to the end. Park along the guardrail. If there's no space, which is unlikely, follow the road down and around to the parking lot near the fountain.

Historical Note

When the Ashokan Reservoir was being constructed in the early 1900s, several hamlets, a railroad and many cemeteries were submerged and destroyed. Some buildings were moved and the village relocated elsewhere. Shokan was one of them.

Several generations of the Winchell family, all successful merchants, had helped realize the dream of their ancestor Lemuel to put Shokan on the map. Winchell's Corners, which eventually became known as the center of town, was moved with a horse and wagon to its present location in Shokan.

Belleayre Mountain

State-operated Belleayre Mountain in Highmount off Route 28 near the Delaware County border has many faces. In the winter it's a ski center. In the summer it's home to the Belleayre Music Festival series (see page 267). Columbus Day Weekend is another big event with crafts, food, music and chairlift rides to the summit. The rest of the time the mountain is the take-off point for several hiking trails.

After passing the magnificent North Woods-like setting west along Route 28 past Big Indian, take Friendship Road to **Belleayre Mountain Day Use Area**. This state-run scenic area, which includes a lake for swimming in the shadow of Belleayre Mountain, locker rooms and a play gym on sand. $5 per car or $1 for walk-ins.

◎ TIP

Route 47, heading south from Big Indian, is very scenic. But first be sure to stock up at **Morra's Market** at the junction of 28 and 47 before heading out.

In 1999, **Belleayre Mountain Ski Center** (☎ 914-254-5600) celebrated its 50th birthday with a dizzy-

Ulster County

ing array of week-long events in late January. Doro-thy "Dot" Nebel, an Olympic skier now in her nineties, was honored. She designed the ski trails and headed the Belleayre Ski School from 1949 to 1966.

Belleayre, at 3,249 feet, is the highest ski-able peak in the Catskills.

Belleayre's vertical drop of 1,404 feet was formed by nature into two mountains – the upper one used by more experienced skiers and the lower by beginners. There are 33 trails open to skiers and snowboarders and nine lifts. Snowboarders also have an obstacle park designed for them.

The snowmaking capacity is 87%, but the high ele-vation means more natural snow. I can vouch for that. Driving along Route 28 in early November, I noticed that it starting snowing only as I ap-proached the slope. The good news is you don't have to drive here. An Adirondack Trailways Ski Bus de-parts daily from Port Authority in Manhattan at 7am and returns at 7:30pm. At this writing, round-trip transportation is $53 and includes lift ticket. (Bus service is also available from Ridgewood, NJ, New Paltz and Kingston on Friday, Saturday and Sunday.) ☎ 800-942-6904; 800-858-8555 for infor-mation; www.belleayre.com. Belleayre is open 9am-4pm during winter.

Kudos For Belleayre Ski Center

Belleayre was named the best place to learn to ski in the East by *Skiing* magazine. An-other source had this to say: "The ski in-structors at Belleayre Ski Center are well known for how well they handle and teach new skiers and those wanting to improve their abilities, and the ski trails are groomed very well all the time."

State Parks

WOODLAND VALLEY
1319 Woodland Valley Road
Phoenicia
☎ 914-688-7647
Open daily, 8am-10pm, mid-May through
Columbus Day weekend

This is a woodsy spot deep in the forest that leads to
the Catskill's loftiest peak, **Slide Mountain**. If you
wish to hike, picnic, fish or camp, follow the road for
five miles to the state campsite. Naturalist John
Burroughs loved the wildness of this region and said
that of all the retreats he found in the Catskills,
"There is no other that possesses quite so many
charms for me as this valley."

The campsites at Woodland Valley can be reached only from Route 28, near Phoenicia.

KENNETH L. WILSON
Wittenberg Road
Mt. Tremper
☎ 914-679-7020
Open daily, 8am-10pm, mid-May through
Columbus Day weekend

This park offers lake swimming (when lifeguard is
on duty), boating, camping, fishing, picnicking, children's play area, sand beach and hiking trails. It's
very picturesque with mountains all around.

*Directional Info: From Thruway Exit 19, take the
first right turn off the traffic circle to Route 28; proceed about 21 miles west on Route 28 to Mt. Tremper.
Turn right onto Route 212 and continue a half-mile
to a four-way intersection. Turn right on Wittenberg
Road (County Route 40). The campsite is approximately five miles on the right.*

Ulster County

Horseback Riding

The **Saddle Up Ranch**, under the auspices of Silver Springs Ranch in Haines Falls, is a new facility 1¼ miles west of Catskill Corners on Route 28 in Phoenicia. Owner Ray Phillips says this ranch is aimed at the Jewish trade, given all the Jewish camps in the area. Horseback riding; petting zoo. ☎ 914-688-7336.

Museums, Theater & Music

TOWN OF SHANDAKEN HISTORICAL MUSEUM
Academy Street
Pine Hill
Open Thursday and Friday, 11am-4pm; Saturday and Sunday, 1-4pm
Free admission

*Hungry? Try the good food at **Key West Café** on Main Street in Pine Hill.*

The museum shows the talented work of local artists. The lovely watercolors of Ralph H. Persons were also on display when I visited, marking the artist's 33rd one-man show. Catskills and New England panoramas inspire his seascapes, selling from $75 to $350. Anyone interested in seeing Persons' work may call **Eagles Nest Studio**, ☎ 914-254-5528.

SHANDAKEN THEATRE
Church Street
Phoenicia
☎ 914-688-7235

The 20-year-old Shandaken Theatrical Society is comprised of local talent that performs in spring (musicals) and fall (drama or comedy), and hopes to start summer productions as well. The theater recently moved into its own building around the corner from the Phoenicia Hotel. The 100-year-old structure now houses this 150-seat theater. Tickets can be either reserved or purchased at the door for $10.

BELLEAYRE MUSIC FESTIVAL
Belleayre Mountain; Route 28
Highmount
☎ 800-942-6904
www.belleayremusic.org

Belleayre Mountain is never silent. In winter the skiers keep it lively, and in July and August this music festival brings top entertainment to the mountain. When the Belleayre Conservatory was founded in 1992, the concert schedule had only one feature performance: The Brooklyn Philharmonic. It now has 10 concerts and a children's series, drawing large audiences to its 800-seat concert tent for classical, folk, opera, rock, pop, and jazz. Previous performers included, in 1998, singer Betty Buckley and jazz pianist McCoy Tyner; and in 1999, Julie Budd and Art Blakey's Jazz Messengers. Also performing were Grammy Award-winner Juice Newton, Shirley Alston Reeves, former lead singer of the Shirelles, and Ben E. King, original lead singer of The Drifters.

Reserve early for tent seating; there is unlimited lawn seating for $9, available on day of concert. Pre-concert dinners prepared by various restaurants and caterers are offered before most performances. Reservations are required a day in advance. Pre-concert prix-fixe dinners at restaurants in the area are also available.

Ulster County

 **Shopping**

EDITIONS

Route 28 (9 miles west of Thruway at Exit 19)
Ashokan
☎ 914-657-7000
www.nleditions.com (includes catalog)
Open daily at 10am, year-round

Editions is a seven-day-a-week bookshop specializing in used, out-of-print, and antiquarian hard- and softcover books. The store opened in 1984, but its mail order business began in 1948. It has some 70,000 uncatalogued books and records other than those found in the catalog. There are about 122 categories, including magic, espionage, the circus, psychology, children's books, American history and foreign language. Stop in and wander the maze of rooms any day of the year.

BERRY PATCH

Route 28 (11 miles west of Thruway)
Shokan
☎ 914-657-2075
Open year-round, Thursday-Monday, 11am-5:30pm; Saturday, 11am-6pm; and Sunday, 10am-6pm. November and December, 11am-6pm daily.

You can't help miss this purple house – a bit garish but fun. I stopped in the Berry Patch a month before Halloween, and pumpkins and garlands were everywhere. The store is attractively packed with miniature items like tiny tea sets, figurines, Christmas ornaments and rubber stamps with every conceivable image or slogan.

Stop in at the fun and bright Berry Patch in Shokan.

WINCHELL'S CORNERS
Route 28
Shokan
☎ 914-657-2177
Open year-round, 11am-5 on weekdays; 11am-6pm on weekends; closed Wednesday

This small, welcoming complex has two floors of collectibles and antiques representing 15 to 20 dealers. The bottom floor also houses a restaurant that serves pizza, hero sandwiches and pasta. The top floor was once a dance hall, and current owner David Kalpakis happens to be a musician. Store items range from Beatles trading cards for 10¢ to $1,000 for furniture.

ASHOKAN ARTISANS
Route 28 (across from Winchell's Corners)
Shokan
☎ 914-657-8772
Open until 6pm on weekends; hours vary seasonally on weekdays. Closed Tuesday.

This fine shop carries fine crafts for the home, garden, body and soul. Six rooms hold jewelry, pottery, woodwork, watercolors and other handmade items by 150 artisans, most of them local. Proprietors and potters Bill and Lesley Reich have exhibited their own work at hundreds of juried craft shows nationwide.

MOOSE CROSSING
Route 28 (next to Winchell's Corners)
Shokan
☎ 914-657-9792

The restored blue clapboard house next to Winchell's Corners now sells antiques and furniture. The original house was ordered from a Sears catalogue for $900 around 1912. Across from the store sits a 19th-century church that once was a meeting house for Baptist ministers. It has no electricity or water. Plans are to convert it to a museum.

CRACKERBARREL COUNTRY STORE

You'll find several stores & restaurants, plus a florist and supermarket on Rt. 28 between Boiceville and Mt. Tremper.

Route 28
Boiceville
☎ 914-657-6540
Open year-round

Here's a wonderful-smelling place with lots of decorative wooden animals, ship models, old-fashioned wind-up toys, deerskin moccasins, candies, and potpourri. Be sure to look up at Ernest, the high wire bear who never stops cycling.

PHLEBUS BOOK SHOP
Main Street
Phoenicia
☎ 914-688-2744
Open year-round

In business for three years, Phlebus specializes in nature books, literary fiction and field guides. According to owner Mark Dorrity, many famous poets and writers have done readings here.

Festivals & Events

Note: Where telephone number is not included, call the Ulster County Tourism Office, ☎ 800-DIAL-UCO.

May

Shad Festival, Hudson River Maritime Museum, Rondout Landing, Kingston. Gourmet dinners, live music, boat rides, craft vendors. ☎ 914-338-0071.

Slabsides Open House, Route 9W, West Park. Third Saturday of every month; also first Saturday in October. Woodland cabin of naturalist/writer John Burroughs. ☎ 914-679-2642.

Woodstock Renaissance Faire, Andy Lee Memorial Field, Woodstock. ☎ 914-679-7148; www.woodstockrenfaire.com.

Woodstock/New Paltz Art & Crafts Fair, Ulster County Fairgrounds, New Paltz. Memorial Day and Labor Day weekends. ☎ 914-246-3414; www.quailhollow.com.

June

Big Indian Car Show, Route 28, Big Indian. Twenty-eight classes of cars, games, drawing, food, craft vendors. ☎ 914-254-4238.

July

Hurley Stone House Day, Hurley. Held second Saturday in July. Tour eight of America's oldest privately owned homes. Country fair. ☎ 914-331-4121; 338-3810, ext. 117.

Music & Art Festival, Benmarl Vineyards, Marlboro. Art exhibit, concert, wine tasting. ☎ 914-236-4265.

Belleayre Music Festival, Highmount. Concerts, dance workshops, children's entertainment. ☎ 800-942-6904; 914-254-5600.

Hudson Valley Triathlon, Kingston. ☎ 914-247-0271.

August

Ulster County Fair, County Fairgrounds, Libertyville Road, New Paltz. Rides, entertainment, horse shows, crafts, petting zoo, livestock auction and judging. $10. ☎ 914-255-1380/1707.

Antique Auto Club Car Show, Cantine Field, Saugerties. Trophies, flea market, judging. ☎ 914-687-0725; 914-679-6810.

Stone House Day, Huguenot Street, New Paltz. Crafts, tours, entertainment. Admission charge. ☎ 914-256-1660/1409.

Corn and Craft Festival, Hurley. Held third Saturday in August. 100 booths of crafts, refreshments, demonstrations. ☎ 914-338-8366.

September

Woodstock/New Paltz Art & Crafts Fair. Labor Day weekend (also see *May*).

Hudson Valley Garlic Festival, Saugerties. Garlic foods, cooking demonstrations, garlic lectures, music, crafts (see story below). Two-day festival held the last weekend in September. $5. Shuttle buses from parking lot. No pets permitted. ☎ 914-246-3090; www.hopefarm.com/garlic.html.

Taste of New Paltz, County Fairgrounds, Libertyville Road, New Paltz. Arts, crafts, tastings of area restaurants and wineries, games, pumpkin painting. ☎ 914-255-0243; 914-255-0411.

Lobster Fest, Rivendell Winery, 714 Albany Post Road, New Paltz. ☎ 914-255-2494.

International Wine Showcase & Auction. Held on different dates at the Culinary Institute of America in Hyde Park and the Would Restaurant in Highland. American and international wineries and find foods of the Hudson Valley are featured. ☎ 914-297-9127; www.mhv.net/~wineshow.

Horse Shows in the Sun (HITS), Kelly Farm, Route 209, Ellenville. Jumping events and competition. ☎ 914-876-3666.

Hudson Valley Garlic Festival

You'll return home with foul breath, aching legs and more information on garlic than you bargained for. All in the name of fun. And fun it is. The huge open-air festival in Saugerties' Cantine Field is part garlic festival and part craft fair. Vendors are required to carry at least 5% garlic-oriented goods among

Ulster County

their wares. Items included garlic spoon rests, garlic holders and garlic presses. Attendees have grown from 125 people in 1989 to an estimated 26,000 in 1998.

It all started a decade ago when Patricia Reppert, who owns Shale Hill Farm and Herb Garden in Saugerties, wanted to promote her herb shop by having a garlic festival. The first two years she cooked all the garlic dishes herself and held the festival in her yard. Five hundred people showed up – 300 more than expected. By the third year, she wisely turned over the festival to the local Kiwanis Club, which is still the sponsor. Kiwanians have proudly tagged Saugerties "the Stinky Breath Capital of the World."

Once asked why a garlic festival is so popular, Reppert replied: "There's a mystique to garlic that attracts people. And garlic is funny. I don't know why." So bring your appetites and funnybone and enjoy.

October

The Country Charm Farm has spectacular views of the Shawangunk Mountains, so be sure to bring your camera.

Pumpkin Patch Harvest Festival, Country Charm Farm, 201 Dubois, New Paltz. Annual event features a giant barn sale, u-pick pumpkins and a now-famous life-size scarecrow display. Runs for three weekends. In the village of New Paltz, take 32S to yellow flashing lights and turn right on Dubois Rd. ☎ 914-255-4321.

Slabsides Open House, Route 9W, West Park. Open first Saturday in October from noon-4:30pm; also third Saturday in May. Woodland cabin of naturalist/writer John Burroughs. ☎ 914-679-2642.

Mum Festival, Seamon Park, Route 9W, Malden Avenue, Saugerties. Thousands of mums in bloom, art show, crafts, bands, live animals, puppets. Noon-5pm. ☎ 914-246-9555.

Headless Horseman Hayrides and Haunted House, Route 9W, Ulster Park. Held weekend evenings in October. Horror hayrides, murder corn maze, tunnel of terror. ☎ 914-339-BOOO (2666); www.headlesshorseman.com.

November

International Pickle Festival, Rosendale Recreation Center, Rosendale. This unusual event conceived by a Tokyo restaurateur, features Japanese chefs bringing such treats as pickled lotus. "Germany" offers pickled red cabbage and other dishes. Live music and a pickle-drawing contest complete the festivities. ☎ 914-658-9649; www.picklefest.com.

Ulster County A to Z

Animal Hospitals

New Paltz Animal Hospital, 230 Main Street, New Paltz, ☎ 914-255-5055.

Hoppenstedt Animal Hospital, Route 32 south of Kingston. 24-hour, year-round emergency care for patients. Toys and treats. ☎ 914-331-1050.

Ulster County

Banks

Ellenville National Bank has branches in Ellenville, Kerhonkson, South Fallsburg, and Woodridge. 24-hour access line: ☎ 800-647-7747/8229; www.ellnationalbank.com.

First Hudson Valley Bank, 1 Twin Maples Shopping Center, Saugerties. ☎ 914-246-1000. **First Union National Bank,** 29 Main Street, New Paltz. ☎ 914-255-6600; **M&T Bank**, 191 Main Street, New Paltz. ☎ 914-255-7100.

Rondout Savings Bank has two locations in Kingston: 300 Broadway and 1296 Ulster Avenue. ☎ 914-331-0073; www.rondoutbank.com.

Sawyer Savings has branches in Saugerties (☎ 914-246-9541) and in Milton (☎ 914-795-2933); www.sawyersavings.com. **Walden Savings Bank** in Gardiner has a 24-hour ATM. **Fleet Bank**, Route 28, Shokan.

Fitness Clubs

28 West Fitness Center, 319 Maverick Road (at the junction of Route 28), Glenford. The club has Nautilus equipment, cardiovascular machines, a tanning salon and personal trainers. Open daily all year. The day rate is $6. A three-month membership is $120. ☎ 914-657-2342

Under the same roof is **Forest Sports**, specializing in snowboards, skate boards, archery and camping equipment.

Hospitals

Ulster County has only three hospitals, but as the *Guide to Mid-Hudson Health Services* (1998-1999 edition) indicates, it has numerous health-related facilities.

Ellenville Community Hospital, Route 209 (next to the Shop Rite mini-mall), Ellenville. Probably no other hospital has a prettier backdrop. I'd like to think that the patients with this glorious view of the Shawangunks heal quicker. The only hospital in New York State to be dedicated by a US President (Lyndon Johnson), it's small (51 beds); and serious trauma cases are airlifted to medical centers in Westchester and Albany. The hospital was recently sold to Westchester Medical Center, who hopes to make it the premier hospital in Ulster County. ☎ 914-647-6400.

Kingston Hospital has facilities in Kingston, Saugerties, Catskill and New Paltz. ☎ 914-331-3131.

Benedictine Hospital, 105 St. Mary's Ave., Kingston. ☎ 914-338-2500.

Call **Emergency One** in Kingston, ☎ 914-338-5600, for immediate medical care. Three emergency medicine physicians are on staff. Open daily at 9am, including holidays.

Liquor Stores

Miron Liquor & Wine, Route 9W, Kingston, ☎ 914-336-5155. **The Wine Gallery**, 52 John St., Kingston, ☎ 914-340-WINE.

Stone Ridge Wine & Spirits, Stone Ridge Towne Center on Route 209. Holds monthly tastings and wine dinners, ☎ 914-687-7125. **Hurley Ridge Wine & Spirits**, Route 375, West Hurley, ☎ 914-679-8444; 800-886-6145. **Trail Liquor Shop** and **Wine & Spirits** are on Route 28 near the Thruway.

Movies

Movie times can be found online at www. newpaltz.org.

All of these theaters show first-run movies. **Hoyt's 12 Screen Cinema** is in back of the Hudson Valley Mall in Kingston, ☎ 914-336-4188. **New Paltz Cinema** in the New Paltz Plaza on Route 299 is a quadroplex. $6, ☎ 914-255-0420. **Orpheum 3,** Main Street, Saugerties, $6, ☎ 914-246-6561. **Rosendale Theatre**, ☎ 914-658-8989, has a single screen.

Newspapers

Daily and Sunday; **Freeman** (Ulster County edition published in Kingston); www.midhudsoncentral.com.

Pharmacies

Dedrick's Pharmacy, 190 Main Street, New Paltz, ☎ 914-255-0310. **Rite Aid Pharmacy**, Route 209, Ellenville, ☎ 914-647-8016.

Religious Services

BAPTIST – First Baptist Church, Partition St., Saugerties, ☎ 914-246-9211.

CATHOLIC – St. Joseph's Catholic Church, 34 S. Chestnut Street, New Paltz, ☎ 914-255-5635. **St. Joseph's Roman Catholic**, 242 Wall St., Kingston.

St. Mary of the Snow, Post and Cedar Streets, Saugerties, ☎ 914-246-4913 (note the magnificent Tiffany window). **St. Francis De Sales,** 104 Main Street, Phoenicia.

EPISCOPAL – St. Andrew's Episcopal Church, 163 Main Street, New Paltz, ☎ 914-255-7116.

LUTHERAN – Redeemer Lutheran Church, Route 32 South, New Paltz, ☎ 914-255-0051.

JEHOVAH'S WITNESSES – Jehovah's Witnesses Kingdom Hall, 7 Sunset Ridge Road, New Paltz, ☎ 914-255-0079.

JEWISH – Congregation Ezrath Israel, Rabbi Eisner Square, Ellenville, ☎ 914-647-4450. **Ahavath Israel**, 100 Lucas Avenue, Kingston, ☎ 914-338-4409. **Kerhonkson Jewish Center**, ☎ 914-626-7260.

METHODIST – New Paltz United Methodist Church, Main and Grove streets, New Paltz, ☎ 914-255-5210. **United Methodist**, 122 Clinton Avenue, Kingston. **Overlook United Methodist Church of Woodstock**, one mile west of Village Green on Route 212, ☎ 914-679-6800. **Saugerties United Methodist Church,** Washington Avenue and Post Street, ☎ 914-246-7802.

PRESBYTERIAN – First Presbyterian Church, Elmendorf and Tremper, Kingston, ☎ 914-331-0633.

REFORMED – Gardiner Reformed Church, Main Street, ☎ 914-255-5210. **Marbletown Reformed**, Route 209, Stone Ridge, ☎ 914-687-7701. **Katsbaan Reformed**, Old Kings Hwy., Saugerties, ☎ 914-246-4008. **Reformed Church of Saugerties** (Dutch Reformed), 173 Main Street, (site of frequent concerts), ☎ 914-246-2867. **Rochester Reformed**, Route 209, Accord, ☎ 914-626-7319.

Ulster County

Greene County

Overview

Washington Irving's legend of the headless horseman and Rip Van Winkle is very much alive in Greene County. But because Irving was not specific about where this harried husband took his extended nap, there are different takes on the location. Palenville, where it's common to find Rip Van Winkle-named businesses,

NOT TO SCALE
N
CANADA
CANADA
VERMONT
NEW YORK
DELAWARE GREENE
ULSTER
MASS
PENNSYLVANIA
SULLIVAN
CONNECTICUT
NEW JERSEY
© 2000 HUNTER PUBLISHING, INC.

claims that it was there. Others contend it was at South Mountain.

The county was named in honor of Revolutionary War General Nathanael Greene, of Rhode Island. Its four original towns were Catskill, Coxsackie, Freehold and Windham. Catskill is the county seat. Henry Hudson, its first recorded visitor, in 1609, found there "a very loving people." Compared to other villages, Hunter and Tannersville incorporated relatively late, in 1894 and 1895, during the railroad-driven boardinghouse boom.

Today, the town of Hunter has a fairly healthy ski business, but its main corridor has been deteriorated for years. The **Hunter Foundation** was recently formed to help reverse this trend and revitalize the town. Its immediate focus is to transform the south side of Main Street into a cultural arts center. The foundation has already purchased storefronts and opened **Catskill Mountain Bookstore and Gallery**, an arts-oriented bookshop with gallery space (see page 344). The existing 215-seat Hunter Theater, adjacent to the bookstore, currently shows Hollywood movies, but plans are to also feature art films. Its stage and lobby are being expanded and dressing rooms and a café are being added. The idea is for theatrical groups from New York City to perform there year-round. The Hunter Foundation also plans to schedule festivals around holiday periods for the benefit of the Mountain Top residents and visitors. Another goal is to create a demonstration farm to teach school-age children about agricultural life.

This non-profit, grass-roots effort was founded by some prominent residents, most notably Hunter Foundation chairman Peter Finn and his wife, Sarah. He is a partner in Ruder-Finn, a global public relations firm based in New York City, a corporate sponsor of the arts and provider of services to arts communities.

The foundation's outreach includes free services to businesses seeking to refurbish their properties. It also helps purchasers of commercial properties to qualify for mortgages. Anyone interested in replicating the plan or joining the Hunter Foundation may call ☎ 518-263-9837 or write to PO Box 486, Hunter, NY 12442.

Directional Info: To Palenville, Haines Falls, Tannersville and Hunter, take Thruway Exit 20 (Saugerties), turn left onto Route 32N, then take 32A to Palenville. At the light, follow 23A west over the mountains. Before reaching Haines Falls, you'll see jaw-dropping vistas that rival those in the Rockies.

⊙ TIP

On the west side of the Hudson River, just off the Rip Van Winkle Bridge (Route 23) near Catskill, there's a cute vest-pocket park with benches for enjoying the view. Restroom facilities are available.

A Monumental Task

Brooks Atkinson (1894-1984), drama critic for *The New York Times* for 35 years, lived on a farm in Greene County. In 1940, a century-old 150-pound monument marking the exact distance from the farm to Catskill, NY was stolen. Atkinson advertised for it in the *Times*. The *New Yorker,* seeing his advertisement, twitted him: "Our advice to Mr. Atkinson is to give up his search. A cold rag on the temples would help, and a little rest, and no newspapers for awhile. There have been too many milestones missing lately, some of them with lettering as ancient as civilization." No trace of the monument was ever found, although reports about it appeared all over the country.

Greene County

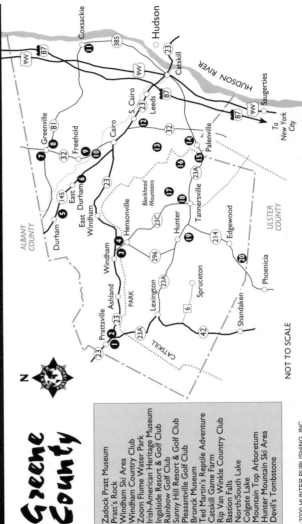

Greene County

1. Zadock Pratt Museum
2. Pratt's Rock
3. Windham Ski Area
4. Windham Country Club
5. Zoom Flume Water Park
6. Irish-American Heritage Museum
7. Ingalside Resort & Golf Club
8. Rainbow Golf Club
9. Sunny Hill Resort & Golf Club
10. Pleasantville Golf Club
11. Bronck Museum
12. Ted Martin's Reptile Adventure
13. Catskill Game Farm
14. Rip Van Winkle Country Club
15. Bastion Falls
16. North/South Lake
17. Colgate Lake
18. Mountain Top Arboretum
19. Hunter Mountain Ski Area
20. Devil's Tombstone

NOT TO SCALE

© 2000 HUNTER PUBLISHING, INC.

Best Places to Stay

The price scale for lodging can be found on page 20.

Resorts

SUNNY HILL RESORT & GOLF COURSE

Greenville

☎ 518-634-7642; 518-634-7693

www.sunnyhill.com

Open mid-May to October (golf course opens earlier)

Deluxe

Ninety-six carpeted bungalow units, each with re-frigerator and TV. Amenities: exercise room, tennis, volleyball and basketball courts; small petting farm; outdoor pool; man-made lake for boating and fishing (stocked with largemouth bass); five playground areas; video game room and entertainment center, day care center. Three meals a day. Theme weekends and side trips offered.

Note that Sunny Hill Resort does not accept credit cards.

One of the few surviving family-owned resorts in the county, Sunny Hill has been owned and operated by the Nicholsen family since 1920. Set on gently rolling hills, the 200-acre property is surrounded by its beautifully landscaped 18-hole golf course (see page 333) with a view of the northern Catskill Mountains that will take your breath away. It's the ideal vacation spot for the family – everyone's needs are met, and the Nicholsens aim to please.

In 1920, Peter and Gurine Nicholsen and their six-year-old son, Arnold, moved from Brooklyn and purchased what was originally called the Edgett Farm. Many of the Edgetts are buried in a small plot beside

Greene County

the petting farm. Gurine renamed the farm "Sunny Hill," probably because many times it rains all around the area but not a drop falls on the resort. The farm became a resort in 1950 under the supervision of Arnold, who planned the landscaping and layout of shrubbery and trees. The many different species create a riot of colors.

PINE LAKE MANOR

Greenville
☎ 518-966-5745
Open Memorial Day through Columbus Day
Inexpensive

Amenities include three meals a day; nine-hole putting green; 30x60 outdoor pool; boating; fishing; tennis and basketball court; volleyball and softball fields; recreation hall with eight-seat snack bar, pool table and video games; playgrounds; wagon rides; and hiking trail. Bring your own fishing tackle, beach towels, tennis rackets and golf clubs.

You won't find a more relaxed and unassuming place than this 75-year-old family resort. The serenity at Pine Lake Manor instills a sense of peace within you. Low-key owners Tom and Joanne Baumann set the mood, and it's definitely not for type-A personalities.

The resort has several artificial lakes and marshes fringing the property. This may explain the preponderance of red-winged blackbirds common to wetlands in spring and early summer. Only one lake is the center of activity, however, with parents and kids fishing off the dock as others go boating. The yellow barn-like buildings have clay-colored roofs, blending nicely with the natural terrain. The lawn is a carpet of yellow birdsfoot and towering conifers, predominantly spruce and pine.

◎ TIP

Rainbow Golf Club adjoins Pine Lake
Manor, which offers a mid-week golf
package in June. This gives you the
choice of playing at Rainbow, Pleasant View, Sunny Hill, or all three.

A historic sign notes that Brandy Hill (just down the
road from the resort) was settled in the 1790s and
was the site of a cider mill, tin shop, church, sawmill
and farms. The renovated building now housing the
wood-paneled dining room was the stagecoach stop,
and the rec hall was the farmhouse.

The resort's relatively flat 222 acres have a camp-
like feel, with people engaging in different activities
and the aroma of the next meal filling the air. The
guestrooms are large but simple, with a TV and telephone.

Pine Lake, which can accommodate 120-170 guests,
draws families in July and August and a mixed
crowd in spring and summer. "We're now into our
third generation," says Joanne Baumann, who at-
tributes the high rate of returnees to the comfortable and at-home atmosphere.

If guests return for the home-cooked meals alone, no
one could blame them. Some dishes – such as the
Friday night buffet of lasagna (vegetable and meat),
stuffed cabbage and meatballs – could be deemed
home cooking at its finest. Portions are plentiful.
The only drawback is that there's no menu. You eat
what is served. If you're on a restricted diet or aren't
a heavy meat eater, let Pine Lake Manor know in advance.

Greene County

Inns/B&Bs

WASHINGTON IRVING LODGE
Route 23A
Hunter
☎ 518-589-5560
Moderate

This 15-room lodge offers TV and telephone, cocktail lounge, billiard room and outdoor pool.

Washington Irving would have loved this lodge. Judging from Sunnyside, his cottage in Tarrytown, and his distaste for the railroad that rumbled by, the father of American literature cherished comfort, solitude and natural light.

The Washington Irving Lodge offers golf packages with Colonial Country Club in Tannersville.

Situated between Hunter Mountain and the legendary Kaaterskill Falls, Washington Irving Lodge is a magnificent 1890 Victorian inn. This gem retains the original dark woods, handmade bookcases and stained-glass windows. Five of the rooms are on the third floor. If you don't mind climbing stairs, you'll be rewarded with a very private and cozy room with sloped ceilings, alcoves and terraces. All are suites, except the corner room ($90), which is perfect for one person. Pastel fabrics contrast nicely with the original wood and each of the five irregularly shaped walls has its own window.

The inn is near ski slopes and hiking trails. Overlook Mountain is not far away. The proprietor, Stefania Jozic, of Yugoslavian descent, is an obliging and gracious hostess who welcomes well-behaved guests and polite children.

FAIRLAWN INN
Main Street
Hunter
☎ 518-263-5025
Inexpensive to Moderate

Offers nine guestrooms, one handicapped accessible and one for a small family. Full country breakfasts are served.

The newly renovated Fairlawn Inn in Hunter.

An extensive 3½-year renovation saved this grand 1904 summer residence from destruction. Kelly Coughlin, a software application developer, and her attorney husband, Sean Byrne, had already renovated two other houses when they fell in love with the oversized porches and original heartwood pine (no knots) wainscoting that covers several walls and ceilings. Using the money they earned from fully restoring and then selling their last house, the couple purchased Fairlawn from the granddaughter of the original owner, a New York City businessman and philanthropist, and opened the inn in the fall of 1996.

A caretaker oversees the house; Kelly lives nearby with her husband and eight-year-old daughter, but she's there for breakfast, whipping up eggs, pancakes or French toast to be served with homemade cakes and muffins. The windowed breakfast room has the most intricate pattern of wainscoting in the house, giving the room a soothing auburn glow.

Directional Info: Look for the cocoa-colored Victorian next to Tequillas restaurant.

DEER MOUNTAIN INN
Route 25
Tannersville
☎ 518-589-6268
Open year-round
Inexpensive to Moderate

Seven double rooms with private modern bath and TV. Two rooms have stone fireplaces. Heaters but no air conditioning. Cocktail lounge and restaurant.

A European flavor pervades this beautiful secluded inn on 15 acres in Onteora Park. A kind host and informed area guide, innkeeper Danielle Gortel is Polish, but has a French name and a Swedish accent. The outside of the inn resembles a Swiss chalet and the rooms have French windows and American wood paneling. Deer Mountain has an excellent restaurant on the premises (see page 304); its menu is best described as Continental.

Danielle and husband, Paul, left Poland 20 years ago, first settling in New York City. Their love of skiing brought them to the town of Hunter. The turn-of-the-century inn – used over the years as a camp and year-round resort called Toppersfield – was renovated and decorated with Danielle's creative touch.

A hand-painted glass shade by Ulla Darni (see page 346) hangs in the bar, where a bullet hole in the mirror reminds patrons of rowdier times.

ⓢ **TIP**

When staying at Deer Mountain Inn, remember to make dinner reservations downstairs.

The Gortels opened Deer Mountain in 1988, naming it for their hometown in Poland – Jelenia Gora (Deer Mountain) – near the Czechoslovakian border. It oozes charm so it's not surprising that weddings constitute much of their business. One couple, married there in July 1996, was featured in the "Vows" column of *The New York Times*.

This is a place where living is easy for contemplating nature from a lounge on the deck or hammock on the lawn. It's perfect for romantic couples, but not for early risers desperate for a cup of coffee. It will be served, but all in good time. Rates are very reasonable spring through fall. Close to ski slopes.

Directional Info: Take Route 23A to the light in Tannersville. Make a right onto 23C and drive two miles to a beautiful stone church perched on an island between two roads. (Special functions, but no services, are held at All Souls, privately owned by Onteora Park.) Turn right and go ¾ of a mile.

Greene County

Onteora Park History

Route 25 is also called Onteora Road. Onteora Park was the first of six self-contained "cottage" communities built in and around Tannersville between 1883 and 1889. The railroad had reached the village in 1882, enabling the upper-middle-class to arrive faster from New York City. Phil Brown wrote that "wealthy gentiles" built the parks "to escape the lower class people of all religions, especially the Jews who were starting to visit the grand hotels."

Candace Wheeler (1827-1923), a textile designer born in Delhi (Delaware County), founded Onteora, an Indian word for "Hills of the Sky." With her husband, a successful wholesale grocer, and her brother, Wheeler established an artists' colony and named many of the roads running through the 2,000 acres of mountain land. An important figure in the decorative arts movement, she entertained such notables as John Burroughs, Antonin Dvorák, Jenny Lind, Oscar Wilde, Mark Twain, and members of the Hudson River School of Artists. Although bent on escaping her Calvinist upbringing, Wheeler reigned over the elite enclave with an iron hand.

In 1927, after attending one of the colony's exclusive social functions, author Hamlin Garland observed that "Luxury such as this may be debilitating." A similar malaise may have come over Mark Twain when he spent the summer of 1890 at Onteora with his wife and daughters. Twain was already a celebrated author of four books and the darling of his hosts, often regaling them with his stories. Yet he failed to finish his sequels to *Tom Sawyer* and *Huckleberry Finn* or write a single word about the Catskills. One can only conclude that all the socialization and adulation clouded his senses.

Of the six communities, the three largest – Onteora, Twilight and Elka – still exist.

ALBERGO ALLEGRIA
Route 296
Windham
☎ 800-625-2374; 518-734-5560
www.AlbergoUSA.com
Moderate

Albergo Allegria is the only B&B/inn in the Catskills with an AAA Four Diamond status.

Sixteen rooms in the main house; five in the carriage house. All have TV/VCR, (with a selection of 285 complimentary movies), CD player, telephone, air conditioning. Some have a double Jacuzzi or whirlpool, gas log fireplace (with one-hour timers) and outdoor deck.

Albergo Allegria means "Inn of Happiness" in Italian, and from all indications guests agree – they are happy with the service, accommodations and hearty breakfasts.

In 1985, the owners completed the renovation of the inn. Created from two of the original cottages of a summer boarding house, it retains the original Victorian trim and moldings. The interior is decorated with period wallpaper and antiques, conveying a blend of old-world charm with 20th-century comfort at surprisingly reasonable rates.

What I found most appealing was the spaciousness of the two beautifully appointed common rooms and the guestrooms. The beds are made in the old Euro-

Greene County

pean style, with a blanket tucked between two sheets under a down comforter, making for one dreamy night's sleep! Each of the rooms is different, but all are cozy. Most of the guests are couples, although there are two family suites. The most popular has a keyhole-window and a door between the parents' and children's rooms.

Located on the Batavia Kill a mile from the ski slopes, Albergo Allegria is on a pretty street with several historic inns, a pizzeria and a pharmacy, and is directly across from **La Griglia Restaurant & Bakery** (see page 304). Vito and Lenore Radelich, who run the inn with daughter Marianna and her husband, Leslie Leman, owned the restaurant for 12 years.

GREENVILLE ARMS 1889 INN
Route 32, South Street
Greenville
☎ 518-966-5219
Moderate

The Greenville Arms was recommended by The Innkeeper's Register in 1999. Member inns must maintain the highest standards of excellence in dining, hospitality and ambiance.

Thirteen rooms in main house and carriage house (some with canopied beds and private porches), 50-foot outdoor pool. Country breakfast and candlelight dinner by reservation; wine and beer available.

This lovely Victorian inn with its Queen Anne gables and cupolas may be one of the only places to accept weekend guests for one night only – Saturday. It works especially well for people who can't get away early on Friday night or for those who prefer driving in daylight. This is the 10th season for innkeepers Eliot and Letitia (Tish) Dalton. He runs art workshops during the week (see sidebar below) and she prepares healthy gourmet meals.

Built by William Vanderbilt as a retreat, the inn's antiques in the common rooms give it a European feel and the renovated guestrooms with their Victorian wallpaper, high beds and original artwork would surely have pleased his illustrious family. A stream runs between the inn and the carriage house under the shade of several huge Norwegian spruces.

Art Workshops at the Greenville Arms

Anyone who has been on a retreat or an extended spa vacation knows the feeling: sleeping under one roof, sharing meals, and working side by side, strangers soon become friends, defenses are lifted, and it's hard to say goodbye.

That's what happens at Eliot Dalton's art workshops, where for his part, Eliot gets as much as he gives. "When you're around creative people, you get a lot of their energy," he says. This is especially true during the week-long workshops held June through October.

Eliot rounds up nationally and internationally known professional artists to serve as instructors for the workshops. When I arrived at the Greenville Arms on a beautiful spring day, the class was already settled on the lawn sketching trees and barns. The group later continued in the well-lighted studio.

The program accepts a maximum of 20 participants of all ages. The package includes lodging and meals. Eliot also organizes workshops abroad. For more information, call Greenville Arms, ☎ 518-966-5219, or visit the Web site at www.artworkshops.com.

Greene County

Farm Vacations

Let the farmer forevermore be honored in his calling, for they who labor in the earth are the chosen people of God.
— Thomas Jefferson

HULL-O FARMS
Cochrane Road
Durham
☎ 518-239-6950
www.hull-o.com
Open year-round
Inexpensive (children under age two free)

Two guesthouses – the Chalet and Rose House – each have a full kitchen. The Chalet is a mile from the farm and sleeps 10. It's designed for one or two families and has a rec room, regulation-size pool table and deck. The Rose House, on the farm's property, has two bedrooms and sleeps six. Two daily meals are included. Country breakfasts of buttermilk pancakes or French toast are made from eggs and milk) courtesy of the hen-house and barn animals); fresh meat is a staple, even at breakfast (sausage and bacon from you-know-where), but vegetarians and others on special diets are accommodated (with advance notice).

Hull-O Farms has been featured in Parents, Hudson Valley & Westchester *magazines, as well as* The Catskill Trumpet.

Hull-O Farms, set in a pristine valley in the northwestern corner of Greene County, is the "only dairy farm in the northeast that takes in guests for a full vacation," according to owner Frank Hull. Although it's well-suited for families (children with parents or grandparents), honeymooners and singles have enjoyed themselves there as well. It's not uncommon for families to return time and again for a weekend or full week.

Guests are free to spend time as they like. The farm has cows, chickens, pheasants, goats, ducks, cats, hunting dogs, lambs, deer and pigs. Streams here are filled with bass. Some guests enjoy watching the cows being milked (twice a day); others never enter the barn. Some gather eggs and feed the goats.

Hull-O Farms' newest additions are a farmer's market and a corn maze.

Guests enjoy the friendly farm animals at Hull-O Farms in Durham.

From September through March, the 330-acre farm serves as a full-service (licensed) game preserve for pheasant, big game, turkey and deer hunts. Tower shoots, releasing 300 birds, are held the last Saturday of every month, October through March, and a free pig roast is offered to all shooters. Hunting dogs and dog handlers are provided.

Greene County

Getting to Know You

Frank Hull of Hull-O Farms was a rough-and-tumble guy fresh from college when he took over the family homestead. Sherry was a college girl from a Syracuse suburb. They met at a dance club, spent their first date shooting ducks, and have been together ever since.

The Hulls opened their home to guests when dairy farming was no longer profitable. While Frank takes the credit for turning the farm into a vacation place in 1993 – an increasingly popular trend called agritourism – he calls his wife "the cog in the wheel."

The Hull property is a National Bicentennial Farm, a federal designation for farms that have been in the same family for at least two centuries. "When I was a kid there were 13 active farms on the road," recalls Frank. "Today we are the last."

Spas

VATRA MOUNTAIN VALLEY LODGE & SPA
Route 214
Hunter
☎ 800-232-2772; 518-263-4919
Rates are Moderate to Deluxe depending on time of year and whether single or double occupancy. Room rate includes three gourmet spa meals, use of spa facilities, lectures, and evening entertainment.

Tennis, volleyball, basketball, swimming pool. Maximum of 30 guests.

If a small spa with a low-key family ambience and a patient, hands-on fitness guru appeals to you, spend a few days or weeks at Vatra. George Borkacki, a Polish-born physical therapist and nutritionist, is general manager. His excellent staff includes a first-rate chef who can turn even bean curd into a gourmet delight. The meals are strictly vegetarian and the only between-meal offering is water with orange slices. You can choose between 750 or 1,200 calories a day. On 750 I would have faded away, but 1,200 managed to keep me satisfied until the next meal. Our dishes seemed like banquets compared to the juice diets of some of our table companions – all middle-aged men and women of assorted shapes and faiths.

★ **FAMOUS FACES**

Monica Lewinsky was at Vatra twice, in the summer of 1996, before she became a household name.

Traditional spa treatments include massages, reflexology and European seaweed body wraps. These can be costly, but there are also many physical activities included in the room rate – power walks, nature walks, stretch classes, water aerobics and exercise machines. George meets with each guest and gives private nutritional counseling, teaching them about the value of exercise and a healthy diet. More than half his guests return, and those who have lost weight and gained stamina enthusiastically attest to his austere regimen.

Opened six years ago, Vatra had a past life as a Polish children's camp; its name means "home campfires." The 24 modern rooms are in a bungalow attached by a walkway to the main house and every-

Greene County

thing is conveniently located. Nestled in the woods near Hunter Mountain, Vatra is open during the winter for downhill and cross-country skiing, when spa treatments and meals are limited. The peak season rate for two nights is about $430 per person.

Dude Ranches

DIAMOND HORSESHOE DUDE RANCH
Dale Lane
Elka Park
☎ 518-589-5197; 800-926-2771
Open year-round
Inexpensive

Two meals daily, 60 rooms, some with oversize bathrooms and freestanding Jacuzzis, indoor/outdoor pools, game rooms, playground, camp-like activities, nightly entertainment, rifle range.

Well-behaved dogs are welcome with advance notice.

First it was Twin Mountain House, named for the mountains overlooking the 150 acres. Then it was Antonio's, an Italian-themed resort, for 28 years. In July 1998, Denny Klein, a Brooklyn-born cowboy who spent his childhood in Florida riding horses, took over. It's now a modern, Old Western-style resort, complete with his mother's watercolor paintings of men on horseback. The resort provides a stagecoach or sleigh ride to its stable two miles away. Riders of all levels are guided. The dining room is run like a restaurant, giving diners 12-14 choices from the menu.

Klein spent his adult life working on dude ranches and participating in rodeos. The resort holds a "City Slickers" Cattle Drive on summer weekends that is open to the public.

Directional Info: Take Route 23A west to Route 16, turning left at Pete's Place in Tannersville. You'll see the stable on the right two miles before the resort. It's next to Redcoat's Return.

Seasonal Rentals

To rent a condo for a weekend, a week, or on a monthly basis within walking distance of Hunter Mountain, contact **Shaw Country Realty** at ☎ 518-263-4723. For daily, weekly or seasonal winter rentals in Hunter or Windham, contact **Jeff Prince Real Estate** at ☎ 518-589-6060; www.jeff-princerealty.com. To rent a home for the summer in the Hunter/Windham area, call **Hunt Realty** at ☎ 518-734-6233.

Recommended Motels

Forester Motor Lodge, Route 23A, Hunter. ☎ 518-263-4555. Large rooms, TV, telephone, swimming pool and gorgeous view of Hunter Mountain.

Greene County

Best Places to Eat

*The price scale for restaurants can
be found on page 21.*

Casual Dining

MOUNTAIN BROOK DINING & SPIRITS
Route 23A
Hunter
☎ 518-263-5351
Open year-round, 5pm-10:30pm; closed Tuesday
Inexpensive to Moderate

In 1998, Zagat named Mountain Brook one of the area's best new restaurants.

Mountain Brook is what you'd call a "find," since owner Wendy Cappello largely relies on word of mouth and does not advertise in many publications. In business for four years, the modern, barn-like restaurant is a wonderful respite for tired skiers and hikers. The pine and cedar paneling is warmed by skylights, Vermont wood-burning stove, and easy listening music.

The artfully prepared Continental dishes reflect Tim Stutz's 16 years of experience in both large and small restaurants in Vermont and Chicago. The grilled tuna with squash, mashed potatoes and carrot crispies (be careful of the fiery green wasabi horseradish) was so delicious and decorative the first time I tried it that when I returned with my husband, I insisted he order it. We had gone a few miles past our destination and he was hungry (read cranky) when we arrived. But after tasting the dish, his unsolicited comment was: "This fish is sensational. I must say you were right. This was worth going out of our way for."

The menu includes à la carte entrées and lighter fare, starting at $6.75 for a hamburger.

CHATEAU BELLEVIEW
Route 23A
Tannersville
☎ 518-589-5525
Open most of the year for dinner and a light Sunday lunch; closed Tuesday. Casual attire welcome.
Moderate

A stone's throw from Washington Irving Lodge, Chateau Belleview is another find. More like a chalet than a château with its mounted wildlife and loft, this charming French eatery has an owner/hostess to match in Josiane. Though born in France, she came to the US at age four and is as American as she is French. While Josiane's busy greeting guests, her husband, Gerard, works his magic in the kitchen. Although his dishes may not be as decorative as Mountain Brook's, his preparation is top-notch.

Chateau Belleview offers children's portions, but the food seems more suited to sophisticated youngsters.

The entrées are huge – mine was served with puréed carrots, wonderfully thin and light scalloped potatoes, rice and a stuffed tomato. The menu contains such French standards as escargots and beef bourguignon, as well as American favorites like pasta, surf and turf, and veal scallopini. There are also a host of daily specials. Although large (200 seats), the mood at this restaurant is intimate. The windows and patio face scenic Platte's Clove, which can best be enjoyed during summer when daylight extends into early evening.

Before purchasing the restaurant from a retiring French couple, Gerard was the chef at Bistro Bordeaux near Madison Square Garden in New York City for eight years. In 1982, Mimi Sheraton, then food critic for *The New York Times*, gave it a favorable review and two stars (meaning very good).

Greene County

DEER MOUNTAIN INN
Route 25
Tannersville
☎ 518-589-6268
Moderate

You don't have to stay at the Deer Mountain Inn to enjoy a romantic dinner at this secluded restaurant. Have a drink on the geranium-filled terrace before settling down to a gourmet dinner in one of two candlelit dining rooms. On the tables, white napkins stand at attention around a vase of fresh flowers.

Chef James Butler, a Culinary Institute graduate, has a way with meat – the rosemary-crusted rack of New Zealand lamb was voted the People's Pick Award, and the sliced roast pork marinated in teriyaki sauce is a guaranteed pig-out. The prix fixe menu, ranging from $21 to $29, includes everything, and portions are more than enough to satisfy even the biggest appetites.

LA GRIGLIA RESTAURANTE
Route 296
Windham
☎ 518-734-4499
Moderate

La Griglia is open 7 days a week during ski season.

The décor of this fine Northern Italian restaurant may look vaguely familiar if you've been to the Albergo Allegria inn. (The inn's proprietors, the Radelichs, once owned the restaurant.) La Griglia's food is good, and service is unhurried but attentive.

THE MILLROCK RESTAURANT
Main Street
Windham
☎ 518-734-9719
Open for dinner year-round; closed Wednesday
Inexpensive to Moderate

Millrock was named for its owners, Millie and Rocky DiPippa, who ran their own catering business – La Mangeria – in Queens before opening this Italian restaurant three years ago. Despite its converted barn-like feeling, the building was built from scratch. The modern interior features tiled floors and a dozen windows. Light steams in and opera plays softly in the background. A wood-fired oven in a faux castle tower is for baking pizza, chops, poultry and steaks.

The Millrock's home-baked bread and pastries accent the restaurant's main dishes.

All dishes are cooked to order. If you're a pasta aficionado, go for it. You're given a choice of 13 shapes and 11 sauces. One guest remarked that this was his third visit and that the restaurant serves excellent food consistently.

The ziti pomodoro features fresh ricotta cheese and tomatoes. Rocky, who is also the chef, revealed that he hand-crushes the tomatoes and adds only garlic and olive oil. Prices are quite reasonable; salads are extra but the portions are ample without one. A children's menu is also available. Millie stops at every table to check on guests, setting the tone for a friendly and competent staff.

FREEHOLD COUNTRY INN
Routes 32 and 67
Freehold
☎ 518-634-2705
Open daily, year-round for lunch and dinner
Moderate

This is practically the only place to eat in Freehold, Greenville or Cairo. Luckily, the ambience and food are pleasing. Have you had your fill of meat? The menu has more chicken dishes than I've noticed in other local restaurants. My chicken breast was prepared well – not dry and yet not dripping in butter – and the vegetables crisp.

Greene County

Service was speedy, maybe too much so. This is my only criticism, however. Attractively decorated in blond woods with highly polished floors and a bar separated from the dining room, it's a welcome addition to northern Greene County. It's hard to believe it was originally an inn built in 1795. The restaurant was closed for two years; Barbara and Ben Buel reopened in March 1999 after extensive renovations. Photographs of how it once looked are displayed.

ⓢ TIP

In my opinion, the Freehold Country Inn is an even nicer place for lunch. The sandwiches and salads are inexpensive and filling, the place more relaxed, and it sure beats gulping down a sandwich in your car.

TEQUILLAS
Main Street
Hunter
☎ 518-263-4863
Open daily during ski season; Thursday-Sunday in fall and spring; weekends in summer
Moderate

For a nice change of pace from the fish and steak restaurants, try Tequillas' excellent Tex-Mex cuisine from north and south of the border. Live music on weekends.

P.J. LARKINS
Route 23A
Tannersville
☎ 518-589-5568
Open daily, year-round
Moderate

Don't be fooled by the bar-like exterior. Celebrating its 10th anniversary this year, P.J. Larkins is large and comfortable, the restaurant far from the bar. It even caters to families, with a children's menu and game room. There's a huge choice of dinners, sandwiches and salads, and nine specials are offered nightly. Although packed in the winter with skiers, P.J.'s is a relaxed place in the off-season and offers good value for your money.

Lite Bites

LA GRIGLIA BAKERY & GOURMET STORE
Route 296
Windham
☎ 518-734-6100
Open daily in summer; weekends in winter
Inexpensive

Have your fresh Danish, donut or vegetable lasagna al fresco at this little place located beside La Griglia Restaurante.

★ TAKE NOTE

If you need a snack on your way to the Catskill Game Farm or Sunny Hill Golf Course, from Route 32 turn onto Main Street in Cairo and make a right at the Mobil Station. **Papa Don's Pizza** and **Mr. Big Stuff's Ice Cream & Grill** will satisfy every member of the family (the ice cream is delicious). Open May to September.

Greene County

JAMS CAFE & PANCAKE HOUSE
Haines Falls
☎ 518-589-6481
Open year-round
Inexpensive

The exterior of JAMS is rather nondescript and could easily be missed by motorists. But if it's breakfast time, it's worth driving slowly when you reach Haines Falls. Two young sisters recently took over the eatery from their dad, Andy DiPalermo, changed the name to JAMS, and are adept at whipping up light and fluffy pancakes filled with fresh fruit ($4.25). The pancakes are named for family members, such as Joey's Pesty Peach and Brianne's Peach Knockout. Eggs, bagels, muffins and freshly-squeezed orange juice are offered as well. Breakfast is served all day, every day, year-round. Andrea's husband, Joe, has just begun preparing pasta dinners on weekends, offered at very reasonable prices. Indoor/outdoor tables and counter service. For lighter pancakes, just ask – Michele or Andrea will happily accommodate you.

SMILEY'S
Main Street
Tannersville
☎ 518-589-6533
Open daily, Memorial Day weekend to Labor Day
Inexpensive

This ice cream parlor, across from the post office, was once a produce stand. During ski season, Smiley's operates as a taxi service.

MAGGIE'S KROOKED CAFE & JUICE BAR
Tannersville
☎ 518-589-6101
Open daily at 7am
Inexpensive

The Krooked Café is so-named because it's inside one of the oldest buildings in town. The café advertises "warm and simply delicious!" and that's no lie. Maggie is warm, and the breakfasts and lunches are not only delicious but also decorative, reflecting her interior design background. The café is cheerfully decorated with art works and wall hangings.

Nothing on Maggie's menu is more than $11.50.

Maggie believes in being open for "three loving squares a day." Start your day with apple-cranberry or oatmeal pancakes or opt for one of the many healthy shakes made with fresh fruit. The breakfast menu is served all day, and the café menu starts at noon and runs through dinner, serving sandwiches, burgers and salads.

LAST CHANCE
Tannersville
☎ 518-589-6424
www.lastchanceonline.com
Open daily at 11am; serves lunch and dinner from late June through March; weekends only from April through June.
Inexpensive to Moderate

Across from Maggie's is another good choice – Last Chance is a combination restaurant, café, and gourmet shop featuring 100 cheeses. Antiques, including musical instruments and farm implements, are used as decoration and all are for sale. Here again, the same menu holds for both meals, the most expensive item a New York strip steak at $19.95. Other hot entrées are chicken pot pie prepared the old fashioned way and homemade macaroni. Lunch offerings include quiches and club sandwiches. And if you need to wet your whistle, you've got your choice of 275 types of beer!

Greene County

YACHT CLUB
Tannersville
☎ 518-589-0039
Open daily at 4pm on weekdays; 11am on weekends
Inexpensive

For a late-night dinner or snack (until 11pm on weekends), try the Yacht Club, under new management. Though its name is a fooler – it overlooks a stream, no marina – service is pleasant and you can enjoy a hamburger or delicious slice of apple pie on deck. The restaurant is across from Last Chance and is set back from Main Street.

RIKARD'S LOG CABIN
Junction of Routes 23 & 23A
Prattsville
☎ 518-299-3182
Open year-round
Inexpensive

After climbing up to Pratt's Rock, you're probably hungry. Nearby is Rikard's Log Cabin, a combination luncheonette, pizzeria and mini-farm market. Nothing on the coffee shop menu (breakfast or lunch) is more than $4, and they don't stint on portions. The pizzeria is open for dinner as well.

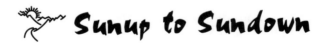

Sunup to Sundown

Sightseeing

Churches

In Windham, you might want to visit **Center [Presbyterian] Church**, listed on the National Register of Historic Places. The stained-glass windows are especially lovely, as is the painting over the piano done by Robert Cepale, a resident of Windham and a "traditional" artist who works from turn-of-the-century photographs. Larry Tomkins, an unofficial village historian, had seen the painting displayed at Key Bank and suggested it be used in Windham's centennial celebration in 1998. (Notice the keyhole in the painting. It was patterned after the window at Albergo Allegria, page 293.) Prints are $15 and available at Windham Pharmacy and Carole's Gift Emporium.

Built in 1834, the church was saved from the wrecking ball and it has taken 20 years to restore it. The public library was built in the back. No longer used for religious services, the church has become a concert hall for all kinds of music. Enter the church through the door next to the library restroom.

Arboretum

If you enjoy a peaceful stroll amid trees and shrubs, the **Mountain Top Arboretum** in Tannersville is good for the soul. The grounds are always open and admission is free. Take a self-guided tour. Most trees are labeled; their goal is to eventually label all the plants. Pick up a self-guided tour brochure that takes you through the beech corner, mountain ash hill, bog plantings, conifers (50 species), shrubs, dawn redwoods, swamp cypress and native woodland.

This non-profit preserve encompasses seven acres of exotic plants that are being tested for their hardiness in this open, windy and cold area on Tannersville's highest point – 2,500 feet above sea level. Another three acres are given over to a shaded wood-

Greene County

land walkway with native, rare and endangered plants.

◎ TIP

Bring a jacket because it's always 10° colder high up at the Mountain Top Arboretum.

The grounds were originally an artist retreat, and among the visitors was Maude Adams, the first actress to play Peter Pan. The dirt road to the Arboretum is named for her. The concept of an arboretum was born in 1977 when Dr. and Mrs. E.H. Ahrens Jr. developed and donated seven acres of their property for an arboretum. The property was transferred to Mountain Top Arboretum, Inc., and in 1981 the board began acquiring plantings of unusual and exotic trees and shrubs.

This living museum relies on grants and member support for income. Manager Christine Story makes a good point for becoming a member ($25 per family, annually): "It's another attraction for the Catskills that's compatible to everyone's goals," she says, since it's non-commercial and committed to the preservation and conservation of nature. Summer events sponsored by the arboretum include a plant sale and auction, lectures and special programs. ☎ 518-589-3903 for a calendar and information.

Directional Info: Turn right at the traffic light in Tannersville onto 23C. Follow for two miles until you see the Mountain Top Arboretum sign.

Animal Farms

ARMSTRONG HOMESTEAD FARM
Hervey Street
Cornwallville
☎ 518-622-8452
Visitors welcome any time free of charge; call first

When you look at an elk, what do you see? A strong, majestic animal with powerful, forward-sweeping antlers? Would you believe that, in the mid-cycle of its growing stage, the antler is soft like velvet? "When you cut it off, it's soft, almost like cartilage," explains Les Armstrong, owner of Armstrong Homestead Farm, and one who practices alternative livestock farming. He removes the antler above the stub and sells it by the pound for use in alternative health supplements under such labels as Vital-Ex and LifeQuest. The animal is electronically anesthetized and experiences no harm or pain, says Armstrong, showing this visitor his surgical lab. "The following year they regrow a new set of antlers."

In 1999, the farm received an Agricultural Accomplishment Award.

★ DID YOU KNOW?

Used in Asia for centuries, velvet elk antler contains essential amino acids. Its use dates back to the Han Dynasty for treating impotence, wounds, pain and arthritis. It is also thought to increase mental capacity and help reduce PMS symptoms. Velvet elk antler is also combined with other herbs, such as ginseng, for peak performance.

The Armstrong Homestead Farm has been in the family since 1863. Les and his wife, Deb, named

Greene County

their two sons and their 18 Rocky Mountain elk after Catskill Mountain ranges (the males) and native flowers (the females). Les, who is also a taxidermist, started with five elk in December 1996, and has witnessed nine births thus far.

Armstrong is trying to reintroduce wild elk into New York State and wants to know how many people want them back in the Catskills. He asks that those interested call him at ☎ 518-622-8452, or write Armstrong's Elk Farm, 143D Hervey Street, Cornwallville, NY 12418.

Directional Info: Exit 21 to Route 23W (approximately 20 miles). Turn right on Hervey Street, bearing to right at bottom of hill. Go about ½ mile to log cabin on left.

Elk Facts

❖   Elks eat one-third more than dairy cows.

❖   Elk meat is low in fat and cholesterol, is nutritious and delicious.

❖   Mature bulls can weigh up to 1,100 lbs.

❖   The American elk is also known by its Shawnee Indian name, "wapiti," meaning white rump.

Family Fun

CATSKILL GAME FARM
Off Route 32
Cairo
☎ 518-678-9595
Open daily, May through October

Catskill Game Farm was begun by Roland Lindemann in 1933 as a conservation project to protect rare and endangered animals from around the world.

Today, however, this attraction does not come cheap: $13.95 for adults and $9.95 for each child over age four. The rides are extra, and only fast food is available. You might as well eat there or bring your lunch because there's no place to eat for miles, except for the **Kaatskill Cider Mill** just south of the farm, where the food is more of same – hamburgers and hotdogs. (The Cider Mill is open March through December, Wednesday through Sunday. The store also sells 32 flavors of ice cream, as well as country gifts.)

Catskill Game Farm was one of the first tourist attractions in Greene County.

But why go to Catskill Game Farm when so many free petting farms exist in the Catskills? To answer that question, I spent a few hours at the farm.

No strollers are allowed into the petting zoo or feeding area of the game farm, which encompasses a large part of the grounds. For parents of cranky toddlers this could be a problem, although with all the sheep, lambs, pygmy pigs, deer and emus to feed, both parents and children keep busy. I didn't hear any crying or whining during my visit, but did see plenty of parents toting their weary kids.

Part zoo and part farm, it has an African section, bird area, equine section and reptile house. It's less commercial than a typical zoo, until you reach the end. The only exit is through the "Wildlife Emporium," a souvenir shop. "Unless you put blinders on your youngsters, they will want everything," one father remarked.

The good news is that the farm is expansive, and the gorgeous woodsy setting means lots of shade trees on a hot day. There are many more animals to touch and hold and feed a bottle of milk than in a typical zoo; signs are kept to a minimum, and it's not crowded like a city zoo. Parking is plentiful and free.

Greene County

Directional Info: From the Thruway, take Exit 21. Catskill Game Farm is located south of Cairo, off Route 32. You can't miss the sign.

ZOOM FLUME WATER PARK
East Durham
☎ 518-239-4559; 800-888-3586
www.zoomflume.com
Open end of June through Labor Day

Features giant winding slides with a miniature version for younger children. Look for coupons in complimentary publications.

Directional Info: From the Thruway, take Exit 21 to Route 23W to 145N; you'll see signs about two miles past East Durham.

TED MARTIN'S REPTILE ADVENTURE
(Previously Clyde Peeling's Reptile Land)
Route 32
Catskill
☎ 518-678-3557
Open daily, Memorial Day to Labor Day
Weekends, May through Columbus Day
Admission is $6.50 adults; $4.25 children

We were met at the ticket window by a staff worker holding a three-year-old alligator. He launched into a short history of the creature before collecting our admission. It's a fun and relaxed way to learn about these fascinating reptiles.

Plans at Ted Martin's are to add an eight-foot king cobra and a turtle pond.

With about 60 to 80 species, the site has a respectable representation of snakes, turtles and alligators, including North America's most dangerous snake – the Eastern diamondback rattlesnake. (The four-inch hissing cockroaches are not reptiles but a tasty lunch for some of the smaller reptiles. They're also on display for their "freaking out" effect on visitors.)

When Clyde Peeling sold the facility to Ted Martin recently, he left only three venomous snakes. (Martin is a breeder and not accustomed to handling deadly snakes.) Martin added some reptiles from his own collection. Peeling is now at the Allenwood, PA location of Reptile Land.

Besides the informational text next to each window, staff workers answer questions and provide hands-on education. For our group, Matt removed the 14-foot, 90-pound python from its slumber for a close-up view. Awesome!

Directional Info: Follow directions to Catskill Game Farm (see page 314) and continue on Route 23 north for two miles.

Swimming

A beautiful place to swim is **Colgate Lake**, which is surrounded by the Blackhead Mountains. The lake is clean and not too cold and there are enough trees to provide shade. You can swim or take out a non-motorized boat. Dogs have fun scooting in and out of the water, chasing one another and shaking water over everyone. The lake is maintained by the state, but there are no facilities or lifeguards.

Directional Info: At the light in Tannersville, turn north onto 23C. Just past Mountain Top Arboretum, across from the East Jewett post office/general store, make a right onto Route 78. Follow the road until you see the sign for Forest Preserve Access Parking on the right. No admission charged.

If you've got kids and feel more comfortable with supervised swimming, head for another beautiful spot, **North Lake Campground**. Swimming is permitted only in supervised areas when a lifeguard is on

Greene County

duty. Animals are not allowed. This campground has two beaches and full facilities – picnic tables, charcoal grills, toilets, hot showers, playing field, organized activities, and boat launch. You can bring or rent a non-motorized vessel. Canoes and rowboats are rented at South Lake only. Admission is $5 per car. ☎ 518-589-5058.

Directional Info: Turn onto Route 18 from Route 23A in Haines Falls and ride to the end.

Paddlers enjoy a peaceful respite on Colgate Lake.

Hiking

Midst greens and shades the Catterskill leaps,
From cliffs where the wood-flower clings;
All summer he moistens his verdant steeps
With the sweet light spray of the mountain
springs;
And he shakes the woods on the mountain side,
When they drip with the rains of autumn tide.
— From *Catterskill Falls*, by
William Cullen Bryant (1794-1878)

Kaaterskill Falls
& Catskill Mountain House

With the possible exception of the Borscht Belt hotels, more has been written about **Kaaterskill Falls** and the **Catskill Mountain House** than anything else in the Catskills. A natural wonder, the falls are still here to enjoy, while the man-made marvel for 140 years is not. Although Niagara Falls has a much greater volume of water, Kaaterskill Falls is the highest waterfall in the East at 260 feet (Niagara is 167). It falls in two tiers; the upper falls dropping 175 feet and the lower falls 85 feet into a rocky basin.

In the Romantic era, painters and poets flocked to Kaaterskill, sharing their impressions with the world. Thomas Cole, Frederic Church and Asher Durand painted the falls, and James Fenimore Cooper's Natty Bumppo called them "the best piece of work I've met with in the woods."

Greene County

⚠ WARNING

Though not restricted, the area near the head of Kaaterskill Falls is dangerous. Truthfully, the falls can hardly be seen at this point. The warning sign about slippery rocks and sheer cliffs should be taken seriously. A memorial bench to a young woman who died at the falls and the three people who died there one recent summer should be enough to deter even the most curious visitor. See page 322 for the best viewing spots.

The Catskill Mountain House was built in 1823 on a sheer bluff overlooking the Hudson Valley. Thirteen Corinthian columns, representing the 13 colonies, supported a long front portico. The vista from there was all but unrivaled in the eastern United States.

This 315-room showplace was the first great mountain resort in the nation. At an elevation of more than 2,200 feet, it was visible for miles. Ads in *Van Loan's Catskill Mountain Guide 1879* touted the health benefits of high elevation, assuring guests freedom from malaria and maladies such as chills and fever, asthma, hayfever, loss of appetite and general debility.

The white palace began as a small inn called Pine Orchard. It was built by Erastus Beach, a stagecoach operator, and was expanded in 1845 by his son Charles. By the end of the century, the property boasted miles of trails and carriage roads, two lakes, a 3,000-acre park, and its own railroad and cablecars from the Hudson River to its doorstep. Two railroads scaled the mountain, competing for business among the well-heeled passengers.

We have only to read the comments of visitors to appreciate its impact. James Fenimore Cooper told his European audience in the 1850s: "If you want to see the sights of America, go to see Niagara Falls, Lake George and the Catskill Mountain House."

Describing his impressions in his 1894 book, *Picturesque Catskills*, R. Lionel De Lisser wrote, "One must see the view to appreciate it. Words fail... I never knew how small I was, until I had stood on the ledges at the old Mountain House."

The summer before David Thoreau went to live at Walden Pond, he hiked in the vicinity of Pine Orchard and stayed at the house of a "saw-miller." In a note written at Walden in 1845, he likened his new abode to that very mountain cabin "so high up in the Caatskill Mountains that all the music... that swept over the ridge of the Caatskills, passed through its aisles."

★ FAMOUS FACES

The Mountain House's guest list is a biographer's dream: Alexander Graham Bell, Henry James, Oscar Wilde, Ulysses S. Grant, Mark Twain, Winslow Homer and Tyrone Power.

Most of all, it was Thomas Cole, leader of the Hudson River School of landscape painters, who popularized the region with his *Catskill Mountain House* and other paintings. This style of landscape painting romanticized nature and lasted from the 1840s through the 1860s. Whereas European artists could look to the ruins of the classical world, American artists had vast expanses of untouched lakes, forest and mountains for inspiration. "The Rhine has its

Greene County

castled crags [but] the Hudson has its wooded mountains..." wrote Cole.

The Catskill Mountain House was in dangerous disrepair by the time of its demise. In 1963, state officials deliberately torched it. The vast ledge is empty now, save for an informational plaque. Not a cinder is left of its glorious past.

Cliffhanger

When I returned to the Mountain House site in mid-summer with my husband, the Tannersville Fire Department Rescue Squad was practicing rappelling off the cliff, with the rope tied to a truck. One guy was visibly nervous but no sooner did he disappear over the ledge did he yell "Whoopee!" with renewed confidence.

Bastion Falls

The best way to view Kaaterskill Falls is to hike from its base at **Bastion Falls** on Route 23A. (The escarpment stretches from here to Route 23 at East Windham, a distance of 24 miles.) Between 23A in Haines Falls and Palenville, you'll see the most dramatic panorama in the Catskills. If you're coming from Palenville, look for the falls on the north side along the horseshoe curve, roughly three miles past the Palenville traffic light. Continue a few yards west to the parking area on the left and walk back down to the falls where the trail begins. Be careful of the cars winding around the bend.

Works in Progress

At of this writing, the Town of Hunter is seeking a **Scenic Road** designation from the New York State Department of Environmental Conservation for the 3½-mile segment of Route 23A from Interim's Bridge outside of Palenville to Haines Falls. The goal is to preserve and protect the Catskill's most famous natural, rugged and undeveloped attraction.

Another walk in the woods that few know about – even people living right across the street from the trail entrance – is in East Durham on Route 145, .4 mile before the turnoff for Zoom Flume and Hull-O Farms. In the summer, the red "6460" sign between two stone pillars marks the trailhead but is hard to find because the pillars are covered with foliage. Look for it directly across from the Vintage Gardens apartments (blue buildings

Bastion Falls.

with a series of mailboxes in front). The trail leads to what some call a "potato hole" – a series of waterfalls. When you hear the first rush of water, don't bother bushwhacking to see them. Continue until you come to the ruins of a house, where a stone platform overlooks the water.

Greene County

North Lake Campground

County Route 18 will take you to the **North Lake Campground,** where six hikes are geared to every level of expertise and the vistas are among the most beautiful in the Catskills. Only the **Mary's Glen/ Ashley Falls Hike** is listed as appropriate for young children since it's an easy hike without any open ledges.

Scutt Road, right before the campground entrance, leads to the most popular hike – the 16-mile **Escarpment Trail** that passes the site of the Catskill Mountain House. An easier route there is to drive to the farthest (gravel) parking lot at North Lake and follow the easy half-mile path to the rock ledge that Natty Bumppo in *The Pioneers* said "looks out on all creation." What he saw was the vast Hudson Valley below and the Berkshire Mountains 100 miles away. The campground closes at the end of October.

Before reaching the campground and North and South Lakes, you'll see Laurel House Road on the right. At the end is the head of Kaaterskill Falls. The Laurel House, an elegant but less expensive alternative to the Mountain House, once stood here. Built by Peter Schutt, and later operated by his son, Jacob, the hotel attracted a middle-class clientele. It ultimately suffered the same fate as the Mountain House. Its doors closed to the public in 1965, and two years later the Conservation Department set it afire, reducing the hotel to ashes.

Pratt's Rock

Whether or not Pratt realized he bore a striking resemblance to Abraham Lincoln, he had his likeness carved into rock along with his favorite things: his son, Col. George W. Pratt (killed in the Civil War); his favorite horse (he had a stable of 1,000); a hemlock tree (representing the tanning industry that made him rich); and an upraised arm (a tribute to the working man).

The Mount Rushmore of the Catskills is an uphill climb, so bring your sneakers. Even if you can't climb, there are interpretive display panels near the parking lot. The gray sandstone rock is estimated to be about 360 million years old. The park has picnic tables and lovely views. Open daily, year-round.

Directional Info: Pratt's Rock Park is in Prattsville on Route 23, a half-mile east of Zadock Pratt Museum (see page 339).

The Cloves

Clove, or kloove, is Dutch for "cleft," or the narrow, steep mountain passes often thought to be the haunts of witches and devils. The three largest cloves are located in the township of Hunter. A two-mile stretch of Route 16 is **Platte Clove**, accessed from 23A in Tannersville. Awe-inspiring, this area is closed from November 15 to April 15 since it's not plowed and has a precipitous drop. The only dirt cutoff can hold about two cars. You can also park at either end and walk along the road, although it's rather hilly. A mile before Platte Clove is the **Devil's Path**, a 23½-mile trail that takes the backpacker over seven mountain peaks, six of which are higher than 3,500 feet. There are many side trails, and day hikes can be done in sections.

Greene County

Treasure Hunt

In *Natural Wonders of New York*, author Deborah Williams refers to the lost treasure of Rip Van Winkle as being located on public land somewhere in Greene County. Anyone who finds the ebony stone inscribed with Van Winkle's initials can claim the secret treasure.

Route 214 bisects **Stony Clove** between Hunter and the Plateau Mountains. In the early days, this was a frightening passageway where the devil was thought to reside. A painter/writer in the mid-1800s termed the clove "the awfulest and most lonely corner of the world that I have ever seen."

On the 12½-mile drive along Route 214 between Route 23A in Hunter and Phoenicia, you can see Devil's Tombstone and Devil's Face. The park maintains a ranger station between the two day-use areas/campgrounds. The 6x7-foot Tombstone fronts the southern campground, which features a grassy area and playground. The theory is that this boulder toppled down from a landslide or glacier centuries ago and landed on its side, resembling a tombstone. To see Devil's Face, drive just north of the northern campground beside Notch Lake (which dries up in dry weather and has no fish). Look up at the rock formations on the same side and you'll see one that resembles a face.

Tannersville

The Huckleberry Multi-Use Trail, a new 2½-mile path that runs along a former rail bed, recently opened in Tannersville. It begins in Cortina Valley on Clum Hill Road opposite the entrance sign at the ski slope, and ends rather abruptly near the village line. The only marker at the entrance is a small fence and a "No Motorized Vehicles" sign. The graveled, 12-foot-wide path is for bikers, hikers, runners and cross-country skiers. The terrain is largely flat and partially shaded. After about ¾ of a mile, you'll come to a red and white house. Continue around it, past the basketball court, and cross the road to the longer portion.

If the powers-that-be in the neighboring villages can agree, the Huckleberry Trail will eventually begin in Haines Falls and extend to Hunter. But skepticism pervades, as expressed by a middle-aged biker on the trail: "It took 12 years to get this [trail] through."

Mountain Top Historical Society runs organized hikes from June to October for members and non-members. To register, call Bob Gildersleeve, ☎ 518-734-9701.

Biking

In Haines Falls, turn onto Route 18 and the first and only store you'll see is **Twilight Mountain Sports**, a combination general store and sports supplier. To rent a mountain bike, snowshoes, ice skates or cross-country skis, or to simply learn more about Greene County's offerings, ask for Joe Cavallaro, the only designated forest preserve official in the region. ☎ 518-589-6480.

Windham Mt. Outfitters is a stone's throw from Albergo Allegria on Route 296 and South Street. ☎ 518-734-4700. A ski shop in the winter, it rents and sells mountain bikes. The shop also sells road

Greene County

bikes, offers bikers its own trail maps, runs one-day guided tours for groups, and provides overnight tuning and repair. One of its other two locations, at 49 Reed Street, Coxsackie, also stocks bikes. ☎ 518-731-9313.

Skiing

In wintertime, Greene County turns white and ski shops abound.

Hunter Mountain has much to boast about. It was the first ski area in the country to offer 100% snowmaking so skiers never have to worry about snowfalls. Because of this, Hunter trademarked the title "Snowmaking Capitol of the World" three decades ago. As a result, the season lasts from early November to late April.

There have been many improvements at Hunter Mountain recently, ranging from replacing some of the chairlifts and expanding the snowboarding operation to adding season-long clinics and programs. In the spring of 1999, Hunter broke ground on its new Learning Center. This was needed because of the advent of shaped skis and the popularity of snowboarding with beginners.

Ski magazine in 1998 named Hunter Mountain the East's Best Day Trip.

Hunter's summit elevation is 3,200 feet; base 1,600 feet. There are 14 lifts and tows, and a single-day lift ticket on weekends and holidays is $44 adult; $28 junior. Inquire about their ski packages, including the mid-week Ski-3-in-4-Days Lift Package, a value you can use at either Hunter or Ski Windham. ☎ 800-775-4641; 518-263-4223; www.huntermtn.com.

The new Snowtubing Park is fun for the whole family. It now features three lifts that carry you up to the top, where there are 12 chutes of excitement.

Directional Info: From the Thruway, take Exit 20 or 21 to Route 23A west.

*Snowtubing at Hunter Mountain is
fun for the whole gang.*
(Courtesy of Hunter Mountain)

Historical Note

Skiing began in the Catskills in the early
1960s when a group of businessmen in Hunter sought an idea to boost the economy. Local contractor Orville Slutzky suggested a
ski area. They placed an advertisement in
The New York Times offering a mountain to
any developer willing to create one. In 1962,
Orville and his brother Israel (Izzy) bought
Hunter Mountain and turned it into a world-class resort.

At **Ski Windham** every event and festival held November through April is centered on this ski area.
And festivities are plentiful – Lifeguard Race, Disabled Skiers Fest and Classic Schnapps Waiters'
Challenge – to name a few.

Greene County

Like Hunter, Windham has a 1,600 vertical drop and came on the scene about the same time. In 1960, a private group purchased 800 acres at Cave Mountain, but their efforts to turn it into a ski resort failed. In 1963, Thomas and Robert Sheridan jointly purchased the ski area, built a new ski lodge costing $150,000, and installed artificial snowmaking machines over 12 acres of beginner terrain. Eventually Windham was hailed as "a little bit of New England in New York," but in 1980 the ski slope went bankrupt. Ski Roundtop took it over in 1981 and has since invested over $30 million in capital improvements.

The Disabled Skier Program at Windham was one of the first of its kind and is now the 2nd largest in the US.

The ski area has seven lifts. A single-day lift ticket on weekends and holidays is $42 for adults, $34 for juniors. New at Windham is a 1½-mile beginner/intermediate trail. Night skiing has been extended to Thursday through Saturday and holidays. The new Mountaintop Adventure Park designed for tubing has six sliding lanes and two tows. The park is open Friday through Sunday, including holidays. A continuous shuttle runs between the park and base area, a quarter-mile away.

For après ski, Windham provides a lounge, a teens-only hangout, a cafeteria and restaurant, movie theater, and fitness center. Its FastTracks reservation service is free. You can reserve valet parking, classes at the Children's Learning Center, day care, lessons, or lodging at a slopeside condo, inn or hotel, including the Windham Arms Hotel just a mile away. ☎ 800-SKI-WINDHAM; www.skiwindham.com.

Directional Info: From the Thruway, take Exit 21 to Route 23W into Windham.

If you find high mountains too intimidating for skiing or snowboarding, consider **Cortina Valley** in Tannersville, recently re-opened under new ownership. The slopes are just that – slopes – with a top elevation of 2,650 and a base elevation of 1,925. This family-oriented operation is primarily for beginners and intermediate skiers. A 20-unit guest lodge is on the premises, 100 feet from the slopes. Daily lift tickets on weekends are $29 adult and $22 juniors. Cortina also has night skiing from 1-10pm at lower rates. ☎ 518-589-7777.

Directional Info: Heading west on Route 23A, turn left at Sportman's Diner.

Golf

Windham Country Club, South Street, Windham. ☎ 518-734-9910. Carries a slope rating of 127 from the back tees and 114 from the front tees. Restaurant, banquet facilities, hand carts and motorized carts, rentals, pro shop, lessons. This public par 71, 18-hole course was originally designed in 1927 by Len Rayner of Cooperstown, NY. One of the highest-rated courses in the state, it's scenic, rolling and challenging. Open April through November.

Directional Info: From the Thruway, take Exit 21, then Route 23W. Make a left onto Route 296 and then turn right onto South Street.

Christman's Windham House Country Inn & Golf Course, Windham. ☎ 518-734-4230; 518-734-3824. Carts are not mandatory. This more challenging regulation length course has a slope of 129 from the blue tees and is fully irrigated. The course at Christman's is open to the public, but only guests have guaranteed tee times. A par 70 regulation course, it offers spectacular mountain views, is walkable, and allows metal spikes.

Greene County

Stanley Christman built the original or "valley" nine-hole course in 1961. Of moderate length, with six holes on flat farmland, it's not as intimidating as the modern nine-hole mountain course designed and built by architect Brian Christman in 1995. The on-site Roland Stafford Golf School has practice areas with covered tee areas in case of rain. Open April 30 through October 15. For further information, including a biography of the golf pro, Stafford, visit their Web site at www.windhamhouse.com.

Directional Info: From the Thruway, take Exit 21, then Route 23W for about 30 miles to the resort.

Rip Van Winkle Country Club, Route 23A, Palenville, NY 12463. ☎ 518-678-9779. Guaranteed tee times on weekends. Motor/hand carts available but not mandatory. Glassed-in restaurant opens in May. This nine-hole, par 36, flat but challenging course has been in the Smith family since 1949. It was designed by Donald Ross in 1919 and was closed for eight years during WWII. The signature hole is #3. "It's amazing to have a flat course in the mountains," says Patricia Smith, who operates the course with her son, Ray Smith Jr. Although flat, the course is scenic and has enough water and sand traps to appeal to seasoned golfers. Opens in April and closes when the snow flies.

Directional Info: Just off Route 23A, about a third of a mile east of the stoplight in Palenville. Look for a gray house.

Pleasantview Golf Club, Route 67, Freehold. ☎ 518-634-7816. Pro shop, restaurant, carts not mandatory, spikeless. Known to locals as a hidden gem, this nine-hole, par 36 course built in 1969 was nearly empty at 9am on a magnificent Sunday in May. (I counted 16 cars in the parking lot.) "Length is one of Pleasantview's best assets," a writer wrote. When another nine holes slated for May of 2000 are complete, the course will be re-named Thunderhart after the corporate owner. (Pleasantview Lodge next to the course is a separate entity.)

Sunny Hill Golf Course, Sunny Hill Road, Greenville. ☎ 518-634-7698. Clubhouse, snack bar, club rental, practice area, pro shop, putting green, lessons. Probably one of the prettiest courses in the Catskills, this public 18-hole, par 66 rolling course is of medium difficulty. The first nine holes were built in 1963 and the tougher back nine were added 13 years ago. One male hacker called it the shortest 18 and least challenging of the local courses, while a female golfer at Pleasantview Golf Club termed the greens at Sunny Hill very tough. Open April through November.

Rainbow Golf Club & Resort, Route 26, Greenville. ☎ 518-966-5343; www.golfrainbow.com. Pro shop, driving range, rentals, restaurant, carts not mandatory, spikeless. Here's another hidden gem. "We come down here because there's never anybody on here," a golfer from Albany said, describing the par 71, 18-holer as a fun course with a lot of water. "It's an ego boost." In another golfer's view, however, "this course (with Lake Otto as a special challenge) can humble you."

The resort is actually six one-bedroom apartments available for daily, weekly or seasonal rental. Inquire about golf packages.

If you prefer a nine-hole course (par 34), head over to **Ingalside Resort & Golf Club**, also in Greenville. Should you find the course too challenging, try your hand at its new 300-yard driving range. ☎ 518-966-5316.

Greene County

Driving Ranges & Mini-Golf

The miniature golf course at **Bear Creek Landing**, overlooking Hunter Mountain and beside Schoharie Creek, is patterned after the adventure sport-course at Myrtle Beach. Complete with water hazards, artificial turf, elevated greens and sand traps, even an experienced golfer will find this challenging, predicted owner Bill Simon. It was the day before the official opening on Memorial Day, 1999, and we were standing among paint cans, building equipment and workers in hard hats. He said the course would be lit for night play and will be booking parties and golf outings. A round on the 18-hole miniature course is $7 plus tax. The **Tom Knowles Golf School** offers individual and group lessons and free clinics. A "SAM 2000" teaching device is on premises. ☎ 518-263-3839. Open daily, April through October.

Directional Info: Located at the intersection of Routes 23C and 214 in Hunter.

High Peak Country Club features a nine-hole miniature golf course and 13-room motel with a pool. Located next to Twilight Mountain General Store in Haines Falls. ☎ 518-589-5221.

Horseback Riding

If you're an experienced rider, **Rough Riders Ranch** in Tannersville is the place to go. ☎ 518-589-9159. While lessons for beginners and children are also given, riders who enjoy the excitement of a Cavalry charge have the freedom to move fast rather than follow other horses. "These are all privately-owned horses, not like regular hack-like horses," a rider named Debbie told me. Preparing to mount one of the five spirited but gentle horses, she lauded the proprietor, Sgt. Joe D'Acunto, for his flexibility: "He lets people he knows go out by themselves. Very few places do that anymore."

D'Acunto is a Civil War buff and US Marine who served with the Army's 1st Cavalry Division Horse Platoon in Ft. Hood, Texas. Nowadays, besides teaching riding and skiing, he entertains at pony parties, dressed in the traditional blue uniform, his horse packed with an authentic McClellan saddle.

Lambs, sheep, goats, piglets and a calf comprise the Rough Riders Ranch petting zoo.

Directional Info: Take 23A to Tannersville. At the light, turn north onto 23C past the Mountain Top Arboretum on the right. Turn right at the sign for Camp Trimount (Boy Scout Road) and go up the hill. Look carefully for the two small wagon wheels on the ground and turn left.

For a guided ride, **Silver Springs Ranch** is on 60 acres in Haines Falls. In business for 30 years, it seemingly has everything for the rider: 40 horses; a shop selling boots, cowboy hats and saddles; a motel and hotel with 11 rooms at $40-$50, double occupancy; lessons; restaurant (for guests only); bar; game room; several packages; and a most personable ranch foreman, Ray Phillips, who says, "we have something to fit everyone's need." Snowmobiling is offered in the winter. Rates run from $25 an hour to $499 for five days/nights with three ranch-style meals per day. ☎ 800-258-2624; 518-589-5559. Open all year. The ranch also has a new facility in Phoenicia called Saddle Up Ranch (see page 266).

Directional Info: Take Route 23A to Haines Falls. At JAMS restaurant, make a right onto Route 25 and continue a quarter mile.

Greene County

Flying

From the outside, **Freehold Airport** looks like a country gift shop, but it's a fooler. When it came into being 40 years ago, there were six airports in Greene County. Today, there are three, and Freehold is the only one open to the public. Clem and Rita Hoovler operate their own flight school and do aerial photography for homeowners who want to know what their property looks like from above. Private planes are also boarded at the airport, which has 11 planes of its own and does airplane maintenance.

Rita Hoovler is an award-winning artist whose work is displayed at the Freehold Airport alongside models of planes.

Conversing with a man who had flown his plane from Orange County, Rita compared her small airport to a larger one. "It gives you a warmer atmosphere than a county airport. You wouldn't go to Newburgh (Airport) and sit on the porch and have yourself a Coke."

The airport offers 15-minute scenic rides daily at $20 per person (minimum of two people) and also long tours. ☎ 518-634-7626. Open April through November.

Directional Info: From Route 32, turn onto Main Street in Freehold, and follow Route 67 until you see the airport.

Museums, Art & Theater 😊😠

> *Art teaches nothing, except the*
> *significance of life.*
> – Henry Miller, *The Wisdom of the Heart*

BRONCK MUSEUM
Off Route 9W
Coxsackie
☎ 518-731-8862; 518-731-6490
Guided tours Tuesday-Saturday, 10am-4pm, Sunday,
1-5pm; Memorial Day through mid-October
$4 admission

This museum contains the Hudson Valley's oldest
home, built by Pieter Bronck in 1663. He was the son
of Jonas Bronck, for whom the Bronx was named.
The stone house and the complex of later buildings
were all part of a working farm operated by eight
generations of Broncks. Among the structures is a
13-sided barn, its roof supported by the walls and a
single center pole. The houses were expanded and
modified as styles changed, but are considered to be
relatively intact and representative of 17th- and
18th-century Dutch architecture.

IRISH AMERICAN HERITAGE MUSEUM
2267 Route 145
East Durham
☎ 518-634-7497; 518-432-6598
www.irishamericanhermuseum.org

Known as the "Emerald Isle of the Catskills," East
Durham houses this interesting museum in a two-
story renovated farmhouse. Although there are no
permanent displays, the revolving exhibits here last
two years. The most recent one focused on the contributions of Irish women to life in America. The li-

Greene County

brary has a fairly extensive collection of books on Irish history, literature and culture, as well as videotapes and genealogy materials. Open Wednesday-Saturday, 11am-5pm, and Sunday, noon-5pm, Memorial Day through Labor Day; Friday and Saturday, 11am-5pm, and Sunday, noon-5pm, Labor Day through Columbus Day. Admission charged.

Directional Info: Driving north on Route 145, the museum is located just past the first flashing light in East Durham.

Celebrating its 61st year, the Kellegher family's **Shamrock House** hosts a full summer season of Irish entertainment. ☎ 518-634-2897 for schedule.

Works in Progress

Will **Irish Village USA** become a reality, bringing in 600,000 visitors annually like its prototype, Bunratty Folk Park at Shannon Airport in Co. Clare, Ireland? Over 44 million people of Irish descent live in this country, and two-thirds of them live within a day's drive of East Durham. The land is already acquired – 33 acres adjacent to the Michael J. Quill Irish Cultural & Sports Center. And, like the idea behind Bunratty (which saved three historic buildings from demolition), the historic Welding House, a motel with 60 units that housed 200-250 people, could be converted to a museum of Irish history. Part of it would serve as a tourism center for Ireland.

The concept is to construct a village depicting life in Ireland over the past 2,000 years. A 900-foot street will be filled with museums, monuments and stores. Each county in Ireland is being given first choice to build, design and finance its own three-quarters of an acre. Each will be given free reign, provided the exhibit is authentic. Should any county decline, second and third choices will go to corporations and individuals. Thus far, 11 counties have more or less committed.

Dennis Meehan, the brainchild behind the village, has completed a four-year feasibility study, which projects 200,000 to 350,000 visitors annually. The village will be the biggest tourist attraction in that part of the state. Meehan is confident the money will come from either the community or from individuals. "It's going to happen," Meehan says. "We plan to open in 2001."

ZADOCK PRATT MUSEUM
Main Street
Prattsville
☎ 518-299-3395
www.prattmuseum.com
Open Wednesday-Sunday, 1-4pm,
Memorial Day through Columbus Day
$2 donation

Pratt's 1828 homestead is celebrating its 40th year as a "look and listen" museum (meaning guided tours only). It's a worthwhile visit. Zadock Pratt was eccentric and beloved, and is largely responsible for turning this northwest wilderness of Greene County into one of the first planned communities in New York State. Situated along Schoharie Creek, the area was founded by Palatine Germans in the mid-1700s and originally called Schoharie-Kill. In 1832 Zadock Pratt (1790-1871), businessman, tanner and politician, named the town after himself, and a year later it officially became Prattsville.

Greene County

Pratt's family, originally from Connecticut, moved to Jewett when Zadock was young. Although he had no formal education, at age 12 he became an apprentice in his father's tannery in Jewett. After opening a general store in Lexington, Zadock Pratt built the entire village of Prattsville and at one point owned the largest tannery in the world. Although the citizens were initially against his installing a tannery in town, Pratt's philosophy was, "I don't want to live on you. I want to live with you." After he built 100 homes from hemlock, most still standing, and planted 1,000 hickory, maple and elm trees along the town streets, objections subsided.

The eccentric Zadock Pratt once donned a fur coat on the Fourth of July, jumped into a sleigh & drove into the village of Catskill, to the surprise of all.

By the mid-19th century, Prattsville had 1,500 inhabitants, three tanneries, four textile factories, three grist mills, five schools, three churches, several hotels and shops and a bank owned by Pratt, who printed currency bearing his own name and likeness. (Pratt's office in the bank is part of the museum, now used as the gift shop.) Pratt also served as a US Congressman for two terms, when he originated the Bureau of Statistics. His most memorable bill was to reduce the 25¢ stamp to 5¢.

The Pratt house was built in 1828, but is representative of the 1850s when Pratt was married to his fourth wife. They were married for more than 20 years (his first three wives died early in the marriage and the fifth outlived him). The museum grounds, located beside the Great American Supermarket, include an herb garden and carriage house containing Pratt's impressive buggy.

Directional Info: From the east, take the Thruway Exit 21 (Route 23W) for 35 miles. From the west, take Route 23 east from Oneonta, off Exit 15 of I-88 (40 miles).

ART AWARENESS MOUNTAIN THEATRE
SCHOHARIE CREEK PLAYERS
Route 42
Lexington
☎ 518-989-6802

The Schoharie Creek Players made their debut in August 1999 with *The Playboy of the Western World* at the Mountain Theater. The group's goal is to present a wide variety of theatrical classics and new plays in the summers to come. It has also developed programs for children. Barbara Sturman, a resident of Lexington, is the founder and head of the new theater group. She has been producing community theater at the Art Awareness Mountain Theatre for two years, and for 20 years was an instructor and director of Dramatic Arts for the New York City Public Schools, the American Conservatory Theater in San Francisco and the University of Delaware. Anyone interested in becoming an active member of this venture may apply; no experience is necessary.

GREENE ROOME PLAYERS
Hunter
☎ 518-589-6297; 914-246-1598

This community group, formed in 1992, performs locally all year round (mostly musicals). They also hold workshops for adults and children in all aspects of theater.

THE CATSKILL MOUNTAIN FOUNDATION
PO Box 924
Hunter
☎ 518-263-4908
www.catskillmtn.org

This newly-formed organization has inaugurated a schedule of events from September to December that includes classical and popular music concerts,

Greene County

foreign film program, literary events and exhibitions.

Shopping

Mountain Top

As you'll see, several businesses use "Mountain Top" in their names. Borrowing author Field Horne's description: "A spur of the Appalachian chain runs northwesterly from a point on the county's south border about seven miles from the river, dividing Catskill, Cairo and Durham and other northeastern towns from those of the 'Mountaintop.'" This leaves Windham, Lexington, Ashland, Prattsville, Hunter, Tannersville and Jewett as the mountaintop townships.

TRAPHAGEN'S HONEY
Route 23A
Hunter
☎ 800-838-9194; 518-263-4150
Open year-round

While in the area, make a beeline here. This is a delightful shop with all kinds of honey blends (including handmade honey/goat's milk bars of soap), jams, teas, maple syrups, salad dressings, chocolate, nuts and fragrances. The store was started in 1945 by Paul Traphagen, a beekeeper and bee inspector who died at age 104. The new owners purchased it in 1978. Purchases can be shipped anywhere.

CATSKILL MOUNTAIN COUNTRY STORE
Main Street (Route 23)
Windham
☎ 518-734-3387
Open daily, year-round

This large country store and café (formerly The Bountiful Basket) carries such items as fur-lined slippers, hand-painted mailboxes, troll habitat and herb teas. It also sells perennials and annuals from its greenhouse and local organic produce.

MOUNTAIN TOP GALLERY
398 Main Street
Windham
☎ 518-734-3104

The gallery shows paintings and photographs by Greene County artists and others, with exhibits generally running six weeks

CAROLE'S GIFT EMPORIUM
Windham
☎ 518-734-4734
Open daily, year-round

Offers gifts for all occasions. For animal lovers, there's the Sandicast collection (replicas of dogs, cats and wildlife) and the county's largest collection of Boyds Bears. Also, chimes, candles, Seraphim angels, and a year-round Christmas shop.

Greene County

MOUNTAIN TOP CLOTHING & GIFT SHOP
Main Street
Tannersville
Open daily (except Christmas Day)
☎ 518-589-6002

This shop, also called Village Candle, Pottery & Gifts, takes the prize for never closing (except for Christmas Day). "We have to be here," says owner Marc Sussman, who splits the hours in the store with his wife, Lillian. "We have become a destination store." His reasoning is that his store sells practically everything and that he never knows who will walk in desperate for clothes, as one couple did when their suitcase was stolen. Popular items include Minnetonka moccasins, handcrafted candles, jewelry and bathing suits (they actually sell more in the winter than in the summer). For aromatherapy fans, check out the hand-dipped incense sticks in dozens of scents.

CORNER COLLECTIONS
Main Street
Hunter
☎ 518-263-4141; 800-315-5790
www.cornercollections.com

Figurine freaks will love this store (especially the Walt Disney collection). It also carries crystals, jewelry, chimes, dolls, stuffed animals, steins, cuckoo clocks, and over 50 different Beanie Babies.

CATSKILL MOUNTAIN
BOOKSTORE & GALLERY
Main Street
Hunter
☎ 518-263-4908
Closed Tuesday and Wednesday

A unique place, which opened in December 1998, Catskill Mountain Bookstore & Gallery runs six-week exhibits of photographs and paintings by artists who are members of the gallery, including members living elsewhere. Each show is linked to books on the same topic. The only general bookstore featuring bestsellers in the county, it also carries a sizable collection of regional books, children's books, cookbooks, classics, and volumes on the performing arts and gardening. The store offers discounts of 10%-50% and will also special order any book not found on the shelves. Prices are competitive with the chains.

EXPANSION
Main Street
Hunter
☎ 518-263-4233
Closed Tuesday

Originally an art supply store, Expansion also has a gallery in the back called "Little Bird." The shop carries gift items, cards, stuffed animals and art supplies.

TERRA BOOKS
Off Route 23A
Between Lexington and Prattsville
☎ 518-299-3171
Open Saturday and Sunday, 10am-5pm or by appointment or by chance

In the market for used, out-of-print or antiquarian books? Be sure to check here.

Directional Info: Follow Route 23A to Mosquito Point Bridge (just off 23A and halfway between Lexington and Prattsville). Turn at Eileen's Snack Bar and follow signs.

Greene County

Acra

ULLA DARNI
Route 23
Acra
☎ 518-622-3566
Open to the public on weekends; by appointment during the week

Lamps take on new meaning after seeing Ulla Darni's museum-like home. A master of "reverse" painting, a process in which paint is applied to the underside of a lamp or chandelier, this blonde dynamo turns out masterpieces that fetch thousands of dollars. For example, a small lamp costs about $5,000 plus $1,600 for the base (which she also designs). Nightlights run about $100-$150 and are sold at her Blue Pearl café (see next page).

"Ulla" designs are represented in 64 galleries worldwide and grace full-page ads in magazines. One museum owner called Ulla "The Tiffany of Tomorrow" because of the caliber of her talent and the exclusivity of her art.

Cher, Melanie Griffith, Goldie Hawn, Al Pacino and Nick Nolte are some of those in possession of an Ulla lamp.

Ulla now works mainly on commission, designing lamps, tiles, marble pieces and fabric swatches for clients that include Disney and Royal Caribbean. Clients can specify the designs but must leave their placement up to Ulla. Flowers are her trademark, and their colorful beauty has a soft illumination and a three-dimensional quality. What's so amazing is that she paints lampshades on their base in their upright position. My wrist hurts just thinking about it!

Directional Info: From the Thruway, take Exit 21 (Route 23) toward Cairo for about 14 miles and you'll see the sign past the Getty Station. On the left is her home and on the right is her new studio.

Shedding Light on Art

Ulla Darni's Victorian home is a showcase of her creativity. But the woman is no museum. A spiritualist with a warm heart, Ulla flits around arranging things while chatting with visitors. "There isn't a thing she doesn't touch," says her friend, June Battisti. Including lives.

An actress and painter in her native Denmark, Ulla (who had given up acting to raise two sons) and her husband moved overseas[1] to the Bronx. In 1980 the couple moved to the Catskills, and the 168-year-old house was converted into a showplace and studio.

Today, Ulla has a thriving business with 24 employees who paint, pack, ship, catalogue and photograph. The four painters do what's called "multiple originals" – painstaking geometric designs that resemble Ulla's style. But only she does the flowers. The multiples, priced from $700 to $1,800, are signed "Ulla," whereas her one-of-a-kind works are also stamped with her fingerprint.

Recently Ulla opened the **Blue Pearl**, a café three miles west of her house. It's open daily, year-round for breakfast and lunch. She recently bought the mountain behind the café and plans to build a village housing a holistic clinic, birthing center and 75-room inn with rates starting at $350.

Greene County

In the last years of Prohibition, Jack "Legs" Diamond moved his gang headquarters to a white farmhouse just north of the village of **Acra**. Hounded by rivals, he came to this isolated spot to raise local stills to the status of an organized business. Mountain bootleggers did not welcome the intrusion and Diamond was shot down in one of the mountain drinking joints. He survived and had the trunks of the trees around his house painted white to make an ambush attack impossible. He was later killed in a cheap rooming house in Albany.

Cairo

For some strange reason, the locals in Cairo pronounce their village "KAY-ro" even though it was named for Cairo, Egypt. Main Street is a mix of empty storefronts, hair salons, tanning parlors, antique shops, and real estate, law, and insurance offices. Cairo also boasts a long list of scheduled events between May and December.

TRADERS OF THE LOST ART
Main Street
Cairo
☎ 518-622-0340

At first blush, this shop looks like a shrine given all the religious articles. Yet on closer inspection it's what the spirited owner Ken Abatayo calls "A bit of

Woodstock outside of Woodstock without the high prices." There are books on spirituality, healing, music, health and philosophy; Tibetan shades; incense; candles; stones; African masks; and so much more. Many of the books are discounted and Ken will take special orders. He gives a free crystal with every purchase – "The larger the purchase, the larger the crystal."

Having Ken tell you your chakra is a kick even if you're not a believer.

CROSWELL'S EMPORIUM
Main Street
Cairo
☎ 518-622-9236; 800-561-5888
Open daily; closed Monday in the off-season

A few doors down from Traders is another crammed-to-the-rafters variety store. Owner Dave Hart waved to me as I walked in. Imagine that happening in midtown Manhattan! Hart sells several discounted items – new and antique – ranging from clocks and figurines to lamps and cigars. Special requests are filled, when possible. Free gift wrapping and daily discounts based on volume of purchase.

East Durham

THE WOOD SHED
Route 145
East Durham
☎ 518-634-7451
Open daily, April until late fall

On Route 145, before entering the village of East Durham from the east, look for a colorful display of wooden ornaments on the lawn to your left. The Wood Shed is the work of Dan Lucente, who builds his birdhouses, signs, Christmas ornaments, lawn decorations, windmills, and Adirondack chairs ("whatever the whim") during the winter for display

Greene County

in the summer. Endowed with a terrific sense of humor, he relates that he was born in Queens and is half Irish and half Italian – Gaelic and garlic. He has also been town judge for eight years.

IRELAND USA GIFT SHOP
East Durham
☎ 800-441-5074; 518-634-2392
Open daily, April-December;
Weekends, January-March

In the Irish enclave of East Durham shamrocks are painted in the street. The largest and most popular variety store – Ireland USA (a.k.a. Guaranteed Irish) – specializes in goods from, or representative of, the Emerald Isle. Billing itself as the largest Irish import store in the United States, its merchandise includes heraldic items in the form of coasters, cups, steins, key chains and the like; a food department selling imported Irish tea, soups, sauces, sweets and drinks; CDs; jewelry; clothing; and sweaters. A nice inexpensive gift is a personalized magnetic notepad for $1.95. Downstairs is an art gallery displaying works by accomplished Irish artists from all over. One wall contains hand-beaten copper decorations that are quite striking. The shop is located at the first flashing light as you approach the village.

APPLE BLOSSOM GIFTS
East Durham
☎ 518-634-7727
Open Thursday-Monday, April through December

This quaint gift shop highlights the Boyds Bears and Friends collection. A Christmas section is in the back.

Works in Progress

Tony Goldman, the man largely responsible for revitalizing SoHo in Manhattan and Miami's South Beach, has another dream. "My biggest vision is to buy the entire Jewett Valley, 12 miles long," he told *New York Magazine* in September 1996. That was about the time he spent $36,000 for Sugar Maples, a 70-acre resort in the hamlet of Maplecrest, famous in the 1950s. The property, a complex of 25 buildings, had been turned over to the county for non-payment of taxes and was auctioned.

A long-time resident of the Town of Windham, Goldman is renovating the building to create an artist colony. Jeff Prince, a real estate agent in Tannersville, who originally showed the property to Goldman, confirms his five-year target completion date. "We have it on line," Prince says, "by 2001 everything will be done."

Festivals & Events

Hunter Mountain: Several festivals are held at the mountain or in the town of Hunter during the year, including **German Alps** (July); **Celtic** (August); **Microbrew** (Labor Day Weekend); **Oktoberfest** and **Craft Expo** (October); **Winterfest** (December); **Winter Carnival** (March). ☎ 518-263-4223.

Windham also has a full winter schedule of activities in February and March. ☎ 800-SKI WINDHAM.

There's an event every fall weekend – classic cars, live bands, carnival games – all including a country barbeque, mountain biking and scenic chairlift rides. Call for a complete calendar. ☎ 800-355-CATS.

July

Athens Street Festival on the Hudson River. Food, entertainment, boat rides, fireworks. Athens Riverfront Park. ☎ 518-945-1551.

Irish Music Festival, Irish arts week, East Durham. ☎ 800-434-FEST; www.east-durham.org.

Great Northern Catskills Black Bear Festival, Tannersville. ☎ 518-263-4524; www.huntermtn.com. This two-day event combines education and fun, and typically draws 5,000 to 7,000 visitors. Its mission is to focus on the natural beauty, wildlife, cultural and historical legacy, music, craft work and folkways of the incomparably beautiful Northern Catskill Mountains. There are exhibits about the NYS Department of Fisheries, bees, bears, and the West-of-Hudson Watershed, to name a few. Music is supplied by Albany's Police Pipes & drums, and there are trained black bears.

August

The Great Northern Catskills Balloon Festival, Greenville. ☎ 518-966-5050.

International Celtic Festival, Hunter. Celtic music, products from the Emerald Isles, handmade crafts, clothing, Irish and Scottish brews, and bagpipe competition. $10 adults. ☎ 518-263-4223.

German Alps Festival, Hunter. German entertainment, foods, crafts, beers, and M.I. Hummel look-alike contest. $7 adults. ☎ 518-263-4223.

September

Eagle Wing Powwow & Art Festival, Hunter. Labor Day weekend. Dozens of tribes from across the nation are on hand with Native American crafts, basketry, clothing, dance products, feather headdresses, Navajo rugs, jewelry and foods. Dance competition with a purse of over $20,000. Admission is $10 for adults. ☎ 518-263-4223.

Leeds Irish Festival, Leeds. Labor Day weekend. Featuring two days of music and dancing. ☎ 518-943-9814/9820.

Autumn A-Fair, New York's largest harvest festival, takes place in Windham at the end of September with historical displays, maple syrup demonstrations, music, wagon rides, petting zoo and dancing. ☎ 518-734-3397.

Greene County A to Z

Banks

Marine Midland, 335 Main Street, Catskill, ☎ 518-943-4400. **Catskills Savings Bank** (☎ 800-993-4CSB) has branches in Catskill, ☎ 518-943-3600, (ATM on Routes 9W/23A); Windham, ☎ 518-734-3991; and Greenville, ☎ 518-966-8244. **Greene County Savings**, Main and Church streets, Catskill, ☎ 518-943-3700, is building a branch in Tannersville. **Trustco**, 345 Main Street, Catskill, ☎ 518-943-2500, 238 Bridge Street (ATM on 9W/ 23A). **Key Bank** has branches in Tannersville and Windham.

Liquor Stores

The Wine Cellar is also a lottery agent at Catskill Valley Plaza, Route 9W, Catskill, ☎ 518-943-4630. **Windham Liquor** is on Route 23 next to the firehouse, ☎ 518-734-3474. **County Wine & Spirits,** Price Chopper Plaza, Route 9W, Catskill, ☎ 518-943-7766. **Boiceville Wines and Spirits**, Route 28, occasionally offers 10% off full cases of wine. **Hurley Ridge Wines & Spirits** has moved to larger quarters in the new Hurley Ridge Plaza, Route 375, West Hurley.

Movies

These theaters all show first-run films: **Greenville Family Drive-In** on Route 32 is open Friday through Monday at dusk, ☎ 518-966-8990. **Hunter Theatre** has a single screen and is open daily in summer and weekends after Labor Day.

Windham Theatre ($6) on Route 32, along with its 18-hole miniature golf course, antique auctions, and genuine D&H railroad caboose (on property once owned by Carson City) are all open daily in summer and part of the ski season; the rest of the year they are open weekends, ☎ 518-734-6110.

Community Theatre in Catskill, ☎ 518-943-2410, is open Friday through Sunday in the off-season.

Coxsackie Drive-In is open spring through summer, ☎ 518-731-8672.

Pharmacies

Windham Pharmacy, Windham, ☎ 518-734-3033. **Greene Medical Arts**, Catskill, ☎ 518-943-1715. **Mikhitarian Pharmacy**, 298 Main Street (near the post office) in Catskill offers 24-hour, seven-day after-hours emergency service, ☎ 518-943-3720.

Religious Services

BAPTIST – Cornerstone Baptist Church, Route 145, East Durham, ☎ 518-797-3927. **Greenville Center Baptist Church**, Route 41, Greenville Center. **First Baptist**, Grandview Avenue Circle, Catskill, ☎ 518-943-3292.

CATHOLIC – St. Theresa's Roman Catholic Church, Windham, ☎ 518-734-3352. **Church of The Immaculate Conception**, Haines Falls, ☎ 518-589-5577. **Sacred Heart Church**, Cairo, ☎ 518-622-3319. **St. John the Baptist Roman Catholic Church**, Route 81, Greenville, ☎ 518-966-8317.

EPISCOPAL – Trinity Episcopal Church, Ashland, ☎ 518-734-4263. **St. Luke's Episcopal Church**, 50 William Street, Catskill, ☎ 518-943-4180.

JEWISH – Temple Israel, Spring Street, corner of Route 23, Catskill, ☎ 518-943-5758; **Congregation Anshei Hashoron**, Tannersville; **Congregation Anshei Kol Israel**, Hunter.

Greene County

LUTHERAN – Resurrection Lutheran Church, at intersection of Routes 23B and 32, Cairo, ☎ 518-622-3286.

METHODIST – Kaaterskill United Methodist Church holds Sunday services (June-July) in Haines Falls, ☎ 518-589-5787, in Tannersville (October-May), ☎ 518-589-5787; and in Hunter (August-September). The thrift shop, ☎ 518-589-5787, is open 10am-2pm every Tuesday, Thursday and Saturday. **Hensonville United Methodist Church**, ☎ 518-734-4149. **Platte Clove Methodist Church**, ☎ 518-589-4787. Bargain Box Thrift Shop open by appointment. **United Methodist Church**, Main Street, Prattsville, ☎ 518-914-734-4122.

PRESBYTERIAN – Greenville Presbyterian Church, Route 32N.

REFORMED – First Reformed, 310 Main Street, Catskill, ☎ 518-943-4405.

Delaware County

Overview

The city has a face, the country a soul.
– Jacques De Lacretelle,
French novelist (1888-1985)

Spanning the western Catskill region, Delaware County is larger than the state of Rhode Island, but has a population density of only 21 people per square mile. Roughly half of its 1,460 square miles are made up of lively trout streams. And it was here among these waters that the father of American fly-fishing, Theodore Gordon,

introduced the techniques that changed the sport of fishing altogether. This rural county is also a hunter's heaven, with thousands of acres of game habitat and an abundance of deer, turkeys and gamebirds.

The six towns in Delaware County were each settled between the late 18th and early 19th centuries. In 1767, the Harper family (for whom the Town of Harpersfield is named) purchased 22,000 acres from Native Americans. The Harpers were the first people of European stock to come into the area. Delaware County was formally designated on March 10, 1797.

In the 19th century, Delaware County boomed and had schools in every district. While most men were farmers, towns such as Downsville boasted a lawyer, surgeon, watchmaker and furniture dealer/undertaker. An entry from the diary of Olneys Smith of Margaretville, dated January 20, 1934, reveals a melding of old traditions with the perils of technology: "Killed beef bull yearling....airiplains [sic] in morning got lost in snow. Storm here. Two came down on Dry Brook. Broke up one of them."

Breakstone is the Town of Walton's largest employer, with approximately 200 employees.

Dairy farming remains Delaware County's most important industry although it has diminished greatly in the last half-century. Back in 1893, Sheffield Farms Creamery in Bloomville was the first in the US to commercially pasteurize milk; the first shipment was sent to New York City from the hamlet of Hobart. In 1955, the county had 2,306 dairy farms, compared to only about 250 today. Among them are Dairylea and Breakstone (Kraft, Inc. Dairy Group).

Local Lore

When Horace Greeley came to the Catskills to show the locals how to make farming pay, a farmer asked what to do with hilly, rocky soil. Greeley replied, "Raise sheep!"

Still, on the region's 750,000 acres of farmland, the queen of agriculture – the dairy cow – is now sharing space with sheep, beef cattle, goats, lambs, emus, llamas and Tibetan yaks. These animals are being raised commercially and are filling several market niches for meat, wool and investment. Just as hog and wool production peaked in the mid-19th century, making way for dairy production, the next century may see other markets taking the lead.

In the towns of Andes, Bovina, Hancock and Roxbury, second homeowners own more than half the land. Non-residents encompass about two-fifths of the properties in the remaining towns. While the county abounds with B&Bs and other accommodations, the village stores are mainly geared for residents. In the smaller villages, one can usually find a post office, hardware store, body shop and/or general store. In the more sizable villages – Margaretville, Walton and Stamford – you'll also find banks, real estate offices, pharmacies and a supermarket.

The county is home to two reservoirs, Pepacton and Cannonsville, and a small portion of the Schoharie. Although the Pepacton Reservoir was not the first in the Catskills, it did not lessen the bitterness of those uprooted. Opened in 1955, it snakes through the towns of Colchester, Andes and Middletown and forced 943 people to leave. Ten cemeteries with a total of 2,369 gravesites were removed and relocated. One resident wrote a verse expressing his grief: "… Man's home was once his castle, he's seen it torn to shreds; The hallowed place where once it stood, will be the river's bed…"

Local Lore

It's said that on a still day you can look down into the Pepacton Reservoir's waters and see the drowned streets of an unfortunate town.

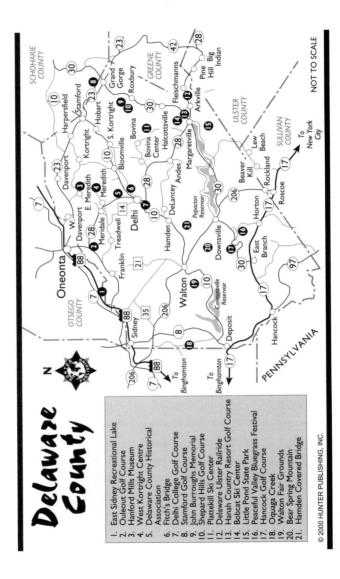

Delaware County

1. East Sidney Recreational Lake
2. Ouleout Golf Course
3. Hanford Mills Museum
4. West Korrtight Centre
5. Delaware County Historical Association
6. Fitch's Bridge
7. Delhi College Golf Course
8. Stamford Golf Course
9. John Burroughs Memorial
10. Shepard Hills Golf Course
11. Plattekill Ski Center
12. Delaware Ulster Railride
13. Hanah Country Resort Golf Course
14. Bobcat Ski Center
15. Little Pond State Park
16. Peaceful Valley Bluegrass Festival
17. Hancock Golf Course
18. Oquaga Creek
19. Walton Fair Grounds
20. Bear Spring Mountain
21. Hamden Covered Bridge

© 2000 HUNTER PUBLISHING, INC.

NOT TO SCALE

Best Places to Stay

The price scale for lodging can be found on page 20.

Resorts

SCOTT'S OQUAGA LAKE HOUSE

Oquaga Lake
Deposit
☎ 607-467-3094
www.scottsfamilyresort.com
Inexpensive to Moderate

Dancing lessons, fishing lessons, canoe trips, cookouts, waterskiing, tennis courts, pitch & putt course, two nine-hole golf courses (no tee times), and nightly entertainment offered.

If you prefer everything under one roof and three meals a day, Scott's is a wholesome environment for adults and youngsters on 1,100 acres. A family-owned, camp-like resort since 1869, it has a beautiful lakefront and incredibly energetic and talented owners. The nine-member, three-generation Scott family (and other performers) entertains nightly, along with serving, instructing, and supervising activities and excursions. Music and dancing is a constant, and daily ballroom dance lessons are very popular. A walk around the lake takes 45 minutes and bikes are available free.

When Doris and Ray (Scottie), married 51 years, sing a duo of love songs, it's more touching than corny. Their involvement with guests is legendary; some families have been vacationing here for 70 years. (I met a woman marking her 51st year at the

Oquaga Lake House resort is all inclusive (no tipping or extra fees). Alcohol is not served.

Delaware County

hotel, who remembers when Scottie was single.) The sense of returning to simpler times pervades. A photo of the lobby taken around 1920 looks pretty much the same as today and a sign over the office door, "Love is Spoken Here," has probably been there forever.

Directional Info: Call for precise directions. From Exit 84, the drive is short but involved; from Exit 82 it's longer but more direct.

★ **WHAT'S IN A NAME?**

The Village of Deposit was incorporated in 1811. Near this site on the Delaware River lumbermen "deposited" their logs to be made into huge rafts.

Inns/B&Bs

RIVER RUN BED & BREAKFAST
Main Street
Fleischmanns
☎ 914-254-4884
Inexpensive

Pets are $10 extra per night at River Run.

River Run is an inviting B&B fronted by a stand of hemlocks. The beige and green Queen Anne Victorian is on an acre of land bordered by a trout stream, past the historic movie theater on Main Street. Guests can laze in a hammock or rest beneath a giant oak in the sylvan setting behind the house. Dogs are more than welcome provided they are housebroken, socialized and well behaved. The owner, Larry Miller, a former Manhattan advertising executive, provides dog owners with his "Canine Code of Conduct" to insure maximum enjoyment for everyone.

THE PINES
Merrickville Road
Franklin
☎ 607-829-8216
Inexpensive

Three rooms with shared half-bath, shower downstairs, country breakfasts.

If you don't mind sharing a half-bath, this is the best bargain in town at $45 per room. The house, on 27½ acres, is the site of the original Merrick Farm, home to Franklin's first white settler, Gad Merrick from Connecticut, in 1782. Caroline Huyck (pronounced HIKE), a kind and helpful woman born in Alsace-Lorraine, France, has lived in the house since 1972. The common rooms are Old World with lots of antiques, while the guestrooms are more modern with thick carpets, plush beds and samples of Caroline's artwork. (Her lovely landscapes and still-lifes are displayed all over and are for sale.)

Breakfast is served beside a big picture window overlooking Huyck's garden and bird feeders. Her flower and vegetable garden is so pretty, in fact, that it was featured in the Spring 1999 issue of *Kaatskill Life*.

After Merrick's house burned down, his grandchildren built the present one in 1886. Caroline's parents bought the house in 1935 and ran a large farm. After they died, Huyck moved up from the city and reared her three children in the house. After her second husband died six years ago, her friends urged her to open a bed and breakfast. "What, strangers in my house?" she responded. Yet no sooner did the first guests leave, she found herself missing them. "They were the loveliest people and I thought, 'Oh my, I'm not ever going to see them again.'" Today, Caroline refers to her time with guests – which include hunters and Europeans – as fun.

Historical Note

In 1983, the Village of Franklin (population 409 in 1990) was placed on the National Register of Historic Places in recognition of the continued preservation of its architectural treasures.

MATTHEW'S POND
Turnpike Road
Delhi
☎ 607-829-5222
Inexpensive

If you're planning to hike the West Branch Preserve, attend the Delaware County Fair or simply enjoy a quiet weekend, this simply furnished B&B is a good bet. Located between Treadwell and Delhi, it has three attractively priced rooms and one shared bath. (The larger double room is better for a couple.) Once a post office and funeral parlor, the 200-year-old federal-style house retains the large "coffin doors," maple banister and shade of a locust tree (shown as a mere seedling in an 1890 photo of the house). Outside is a pond, named for the owners' grandson, Matthew, now seven.

During stagecoach days, the road in front was Treadwell Stage, a toll road, and the local general store, Barlow's, has been around since 1841.

Owners Joyce and Joe Kost, former Long Islanders, are very hospitable. He loves to help guests with directions and will pull out a map in the middle of breakfast. She's apt to send you off with a bag of muffins.

Delaware County

★ WHAT'S IN A NAME?

Shortly after the Revolutionary War, Judge Ebenezer Foote was involved in naming Delhi. Foote was so influential locally that he was nicknamed "the Great Mogul." He wanted the town named Delhi after the capital in India, the city of the real Great Mogul. Another early settler, Gen. Erastus Root, wanted the town called Mapleton because of all the beautiful maple trees. When the town voted in Delhi as the name, Root is said to have cried, "Delhi, Hell High, might as well be 'Foote high.'" This is probably the reason the village is pronounced "del-HI."

THE OLD STAGE LINE STOP
Catskill Turnpike Road
Meridale
☎ 607-746-6856
Inexpensive

Four large rooms, one with private bath. Plush beds. Full country breakfast.

Try to imagine yourself disembarking from a stagecoach into the care of an inviting hostess, attentive to your every need. This B&B was built in the 1930s on the stagecoach route – the Susquehanna (Catskill) Turnpike – opened in 1800. Not much has changed except the mode of transportation.

The rooms are beautifully decorated in what could best be described as country comfortable – all florals, lace and straw hats. It's the mood set by proprietor Rose Rosino, mother of five grown children. "Are you allergic to anything?" she asks upon my arrival. "Do you drink regular coffee in the morning?" In her unassuming way, she wants guests to feel at home and she succeeds. To remain free from worry about damage, she keeps antiques to a minimum. Rose also makes and sells delicious jams that you can sample at breakfast.

Directional Info: From Delhi, take Route 28W to Meredith sign (after one for Town of Meredith). Turn left onto Catskill Turnpike and follow for 1.2 miles. House is on the right.

Local Lore

All of Meridale is on what once was Meridale Farms, a farm conglomerate that was a major supplier of dairy products. Eventually the farms were turned over to the owner's employees – Norwegians – who proved to be good farmers.

BREEZY ACRES FARM
Route 10
Hobart
☎ 607-538-9338
www.delawarecounty.org
Inexpensive

Three rooms, two with private bath. Shared bath is for families or close friends (room without bath has adjoining private room with pullout sofa). Full country breakfast features the farm's own maple syrup. Plush beds and a fully stocked medicine chest that includes toothpaste and toothbrush, floss, shaving cream, disposable razors, Q-tips, bandages, aspirin and even Maalox.

Breezy Acres is an 1830s farmhouse with two columned porches and a garden, totally modernized within. The spacious kitchen alone is something you'd see in a decorating magazine. Blond wood throughout the house and an ash floor give the B&B a cheerful glow.

When Joyce and David Barber – both raised in Delaware County – married in 1972 they moved into the house on 300 acres. They had a dairy farm and then a crop farm, but when the barn burned in 1988, they abandoned farming. Only maple syrup is now made and sold, both for wholesale and retail.

Joyce is a veteran innkeeper, with a master's degree in home economics. Running the B&B for 16 years, she has some longstanding guests. The four who have joined her 100-Nights Club have gotten gifts. One received a monogrammed bathrobe. Another guest, who "streaks" from his room to the bathroom, received a bathsheet. Several guests have become good friends. "We now have as many friends who live here (in Delaware County) as don't live here. That's become a real perk."

Directional Info: From Delhi, take Route 10N. When you reach Hobart, go past the stores and the two silos. Look to your left for the sign.

⊚ TIP

Joyce keeps a file of brochures and clippings to help guests choose nearby activities. One of the categories is *Stay Another Day.* If time permits, why not combine a trip to Delaware County with a visit to Cooperstown and the National Baseball Hall of Fame, Fenimore Art Museum, or the Farmer's Museum?

Finding Room at the Inn

When there's no room at the inn, where do you turn? Left or right? Contact the **Delaware County Bed & Breakfast Association** at 800-DEL-INNS (335-4667) for B&B recommendations and directions. Or visit their Web site at www.delawarecounty.org.

Motels

DOWNSVILLE MOTEL
Routes 30 & 206
Downsville
☎ 607-363-7575
Inexpensive

Spacious rooms with TV, terrace, decent size towels, and coffee server.

Canoes can be rented at the Downsville Motel, which offers paddlers easy access to the river.

This is not your cookie-cutter motel, thanks to the multiple talents and housekeeping fussiness of Melanie Carpenter. A native of Holland, she and her Catskill-reared husband, Al, run the motel and sports shop. In the winter, the couple makes wooden signs, boxes, ink stands, birdhouses and clocks for sale in the shop. Licenses can be obtained at the store, which caters to fishermen and hunters.

The East Branch of the Delaware River runs behind the motel where rental canoes and a picnic table are available.

Fluent in five languages, Melanie has attended interior design and photography school. (Ask to see the postcard with her exquisite photo of Al canoeing by the recently reopened Downsville Covered Bridge.) Melanie takes great pride in designing the guestrooms at the Downsville Motel and keeping them clean.

Al's Sport Shop is devoted to sportsmen, and the Carpenters' wooden items are perfect gifts for your favorite fisherman or hunter. A sign on one plaque says it all: "Some men would rather be photographed with their fish than with their wives."

⊚ **TIP**

An avid walker and member of the local Chamber of Commerce, Melanie (from the Downsville Motel) knows nearly every trail in the area, including the one up to the grave of Col. George W. Downs. "They say he was buried standing up to overlook his town," she says. Downs, who died January 15, 1861 at age 44, owned a tannery and gristmill in what was then a booming town. An atlas from 1869 shows a school in every district, and residents included a surgeon, watchmaker, blacksmith and lawyer.

Downsville Motel and Al's Sport Shop are open all year.

BUENA VISTA MOTEL
Route 28
Delhi
☎ 607-746-2135
www.buenavistamotel.com
Open year-round
Inexpensive

AAA-approved motel with 33 rooms, TV, telephone and writing desk.

A continental breakfast, included in the price, features muffins and cold cereal. Checkered tablecloths and a fireplace in the breakfast room give it the feel of a cozy inn that costs three times as much.

*Looking in on the cozy breakfast room
at the Buena Vista Motel in Delhi.*

REXMERE LODGE
At Junction 10 and 23
Stamford
☎ 800-932-1090
Inexpensive

A good place to stay, especially if you're alone or with kids. I lucked out with the cheapest room ($40) and had a TV, telephone, comfortable double bed, small porch and shampoo. The lodge has an outdoor pool, restaurant, children's activities, live bands, movies, games and room service.

Best Places to Eat

*The price scale for restaurants can
be found on page 21.*

Casual Dining

Delaware County

RIVERSIDE CAFE & LODGE
Exit 92; turn right
Horton
☎ 607-498-5305
Open all year; restaurant closed Tuesday
Moderate

From this roadhouse restaurant beside a gas station
the view outside looks like one of Winslow Homer's
watercolors. Non-smokers are rewarded here, because the wood and glass atrium is reserved for
them (smokers must eat inside next to the bar).
Diners can watch the fly-fishermen on the Beaverkill
just as the Hudson River painters did a century ago
– possibly even Homer, who spent at least a summer
in the Catskills.

Owner/chef Tammy Sherwood is a CIA graduate
who earned her stripes at two high-end resorts,
Greenbriar in West Virginia and the Beaverkill Valley Inn. The cuisine reflects her talents as well as
that of the previous chef. When she bought the property a year and a half ago, the Silver Fox had been
closed for two years. Daily News columnist Jerry
Kenney, who now dines at Riverside, often wrote
about the Silver Fox, and the atrium room is named
for him.

*A motel with
11-rooms (six
efficiencies) ad-
joins the River-
side Café.*

Meals always begin with a basket of homemade
bread – we had tomato bread with poppy seeds. Her

other breads include raisin, French, and baking powder biscuits with cheese. A huge salad followed, with a variety of lettuces grown locally. Tender and flavorful roast pork slices served with sweet and sour red cabbage and potatoes filled the plate, as did my husband's scrumptious Southwestern chicken.

STAMFORD CAFE
122 Main Street
Stamford
☎ 607-652-3530
Open all year, Thursday-Sunday
Reservations recommended
Moderate

This is another fine restaurant that isn't aesthetically perfect. Currently, eight plastic-covered tables and the kitchen are crammed in a small space. Chef/owner Larry Lowndes, a graduate of the Culinary School at Kendall College in Illinois, opened the restaurant in 1993 and hopes to expand soon.

Patrons may bring their own wine to the Stamford Café until the restaurant gets a liquor license.

The one crackerjack waitress buzzes from table to table as if she were in a Manhattan bistro. The two rolls and salad are nothing to rave about, but when the main dish appears in a blaze of color, everyone forgets the negatives. "This place should get 12 stars," volunteered the man at the next table, thinking I was a food critic. "Don't tell anyone about this place," his wife half-joked.

My spice-rubbed shrimp with roasted chili-garlic sauce, displayed like a necklace on the plate, was fabulous, but the man insisted I have rack of lamb next time, given that he's sampled it from one coast to the other and it's never been as good as the Stamford Café's. The menu is small, but there are lots of specials. Scrumptious selections include jerk chicken, Thai shrimp, and dark chocolate mousse with coffee-soaked genoise.

HIDDEN INN
Main Street
South Kortright
☎ 607-538-9259
Inexpensive to Moderate

Culinary awards aside, some entrées served here are disappointing. There is a nice shrimp bar and the steak fries are special. The ambience is country; the service good. Dinner for two with wine was $37, not including tax.

Directional Info: From Delhi, take Route 10 to South Kortright; turn right at stone bridge.

THE OLD SCHOOL HOUSE INN & RESTAURANT
Main Street
Downsville
☎ 607-363-7814
Open year-round for lunch and dinner
Closed Monday
Moderate

This is a nice family restaurant with an extensive wine and beer selection. As the name implies, it was a school from 1903 to 1939 for grades 1-12. The dilapidated wooden schoolhouse underwent a meticulous interior restoration after Tom and Julie Markert purchased it in 1987.

Today, the décor of the rectangular dining room, where high school classes once met, is a mix of early American and art deco furnishings with tables and booths. A shrimp salad bar sits where the teacher probably stood. My center-cut pork chops ($12.95) were succulent, well-done as ordered but not dry. The mashed potatoes were deeply satisfying, but the soggy string beans, which I didn't order, were not. They tasted canned despite the waitress's contention that they use frozen vegetables. Go there with your kids – there are no grades or detention in this schoolhouse!

Directional Info: The restaurant is on Route 206W, 15 miles from Route 17, Exit 94.

HAMDEN INN
Route 10
Hamden
☎ 607-746-7203
Open year-round, Tuesday-Sunday
Inexpensive to Moderate

The Hamden Inn was recently sold to Christina and Danny Zale and the restaurant leased to Frank and Mary Jeanniton. The imposing visage of this 19th-century building is deceiving. The restaurant is ultra casual with very reasonable prices. The menu is small, but specials are numerous. Lunch choices include burgers, club sandwiches and salads, and the four-course dinner choices are equally simple but good. Complimentary softcover books are available for reading at the table.

SHIRE PUB & KITCHEN
Main Street
Delhi
☎ 607-746-6202
Open year-round for lunch and dinner. Restaurant closed Sunday and Monday; bar open daily
Inexpensive to Moderate

Casual place for burgers (huge and scrumptious), hot and cold sandwiches, salads or full dinner. In business for 20 years, so they've got it right.

Lite Bites

THE RESTAURANT
82 Main Street
Delhi
☎ 607-746-7170
Inexpensive

You can't go wrong with The Restaurant, a.k.a. Village Seafood. Forget ambiance. It's open daily for breakfast, lunch and dinner and the meals are simple, hearty, inexpensive and tasty.

QUARTER MOON CAFE
53 Main Street
Delhi
☎ 607-746-8886
Open year-round for lunch, Monday-Saturday
Inexpensive

Here's another good lunch option, which is in back of **Good Cheap Food**, a cooperative store that's part grocery/bookstore/boutique/pharmacy. The menu is vegetarian and portions are generous. Offerings include tuna sandwich, TLT (tofu instead of bacon), pan-fried trout and chicken-avocado burger.

MAIN STREET BOVINA
Bovina Center
☎ 607-832-4300
Open for breakfast and lunch, Wednesday-Sunday
Inexpensive

A renovated warehouse on a super quiet street, this cheerful café and gourmet grocery is a welcome surprise and a real treat. Paula and husband, Tom, arrived from Michigan with backgrounds in the culinary arts and serve as the managing partners. The owners, Dave and Carol, weekenders who work in the fashion industry, opened the restaurant three

There's a tiny museum in Bovina Center next to the fire department. If it's open, it's worth a peek.

years ago but had to shut down when the chef left. Nowadays, though, you can be assured of homemade and fresh food. The meat is from a Bovina butcher who raises his own cattle and Tom (who teaches culinary arts at SUNY Delhi) makes sausage every Friday. On Sunday, dishes are packed on ice for city folk. Soup, sandwiches and pasta are $3-$8. "We're thinking about starting dinners on Saturday nights," says Paula, "since the locals are clamoring for it." Plans are to have a different menu every weekend.

Directional Info: Exit Route 28 at Bovina Center and follow road into town.

★ **WHAT'S IN A NAME?**

Bovina, a pioneer town in the dairy industry, was named in honor of the cow (in Latin, "bovinus" means cattle). It's the county's smallest and most sparsely populated town.

ANDES PIZZA PLACE
Route 28
Andes
☎ 914-676-3703
Inexpensive

*For fast food addicts, there is a **McDonald's** in Walton.*

It's fun having pizza on a magnificent cherry wood counter under Tiffany lamps and a high ceiling. Proprietor David Frontera made the counter himself and serves up a mighty good pizza to boot. A favorite watering hole for locals, the restaurant shares its ceiling with the general store (opened in 1864), which once occupied the entire space.

DANNY'S RESTAURANT & LOUNGE
14 Gardiner Place
Walton
☎ 607-865-7811
Inexpensive

Hungry for a burger? Danny's makes juicy and flavorful eight-ounce BBQ burgers topped with grilled peppers and onions and other combinations. As its ad boasts, it's "A place to meet and eat," with wooden booths and Tiffany lamps. You can also get cold and hot sandwiches, and seafood and steak dinners from $9.95 to $16.95.

Sunup to Sundown

Sightseeing

Historic Sites

In his day, **John Burroughs** was a revered figure and one of the country's most widely read authors. Unlike Henry David Thoreau, whose work was not generally known until after his death, Burroughs enjoyed popularity during his lifetime.

He was instrumental in establishing the nature essay as a literary genre and counted among his friends Theodore Roosevelt, Thomas Edison, Harvey Firestone, John Muir, Henry Ford and Walt Whitman. In 1867, Burroughs wrote the first of his 31 books, *Notes on Walt Whitman as Poet and Person*. The two initially met in Washington, DC during the Civil War, when Burroughs was working at the Treasury Department and Whitman was volunteering at a military hospital. Burroughs was widely traveled but throughout his nearly 84 years always returned to his beloved Catskills. After turning 70, he spent every summer at Woodchuck Lodge, a rustic residence built by his parents that still stands. The house is only open twice a year – on the third Saturday of May and first Saturday in October. It's not his birthplace – that house is gone.

To me, the gravesite is more interesting. Just .2 mile from the house is the sign for **John Burroughs Memorial Field Historic Site**, owned by New York State. (Henry Ford, who also romanticized his own rural past, presented Burroughs with a deed to the three acres in 1913. That plot became his burial site.)

Burroughs' stone-encircled grave is on a sweeping rise, but is well worth the climb. A glance around, and at the logbook entries, reveals why. "Always an experience of spiritual renewal," a man penned. "How many places are there left in this country where you can have this experience?" A distant relative of Burroughs pleaded, "Please don't restore [the lodge] – its beauty is in its simplicity." A couple from the Netherlands, apparently struck by the idyllic spot, wrote: "How we wish to be buried in a place like this!"

It was Burroughs' wish to be buried beside the rock on the hill above Woodchuck Lodge. It was here on "Boyhood Rock" that he would often retreat to revel in the "wealth of the universe." A bronze plaque contains lines from one of his poems: "I Stand Amid the Eternal Ways and What is Mine Shall Know My Face."

Directional Info: Take Route 30 from Margaretville to the sign in Roxbury for Burroughs Sanctuary, and continue until you see Burroughs Memorial Road. Follow it for a few miles to the site.

★ FAMOUS FACES

Yoko Ono, Dan Ackroyd, and married couple Pam Dawber and Mark Harmon all have homes in Delaware County.

Covered Bridges

Robert Murray, a Scot who came to this country as a boy and lived in Andes, was Delaware County's most famous bridge builder. Between 1854 and 1859 he built four long truss bridges over the East and West Branches of the Delaware River.

There's not much left of the original **Downsville Covered Bridge** save a few inside beams. The second-longest single-span covered bridge in the world, it was closed for several years for repair. Spanning the East Branch, it was built by Murray in 1854 at a cost of $1,700 and was restored in 1998 for $1 million.

The **Hamden Covered Bridge**, also built by Murray, in 1859, cost $1,000 to construct. The bridge is set back from Route 10 and is easy to miss. Heading north after the village of Hamden, look for the street sign: Basin Clove Road.

Also accessible from Route 10 further north in East Delhi is **Fitch's Bridge**, built by James Frazier and James Warren on Kingston Street in Delhi. It was moved three miles up the West Branch sometime around 1885 to make way for a modern iron bridge. Richard Sanders Allen in *Covered Bridges of the*

Covered bridges were called "kissing bridges," as they provided lovers with a private spot for a smooch.

Northeast (Stephen Greene Press, 1974) notes that the old lattice timbers retain the letter and number markings, but that the bridge is in the opposite direction than it was in Delhi and the markings incorrectly placed.

Set back from Route 10, the Hamden Covered Bridge is easy to miss.

Bridging the Gap

New York State once had more than 250 covered bridges and Delaware County was endowed with at least 57. No one knows why covered bridges were so popular in the 1900s. Theories are that horses felt safer entering them – thinking they were barns – or that the roof protected the bridge floor. Whatever the reason, those remaining need to be protected. In 1942, 18 of the 46 remaining covered bridges in New York State were in Delaware County. Today, only three are left.

Animal Farms

The farther we get away from the land, the greater our insecurity.

— Henry Ford

EAST BROOK FARMS
East Brook Road
Walton
☎ 607-865-7238
www.eastbrookfarms.com

Ever think to try llama trekking? Then visit this huge alpaca and llama farm, which rents llamas for packing or play. The 75 acres have several trails where adults and children can go out for a half-day at $50 or $60 per llama. Gordon Cuculli started with 81 animals and at last count had 330. His alpaca business, he claims, has already grown into the largest operation east of Ohio. On a recent visit, his "maternity ward" had 140 pregnant females.

East Brook has two kinds of alpaca – Huacaya, the most common kind, and Suri, a rare breed. According to Cuculli, the Catskill terrain and climate are ideal for raising alpacas. The beasts are easy to maintain and are not slaughtered, so interest is growing from urban dwellers seeking a lifestyle change. "They're a good investment; you can utilize the fiber and you don't have to eat them," adds his farm manager, Jeff Tucker.

An alpaca can cost anywhere from $13,000 to $150,000 per animal.

Alpacas are about half the size of llamas and produce roughly twice the fiber. Alpacas are sheared once a year – yielding three to five pounds of fiber – and their fur is spun into wool for sweaters and scarves. A sweater uses about two pounds. That's why alpaca is often mixed with other fabrics. The few items on hand at East Brook (they hope to open a gift shop) include a $150 scarf that is 50% rayon and chenille.

The first Catskill Llama Festival was held at East Brook in 1998. There were 21 ranches represented and 1,000 visitors. The second was held the third weekend of June. Call for dates of the next festival.

Directional Info: From Route 17, take Exit 94 Roscoe. Take Route 206 west to Walton and turn right at Country Emporium. Go two blocks to East Street and turn right onto East Brook Drive; continue three miles. The farm is just after the bridge.

Alpaca Info

Like llamas, vicuna, and the guanaco, alpacas are members of the cameloid family and resemble small camels without the hump. Treasured by the ancient Incas, they've been domesticated for some 5,000 years. Alpacas were first imported to the US from the Andes region in South America in the early 1980s.

Because of their pleasing dispositions (as quiet and placid as cows), easy care, and soft coat (under the coarser outer fur), alpacas are considered a good investment for breeders. They can be black, grey, white, reddish and sometimes two-toned. Farm manager Tucker tells the story of a woman who purchased an alpaca and entered it in a competition. It won first prize, which raised its value right away. "The investment outright is high, but the price does tend to go up," he said.

STONE & THISTLE FARM
Kelso Road
East Meredith
☎ 607-278-5773

Animals here are raised on pasture without the use of chemicals and are gentle creatures. Dogs, cats, chickens and hogs join the fun of the day. The best time to visit is between April and November, but call ahead. Read more about Stone & Thistle Farm and its owners, Tom and Denise Warren, on the next page.

Directional Info: From Delhi, after crossing bridge, turn right onto Route 10 to Elk Creek Road (immediately after parking area). Turn left onto Elk Creek Road. Drive 9.8 miles where you'll see a road with a stop sign on your right. Make a sharp right onto it; bear left at fork. Stone & Thistle Farm is the second farm on the road.

The Warrens (and friends) greet visitors at Stone & Thistle Farm in East Meredith.

Trading the Rat Race for Rural Living

Some people are fortunate to realize their dreams while still young. It takes guts, belief in yourself and financial security. Tom and Denise Warren, owners of Stone & Thistle Farm, had the first two traits when they left Brooklyn four years ago to permanently settle in their weekend home in Delaware County.

Tom had a thriving design construction business (he built Bill Cosby's house on 71st Street). One day he announced that he wanted to quit the rat race to become a farmer. Denise, who worked for a Wall Street investment-consulting firm, needed only to get her boss' permission to telecommute. "Leaving was an emotional decision," she says. Thus far, she's the primary breadwinner in the house.

An engaging couple, the Warrens knew nothing about raising livestock. When Tom milked his first goat, he held a copy of *Raising Milk Goats the Modern Way* in his other hand. Now he's quite the expert and has even developed a niche. "What we sell is lamb and kid goat – not typical food," he explains. "We market to a large ethnic population. The demand for goat in urban areas of the northeast is enormous."

The couple have three young children, 175 breeding animals, fresh food daily, and no TV. This year they finally broke even. "I think it's a wonderful cure for midlife crisis," says Denise, who misses only take-out food and pizza delivery.

Family Fun

DELAWARE & ULSTER RAIL RIDE
Route 28
Arkville
☎ 800-225-4132; 914-586-DURR
Open weekends and holidays,
Memorial Day through October

A fun way for a family to experience history is a one-hour ride aboard this rail ride. The train departs from the restored Arkville depot on Route 28 and rides along one mile of the Catskill Scenic Trail. It's the same route that drew hundreds of thousands of vacationers a century ago. Special events, such as train robberies, are held June through October.

★ WHAT'S IN A NAME?

Arkville was named for Noah's Ark because it was the only local village to escape a flood.

Fishing

*Large streams from little fountains flow
Tall oaks from little acorns grow*
– David Everett (1769-1813)

In his book, *Good Fishing in the Catskills* (Backcountry Publications, 1997), Jim Capossela terms the 20-mile-long Pepacton "the best brown trout reservoir in the city chain" and "one of the best in the entire northeast." He writes that it's stocked annually with about 8,000 browns, accounting for some 30% of all fish taken by anglers.

Reservoir fishing requires a permit, which can be obtained by calling ☎ 914-657-2213.

Delaware County

Another resident called the Pepacton a well-guarded secret. I guess the secret is out now!

Attention Trout Fishermen

The **Catskill Center for Conservation and Development** sponsors various activities during the year related to trout fishing. To add your name to its mailing list, ☎ 914-586-2611.

Swimming

The **town pool** on Wagner Avenue in **Fleischmanns** may look private, but it's open to the public, heated and beautifully maintained. Open July 4 through Labor Day. Admission is $2.50 adults, $1.50 children. Hours are 11am-6pm, Monday through Friday, and 10am-6pm on weekends. ☎ 914-254-5514.

Historical Notes

Fleischmanns was named for Julius Fleischmann, the yeast magnate, in 1913, after he donated a village park. It was originally called Griffin's Corners after businessman and lawyer Matthew Griffin. In the late 1800s, the Fleischmann Family, led by Charles, began extending its holdings in the area. Fleischmanns Park was a gift to the village from son Julius, who stipulated it was to always remain a park and athletic grounds.

Delaware County

The **East Sidney Lake Recreation Center** is a
popular place for swimming, boating and camping.
The East Sidney dam was built in 1948 to control
floods. An old timer there said that once a year
there's a tour of the dam but no one knows when it
will be. The entrance fee for a day is $5. Take Route
357 west until you see sign.

Another option is **Bear Spring Mountain Wildlife
Management Area**, between Walton and Downsville on Route 206. Since the area is almost entirely
forested, it's ideal for campers, horseback riders,
fishermen, hunters and bird watchers. Swimming is
permitted, but only at Launt Pond Beach, one of the
three largest of 26 ponds. ☎ 607-652-7364 (wildlife)
or ☎ 518-357-2234 (operations).

Hiking

*The woods are lovely, dark and deep. But
I have promises to keep. And miles to go
before I sleep.*
– Robert Frost (1874-1963)

South toward Hamden on Route 10 is the **West
Branch Preserve**. My husband and I followed the
Orange Trail, which was well marked until we de-
scended to the stream. It was near the end of a rigor-
ous 1½-hour hike and Ron correctly surmised that
we cross the stream and walk straight to the path. A
few hundred yards from the entrance is a giant oak
tree – a mastodon among modern-day mortals. It
would take several adults to encircle its belly.

In 1962, a committee was formed in Penn Yan, NY to
promote and coordinate the building and maintenance of the Finger Lakes Trailway, as it was known
then. It's a credit to the vast number of volunteers

who have worked to bring about this continuous footpath from the Allegheny Mountains through Delaware County that a legally blind 70-year-old man was able to negotiate the 550-mile trail in 25 days. He joined the roster of 70 other end-to-enders who have walked from the New York-Pennsylvania border to Denning Lean-To near Margaretville.

A booklet published by the Finger Lakes Trail System lists 63 sponsors, most of them non-paid volunteers. Some are individuals and others are clubs or Boy Scout troops. Each of the volunteers is responsible for maintaining one or more sections of the trail. Among other things, they clear dead trees from the path and cut the grass.

Some also serve as car spotters, or trail angels. Their job is to pick up long-distance hikers at the end of the trail, where they park their cars, and drive them to the start. Ed Sidote of Norwich, an 81-year-old who completed the trail in 1990, is the coordinator for end-to-end hikers. Call him at ☎ 607-334-3872 if you plan to hike a considerable portion of the trail.

A dozen trail sections are still in need of regular maintenance. If you wish to adopt a trail, contact Tom Reimers at ☎ 607-272-8679.

For membership information in the Finger Lakes Trail Conference, write FLTC Service Center, PO Box 18048, Rochester, NY 14618-0048, or obtain forms at www.fingerlakes.net/trailsystem. E-mail: fltc@axsnet.com. Annual membership is $15.

An easy hike is the 1.3-mile **Campbell Lean-To Trail** off Route 206, about four miles east of Downsville. The wide path winds through a forest of tall oaks and maples before reaching a spruce grove near the first of several stone foundations. According to Fred Salvante of Downsville, a FLTC volunteer who tends 23 miles of state land from Campbell

Brook Road to Alder Lake, these are probably remnants of old farms. The path runs along old wagon roads where several farm communities were located.

A hike can surprise you with beautiful vistas such as this overlook of the Delaware River.

If you prefer walking on a flat, hard-packed surface, the **Catskill Scenic Trail** takes you through beautiful countryside. The former railbed of the Ulster and Delaware Railroad is now a walking/biking, horseback and cross-country skiing trail extending 19 miles from Bloomville to Grand Gorge. I picked up the trail in Stamford at Railroad and South Street near the old Stamford Station. One way is the path to Grand Gorge, but I headed toward Hobart, passing meadows, streams and distant mountains. It was just me and the birds one summer morning. ☎ 607-652-2821; www.railtrails.org.

Skiing

There are two ski locations in Delaware County. **Bobcat Ski Center**, on the county's highest peak, has 19 trails, and is open Friday through Sunday and holidays. It's located three miles off Route 28 in Andes. ☎ 914-676-3143.

On weekends from April through November, **Ski Plattekill** has more than 60 miles of terrain. The site also has chairlift skyrides. They recently added two new runs, expanded snow-making coverage and a new chairlift. It's also a premier mountain biking destination. Buses leave every weekend from NYC and New Jersey. $49 includes round-trip fare and lift ticket. Route 30, Roxbury. ☎ 607-326-3500; www.plattekill.com.

Golf

Delhi College Golf Course, Arbor Hill Road, Delhi. Full service 18-hole public course, pro shop, new clubhouse. Soft spikes and tee times required. ☎ 607-746-GOLF (4653).

Hanah Golf & Country Club, Route 30, Margaretville. 18-holes. Clubhouse, club rentals, restaurant, pro shop. Carts and soft spikes are mandatory. Unlimited golf packages include cart, meals, two nights' accommodations and 20-25% off lessons at the golf school. Considered a tough course. ☎ 800-752-6494 for tee times; ☎ 914-586-4849 for information.

Ouleout Creek Golf Course, intersection of Routes 357 and 28 in North Franklin. Public nine-hole course has pro shop, club rentals, restaurant, ice cream parlor. Fairly flat terrain surrounded by farmland. Carts are not mandatory. Tournaments are sometimes held on weekends so call ahead. Open April through November. ☎ 607-829-2100.

Shephard Hills Golf Course, Roxbury. nine-hole, public course. Call Thursday for weekend tee times. Pro shop, clubhouse, restaurant. Mountain course is very hilly and carts are recommended. Spikeless. Open April through November. ☎ 607-326-7121.

Stamford Country Club, Taylor Road, Stamford. Premier 18-hole public golf course. Pro shop, restaurant. No tee times required except on holidays. Spikes allowed. Carts not mandatory. Easy to walk and easy to play. Open April through October. ☎ 607-652-7398.

Horseback Riding

Ken Seiferth (whose son runs Country Emporium, see page 401) gives riding lessons at his 500-acre **Sagamore Stables** in East Branch, where he trains and breeds Morgans and Dutch warmbloods. About half the 40 horses are his; the rest are boarded. He also raises cranes as a hobby and there are ducks and chickens roaming around. The public is welcome to drive in for a look. ☎ 607-865-4715.

Several horse shows are held in summer. Call the Tri-Valley Horsemen's Association, ☎ 607-746-6990, for an event schedule.

Directional Info: Take Route 30 to Houck Brook Road (next to Harvard Schoolhouse Theatre) and follow for 3.1 miles.

On the way back from Sagamore Stables I left Piney Point Road for Route 28A, which runs along the other side of the Pepacton Reservoir. This region is largely undeveloped and the ride seems to go on forever. I spotted several deer, but only glimpses of the reservoir.

TIP

If you're on Route 30, which runs along the Pepacton Reservoir, be aware that the only place to eat is on the south end, at a country store in the Sunoco station.

Museums, Art & Theater

Give me a museum and I'll fill it.
— Pablo Picasso (1881-1973)

MUSEUM OF MEMORIES
Main Street
Fleischmanns
☎ 914-254-5514
Open weekends, 11am-3pm,
Memorial Day through Labor Day
Free admission

Worth visiting in the once posh and wealthy destination of Fleischmanns is the Museum of Memories, which celebrated its 20th anniversary in 1998. Located behind the library, the old barn is a gold-mine of memorabilia: postcards, scrapbooks, documents, implements, and photographs. The museum is popular with architecture buffs and people tracking down relatives, says volunteer Susan Ferraro, boasting that "This is one of the best-documented towns in the Catskills."

CATSKILL CENTER & ERPF CULTURAL INSTITUTE
Route 28
Arkville
☎ 914-586-2611
www.catskillcenter.org
Open weekdays, 9am-5pm; Saturdays, 11am-6pm
Free admission

The center is an advocate for the environmental and economic health of the entire Catskill Mountains, and is a good place to pick up information on Delaware County.

The center houses the **Erpf House Gallery** featuring the work of regional artists. Exhibits rotate every six weeks. The institute also holds workshops, lectures and field trips on cultural heritage all year, most of them free. I attended one in March on the geology of Platte Clove with Catskill geologist Robert Titus – it was fascinating. Thanks to him, I am able to share some of the stories behind this unusual formation. His lecture coincided with the closing of Platte Clove landscape paintings. Other interesting workshops were Catskill cooking, winter animal tracking, and a sledding party and ice-fishing derby.

DELAWARE COUNTY HISTORICAL MUSEUM
Route 10
Delhi
☎ 607-746-3849

This museum spans 60 acres with seven historic buildings. The main building has three galleries, including a large exhibit hall. A show on family farms runs through 2001. Director Liz Callahan says new photographs will be added from time to time because "with so many aspects of family farming, we couldn't do it all in one exhibit."

Most of the historic buildings were moved to the site from other places in Delaware County. The majority are pretty much intact, such as a tollhouse from the Stamford area that now houses the gift shop, and a blacksmith shop that served three generations of the Woodin family in Andes. Some contain artifacts that are representative of the era. The Amos Wood Gun Shop, for instance, belonged to a postmaster and gunsmith from the late 19th century and the gun collection is similar to those found on many farms.

Gideon Frisbee, a judge, tavern keeper, farmer and entrepreneur, originally settled this property. It was donated to the historical society in 1960 by the Frisbee family. His Federal-style house, built in 1797, is the most complete and architecturally perfect. It underwent few changes and retains the original furnishings. However, each room reflects a different time period, beginning in the early 1800s when it served as a tavern. "We are in the process of reinterpreting the house," says Callahan. "Visitors will see this house in transformation."

The Delaware County Historical Museum requests a $5 donation from non-residents.

The exhibits and library are open year-round. The museum is open Tuesday through Sunday from 11am-4:30pm; $3 admission fee. The library is open Monday and Tuesday from 10am-3pm, or by appointment. The historic buildings are open Memorial Day through Columbus Day.

TREADWELL MUSEUM OF FINE ART
54 Main Street
Treadwell
☎ 607-829-5812
Open daily, 10am-6pm, June through September

Housed in a former dance hall built in 1867, this must-see museum has floorboards that seem a bit shaky, but I'm assured I won't sink. Perhaps it sags from owner Joe Kurhajec's many sculptures, ceramics, wooden toys, and African masks. Opened in 1971, the museum houses a collection of 4,000 works of art representing over 100 artists. It's also a shop with almost everything for sale. Joe, a sculptor/painter, gives individual instruction, runs workshops, and hosts programs at the museum. His annual **Treadwell Stagecoach Run Art Festival** at the beginning of July invites participants to tour open studios and galleries of a dozen artists in the area.

Historical Notes

The Delaware County Historical Association has a vast list of local books that can be ordered by mail. The histories, cookbooks, folk arts, genealogies, and literary works are listed in a catalogue with brief descriptions and prices. One of them is a recipe book, *Memories from the Kitchen*, with contributions from Delaware County cooks and diary entries from turn-of-the-century residents. A notation from 1897: "Liz and father went to Hamden. They sold some chickens to George Green at 8¢ a pound."

HANFORD MILLS MUSEUM
County Routes 10 and 12
East Meredith
☎ 607-278-5744; 800-295-4992
Open daily, 10am-5pm, May through October
$5 admission

Hanford Mills Museum has special events and workshops nearly every weekend.

A couple visiting the museum from Missouri remarked that it's the best mill they've seen (her family had five mills in Delaware and North Carolina).

Can you believe they were talking about a 150-year-old mill that still harnesses the waters of Kortright Creek to power its sawmill and gristmill? A 10x12-foot waterwheel has kept churning all these years, driving 19th-century machinery through a belt-and-pulley power transmission system. It reminds us of the time industry was dependent on waterpower – at one time the mill powered electric lights in the village.

As one of the last 19th-century mills to survive intact, Hanford Mills earned a place on both the State and National Registers of Historic Places.

For most of its life, the mill has been owned and operated by the family of David Josiah Hanford. He purchased it in 1860 and the mill grew into a rural industrial complex with a saw, grist and feed mill, woodworking shop and hardware store. In 1967, the mill closed and re-opened as a museum. The complex of buildings is clustered around a scenic mill pond.

During a tour of Hanford's late Victorian house on the museum's property, the guide pointed out that the kitchen was built as a creamery and that people would bring their cream to be churned into butter. If you opt for the guided tour, which is given every hour, visit during the week when it's quiet.

Directional Info: Take Route 28 from Delhi to Meridale and make a sharp right at the post office. Follow the sign and turn right onto County Route 10.

OPEN EYE THEATER
Margaretville
☎ 914-586-1660 (for schedule and location)
www.tchouse.com (click Art Centers)

Presents plays and classics for all ages. The theater was founded in New York City, and in 1991 moved up to Delaware County. Professional actors and local artists and playwrights combine to develop new work and hold performances and readings all year in 15 different locations, including NYC. In summer, the

Open Eye is in residence with the Roxbury Arts Group and many shows are performed at Roxbury Arts and Community Center on Vega Mountain Road. Tickets are $10 for adults; $5 for children and seniors.

LITTLE VICTORY PLAYERS
Harvard Schoolhouse
Route 30
Between East Branch and Downsville
☎ 607-363-2819

This new professional theater group offers mostly comedies and some mysteries. Their season starts in May.

WEST KORTRIGHT CENTRE
Turnpike Road
East Meredith
☎ 607-278-5454
www.westkc.org

Denise Warren of Stone & Thistle Farm calls the West Kortright Centre the "lifeblood" of second home-owners from New York City. Now in its 25th year, the cultural and community center is housed in a restored 1850 church. It presents a world-class performing arts series of music and theater from around the globe, May to October. The acoustically fine auditorium, original woodwork and intimate, pastoral valley setting of the former church make it an ideal venue for theater, workshops, gallery exhibits, and community gatherings. Nature walks fill out the season. Artists have included composers John Cage, Virgil Thompson and Meredith Monk, poet Allen Ginsberg and singer Richie Havens.

SEMINART & MOVIES THAT MATTER
Bovina
☎ 607-832-4889; 607-832-4278

Dr. Ed McNulty, an ordained Presbyterian minister and film reviewer, has been running what he calls **"Seminart"** since 1998. He grew up watching and loving films and has organized film series in theaters in three cities. He writes for *Presbyterians Today*, *Delaware County Times*, and *Visual Parables*, a monthly exploration of film from a theological perspective.

The discussions deal mainly with spiritual themes and, to a lesser extent, how the films can be used in church or synagogue. Recent offerings included *Diary of a Country Priest, Jesus of Montreal,* and Woody Allen's *Crimes & Misdemeanors.*

Dr. McNulty has written several books on media and film.

Dr. McNulty also runs a monthly film series year-round, usually on Friday nights, called **"Movies That Matter,"** sponsored by the Bovina church and library. "Thanks to grant money, we watch significant films and discuss them," Dr. McNulty explains. "The audience ranges from age 15 to 50, consisting of a few church members and a wonderful mixture of Christians, Jews, an atheist or two, and others."

Participants receive an information sheet listing nearby B&Bs and motels. The fee is $100-$125, depending when you pay. You can also enroll in a portion of the seminar and pay a reduced rate. (Most of the proceeds benefit the Bovina Presbyterian Church.) For more information, phone or e-mail Dr. McNulty at mcnulty@catskill.net.

HONEST BROOK FESTIVAL
Honest Brook Road
Meridale
☎ 607-746-3770

This festival celebrates its 10th season of chamber music concerts under the direction of Michael Cannon, a Juilliard-trained pianist and teacher. The series is held in July and August in a converted barn with wonderful acoustics in an area where collapsing barns are all too common. Tickets $12; $10 seniors/students.

Shopping

Fleischmanns

The first Delaware County village on Route 28 is Fleischmanns, one of the first all-Jewish resorts. Walk to the old train depot and try to imagine passengers from New York City disembarking in their finest duds and heading down to the village to see and be seen.

ROBERT'S AUCTION
Main Street
Fleischmanns
☎ 914-254-4490

On Saturday nights this traditional country auction draws dealers and visitors from miles around to bid on antiques and collectibles.

Margaretville

Margaretville is a village on the move, where stores are open daily, year-round.

THE COMMONS
Main Street
Margaretville

Anchored by **The Café**, The Commons has been renovated and now houses several gift shops, including **Bookmark** (☎ 914-586-2700), a cheerful book store. Upstairs is the office of **Catskill On Line**, which provides local Internet access for residents, ☎ 800-444-9338.

EXPRESSIONS
Bridge Street
Margaretville
☎ 914-586-3344

If you haven't found the right gift yet, the A&P shopping plaza has Expressions, with its perfumed scents and plentiful assortment of Pooh items, Puffkins, candles, figurines, cards, chimes and stuffed animals.

★ FAMOUS FACES

Kelsey Grammer, of *Frasier* fame, has a home in Margaretville. And Amelita Galli-Curci, a well-known opera singer, had a mansion nearby.

MARGARETVILLE ANTIQUE CENTER
Main Street
Margaretville
☎ 914-586-2424
Open daily, 10am-5pm, year-round

Next door to The Commons is this 5,000-square-foot antique center in the former Galli-Curci movie theater. The 37 booths contain items ranging from primitive to Victorian and beyond. Prices range from 50¢ to $25,000.

Walton

Feel like browsing some more? Then head to downtown Walton – a lively village.

COUNTRY EMPORIUM
134 Delaware Street
Walton
☎ 607-865-8440
www.countryemporiumltd.com
Open daily at 10am, year-round

This is a 17,000-square-foot one-stop marketplace, with the biggest sellers being furniture, collectibles and gourmet food. The store also carries scarves made from baby alpacas and adorable toy alpacas made from the fur. One room is for fishermen (with fishing-related gifts); upstairs are five rooms devoted to Christmas. When you climb the first three steps from the main floor into the artifacts room, before marveling at the record- holding moose head, notice the barn-like walls. This portion of the store has been dated to the early 1700s.

*If your camera needs a battery, Walton has a **Radio Shack**.*

The four-story building opened as a center of trade in 1892 and it has since housed a pharmacy, bakery and other businesses. Two years ago, the Seiferth family opened the building as the Country Emporium. Young Eric Seiferth is a gung-ho proprietor with lots of ideas to keep the business upscale and up-to-date. With each season, he changes the theme – soup in winter, jams and jellies in the fall, and cheese at Christmas. As a former restaurant owner and chef (at the Ole Cotter Restaurant in Hancock), he has an understandable passion for food and a restaurateur's graciousness.

Directional Info: From Route 17, take Exit 94 (Roscoe). Turn left on Route 206/7 to Walton. At the stop sign, turn right and you'll see the red brick Georgian building ahead.

Historical Note

Lumbering and stone-cutting were the first major industries in the county. The trees stood so tall and straight, in fact, that they were in demand for shipbuilding. The main mast of the famous Constitution (*Old Ironsides*) came from a hilltop near Walton.

Delhi

PARKER HOUSE GIFTS & ACCESSORIES
74 Main Street
Delhi
☎ 607-746-3141; 888-263-5573
Open Monday-Saturday, year-round

Parker House is not a store as we know it. It's a Federal-style 1820 mansion with eight rooms of merchandise, selling everything from handbags to reproduction Tiffany lamps. Although renovated, the house retains its six fireplaces and original plaster and windows. Owner David Smith likens Parker House to shops in historic Williamsburg.

Parker House offers free gift wrapping. Pick up something special in their year-round Christmas room.

Looking for jewelry? You'll find it here in sterling silver, along with semi-precious necklaces and an expert appraiser, watchmaker and repairman. Kitchen items? You name it – there's Oneida stainless flatware, biscuit baskets, oven-proof porcelain, bone china. China is always 30% off regular price.

According to Smith, Parker House owns the designs to its Delhi plates and is the only shop to carry them. The biggest sellers are those of Fitch's Bridge and the Delhi Courthouse. It may be gone by now, but the store had a beautiful Delhi throw that was as soft as a kitten. It was selling for $48, while the original holey blanket it was patterned after sold for $2,700 in an auction.

MEREDITH MOUNTAIN FARMS
Honest Brook Road
Delhi
☎ 607-746-3857; 800-828-3422
www.catskill.net/cheez

For 15 years, Arnie Weiss has been perfecting his cheeses and mustards. He uses ale in some of them and blends some cheeses "so you can actually taste it and not go crazy from the heat." Still, some of them sure can put fire in your belly. Take his "Mother of Kong," the mother of all horseradish cheddars, or "Furnace Gulch" with whole jalapeño peppers that could "burn your kishkas out." The mustards also range from very mild to devastatingly hot, making use of flavoring from fruit, ale, honey and molasses.

What's the biggest seller at Meredith Mtn. Farms? "Whatever we're sampling," says Arnie with a big smile.

Julee Rosso and Sheila Lukins, authors of *The New Basics Cookbook*, write that Meredith Mountain Farms' smoked cheddar is "permeated with the flavor of Apple Wood: we found it quite extraordinary."

Weiss, who has an engineering degree, was living in Bergen County, NJ. He liked smoked cheese and developed a process of his own. Friends who tasted his cheeses wanted more. He said to his wife one day, "Maybe there's a business here." They moved to a 33-acre parcel on the eastern slopes of Honest Brook Valley just outside of Delhi and converted the two-car garage into a factory. Weiss turned an airline oven into a smoker and designed a computer to operate it. He's continually inventing new products and designing his own labels. "I get a kick out of naming new things," he says. "No one can ever catch me. I'm moving all the time."

He ships all over the US and Canada, and has several gift packages. "Last year we shipped to 40 states," he says proudly. "The food business is very exciting. There are absolutely no boundaries." If you can't personally visit, you can order by phone or over the Internet. The farm also participates in the farmers' market in Delhi on Wednesdays from 9:30am-1:30pm.

Directional Info: From Delhi, take Route 28N for 2.7 miles and turn right at the sign. Follow Honest Brook Road for two miles.

Downsville

COVERED BRIDGE GIFTS & ANTIQUES
Intersection of Routes 206 and 30
Downsville
☎ 607-363-7712
Open at 8am, year-round; Sunday in season

A glance at the Covered Bridge's guestbook reveals it as a popular place for tourists from West Virginia to Singapore. Located near the covered bridge, this newly constructed barn sells novel items such as wooden houses and villages with miniatures to fill them, and Amish wrought iron, along with Gund toys, candles, handmade dolls, shrubs and trees.

Stamford

BOOKS OPEN
7 Harper Street
Stamford
☎ 607-652-7158
Open year-round; closed Wednesday

At this book shop, also known as Sometimes A Great Notion, personable Pat Parks buys and sells used hard- and softcover books. If she accepts your trade paperback, you'll get a 25¢ credit toward your purchase of another book. The 12,000 shelved books include used cookbooks, garden books, literary biographies, fiction, military history, religion, science and math. Some of the hardcovers have never been read.

◎ *TIP*

If you're looking for a book on line, try searching www.bibliofind.com; www.abebooks.com; and www.book-finder.com.

O'CONNOR PHARMACY
81 Main Street
Stamford
☎ 607-652-3636

Need a last minute greeting card or gift? This pharmacy has a separate gift shop. Both are open daily year-round at 8:30am, except Sunday.

South Kortright

BIBLIOBARN
627 Roses Brook Road
South Kortright
☎ 607-538-1555
Open daily, year-round

Have you been looking for an out-of-date or rare book for years? If you can't find it at Bibliobarn, Linda will direct you – at no charge – to the dealer most likely to carry it. Asked about a store catalogue, she quipped, "We're the catalogue." Mind you, according to Linda, there are 198 book dealers in New York State, 142 of them dealing in rare books.

Linda and husband H.L Wilson had a bookstore in their native Norfolk, Virginia for 12 years. Three years ago, they packed 38,000 pounds of books and made their way to this heated 19th-century barn, where they now live and work. It's a wonderful place to spend a few hours perusing the new and used books, including those on regional history. Linda is also a wonderful source of information on local attractions. "People come here who might not be book people," she says. "They want to see what's going on."

The oldest tome in stock at this writing is an illustrated guide to Rome, printed in 1643 in Italian.

An African man reluctantly visited the store looking for a book on Sanskrit grammar. When she handed him one, he almost fainted. Now he comes up (from New York City) all the time and goes away with box loads.

Another customer, thrilled that he'd found a book he'd been searching for all his life, remarked, "and you're only charging $2 for it!"

The genres carried range from literature and detective fiction to gardening and books by local authors. The store also does appraisals, grows and sells organic vegetables, and is a bindery. "My husband restores books in the old medieval way and teaches it here," Linda explains, adding that he'd like to teach hand bookbinding to private students. The Wilsons plan to expand operations by restoring the 19th-century Grace Episcopal Church in Stamford and filling it with books on religion and philosophy. The couple is also encouraging New York City dealers to relocate to the area in order to create a "book village." Asked what the chances are of these dealers moving to the Catskills, Linda responds with flinch-

ing, "Hey, I'm a Southern woman – with Irish genes."
To illustrate her persistence, she describes the effort
it took to get one Manhattan book dealer to visit. Af-
terward, he told her, "You're right. This is gorgeous
(country). I can breathe."

*Directional Info: From Stamford or Delhi, take Route
10 to the South Kortright stone bridge. Turn right
and follow for about one mile. Turn left onto Roses
Brook Road and continue to sign.*

Festivals & Events

For more information, Margaretville has a calendar
of events on its Web site at www.margaretville.org,
or call the Greater Margaretville Chamber of Commerce at ☎ 800-586-3303. The Delhi Chamber of
Commerce Web site is at www.delhiny.com.

July

Bluestone Festival & Summer Celebration. Hancock. Craft fair, 5K run, parade, duck races, live concerts, stone-cutting competition. ☎ 800-668-7624;
www.hancock.net/~chamber.

Peaceful Valley Bluegrass Festival. Downsville.
For four days in mid-July bands perform 10 am to
midnight on the campground in Shinhopple along
the Delaware River. Fans can fish, hike, swim in a
pool, or shower while enjoying the music. $15-$25.
Four days with camping is $60 per adult; half-price
for children 12-16. ☎ 607-363-2211; 888-413-0137;
www.peaceful-valley.com.

*Over 6,000 peo-
ple attended the
Bluegrass Fes-
tival in 1999.*

August

Lumberjack Festival. Hanford Mills Museum, East Meredith. ☎ 607-278-5744; 800-295-4992.

Delaware County Fair (see story below). Walton fairgrounds. Annual six-day fair. Admission $5; children under age 12 free. Wednesday is children's day with reduced prices on rides; Thursday is senior citizens' day with admission at $3. Ample parking for cars and campers; a tram runs from the parking lot to the grounds. ☎ 607-865-3105/6414.

Delaware County Fair

Every August, Delaware County stages an old-fashioned fair and has been doing so every summer for 112 years. There's something for every age and interest here. You can watch pink and brown sows kicking up sawdust during the swine competition (handlers use canes and sticks to keep the pigs in line). Local farmers and others love the tractor and truck pull contests and the horsey set swoons as the riders jump the hurdles. You can see a sheep Olympics, goat show, demolition derby, Western square dance demonstration or attend a concert featuring a well-known country artist. Besides the animals, there are pony rides for the kids, clowns making balloon hats and, of course, plenty to eat.

With so many dairy farms in the area, including Breakstone, it's no surprise to find cows competing, their owners in black and white to match the Holsteins. (Holstein and Jerseys constitute most of the county's milk production.)

The fair offers farmers a chance to network and keep abreast of agricultural advances. It's not a commercial event, except for some vendors selling items like cow-embossed T-shirts and 4-H members pitching raffle tickets. The 4-H Club's prize-winning projects are on display – handmade wooden benches, baked goods, dolls, and vegetables so perfect they look like wax.

Even competition is relaxed. Jeri Brayman of Mormon Hollow Farm in Masonville takes home blue ribbons every year for her breeding cows and sows. But with only one other competitor, who sometimes buys piglets from the Braymans, her hogs can't lose. "That's fine, I don't mind," she says. "It's all for fun as far as I'm concerned."

Promoters of the fair hope to encourage young residents to value their area's traditions and consider a career in agriculture. With more and more area farms being sold and converted into vacation homes, the display of new farm technologies and comradery with other farm youngsters help foster that commitment.

When the Delaware Valley Agricultural Society staged the first fair in Walton in 1887, it featured cattle, horse, sheep, swine and poultry judging. Not much has changed, except that the horses have their own shows, and an enormously popular Demolition Derby was added two decades ago. One new event is the All-American Rodeo, a sell-out at the New York State Fair. Residents eagerly await this end-of-summer event, claiming it gets better every year.

September

Antique Engine Jamboree & Fall Harvest Festival, Hanford Mills Museum, East Meredith. ☎ 607-278-5744; 800-295-4992.

October

Octoberfest, Deposit. Columbus Day weekend.
☎ 800-467-3190.

Octoberfest, Ski Plattekill. Live music, German
bratwurst and brew, chairlift rides. ☎ 607-326-3500.

Delaware County A to Z

Animal Hospitals

Grand Gorge Animal Hospital, Stamford Road,
Grand Gorge, ☎ 607-588-7011.

Banks

National Bank of Delaware County has branches
in Walton (☎ 607-865-4126), Andes (☎ 914-676-3115),
Franklin (☎ 607-829-5200), and Hamden (☎ 607-
865-4170; 607-746-6700). **Delaware National Bank
of Delhi** (www.delhibank.com) has two locations in
Delhi: 124 Main Street and Ames Plaza (☎ 607-746-
2356), and on Route 28 in Margaretville (☎ 914-586-
1200.

National Bank of Stamford (www.nbstamford
.com) has branches in Stamford (☎ 607-652-7545),
Roxbury (☎ 607-326-4100), and Sidney (☎ 607-563-
7770). **Wilbur National Bank** (www.wilbur-
bank.com) is in Fleischmanns (☎ 914-254-5252),
Delhi (☎ 607-746-2162), and Downsville (☎ 607-363-
7211).

NBT Bank (www.nbtbank.com) has branches in Deposit (☎ 607-467-2195), Grand Gorge (☎ 607-588-7513), Hancock (☎ 607-637-2611), Hobart (☎ 607-538-9141), Margaretville (☎ 607-586-2623), and Sidney (☎ 607-561-2800); all have ATM machines except Hobart. **Marine Midland Bank**, 124 Delaware, Walton, ☎ 607-865-6555.

Hospitals

Delaware Valley Hospital, 1 Titus Place, Walton, ☎ 607-865-2100. **Margaretville Memorial Hospital**, Route 28, Margaretville, ☎ 914-586-2631 (ambulance and emergency, ☎ 914-586-2929).
O'Connor Hospital, Route 28, Delhi, ☎ 607-746-0300. **The Sidney Hospital**, Pearl Street, Sidney, ☎ 607-563-3512.

Liquor Stores

Acme Liquor Store, 36 Main Street, Stamford, ☎ 607-652-4080. **County Wine & Liquor**, 13 Harper Street, Stamford, ☎ 607-652-WINE. **Ray's Fine Wines & Spirits**, 70 Main Street, Delhi, ☎ 607-746-3775; www.empirewines.com. **Delhi Liquor Store**, 55 Main Street, Delhi, ☎ 607-746-2321.

E&D Spirit Shop, Route 28, Margaretville, ☎ 914-586-2835. **Margaretville Liquor Store**, Main St., Margaretville, ☎ 914-586-4314. **Uhorchak Bros. Wines & Liquors**, 9 Cartwright Avenue, Sidney, ☎ 607-563-2704. **Corky's Wines & Spirits**, 58 Main Street, Sidney, ☎ 607-563-3233.

Walton Liquor Store, 18 Gardiner Place, Walton, ☎ 607-865-6456. **Breakley's Liquor Store**, 11

Bridge Street, Walton, ☎ 607-865-5997. **Hancock Liquor Store,** 9 W. Main Street, Hancock, ☎ 607-637-5364.

Movies

Walton Theater (on National Register of Historic Places), Gardiner Place in Walton, ☎ 607-865-6688. Single-screen, first-run films shown April through September; $5. **Fleischmanns Theatre**, Main St., ☎ 914-254-4666. **Sidney Cinema**, 61 Main Street, Sidney, ☎ 607-563-1956. **State Theatre,** 148 Front Street, Deposit, ☎ 607-467-2727. **Capital Theatre**, 50 E. Front Street, Hancock, ☎ 607-637-3400.

Newspapers

It's really not surprising that in a rural community, especially, newspapers have thrived. Since 1819, Delaware County has published a total of 38. Even now, in the age of on-line communication, several communities still support a weekly newspaper. *The Daily Star* (www.thedailystar.com) published in Oneonta, covers news of Delaware and Otsego counties. *The Walton Reporter*, a weekly sold by subscription, has been serving Delaware County and surrounding areas since 1881.

Pharmacies

Eckerd Drug Store, Main St. and Steiner Rd., Sidney, ☎ 607-563-2166 (pharmacy); 607-563-7212 (store). **O'Connor Pharmacy**, 81 Main St., Stamford, ☎ 607-652-3636. **Stamford Pharmacy**, 119 Main Street, ☎ 607-652-7233.

If you're not as close to God as you used to be, guess who moved.
– Sign on a church

BAPTIST – **First Baptist**, Corner of Division and Second Streets, Delhi, ☎ 607-746-3115. **First Baptist**, 139 Second Street, Deposit, ☎ 607-467-3381. **Hancock Baptist Church**, ☎ 607-637-2601. **Clovesville Bible Baptist**, Old Route 28, ☎ 914-254-5305. **First Baptist Church**, Townsend and Platt streets, Walton, ☎ 607-865-5724.

CATHOLIC – **Sacred Heart Church**, Main St., Stamford, ☎ 607-652-7170. **St. Paul's Roman Catholic Church**, 60 West Main Street, Hancock, ☎ 607-637-2571. **Sacred Heart Rectory**, Academy St., Margaretville, ☎ 914-586-2665. **Sacred Heart Rectory**, 15 Liberty Street, Sidney, ☎ 607-563-1591.

CONGREGATIONAL – **First Congregational**, UCC, Bridge and Main Streets, Sidney, ☎ 607-563-1329. **First Congregational**, UCC, Corner of North and Mead Streets, Walton, ☎ 607-865-4066.

EPISCOPAL – **St. James Church**, Lake Delaware (Route 28 between Andes and Delhi), ☎ 607-832-4401; 607-832-4205. **St. John's Episcopal**, Main Street, Delhi, ☎ 607-746-2826. **Christ Episcopal**, 14 Monument Street, Deposit, ☎ 607-467-3031. **St. Paul's Episcopal**, Main Street, Franklin, ☎ 607-829-6404. **St. Paul's Episcopal**, River St., Bloomville, ☎ 607-865-4698. **St. Margaret's Episcopal**, Margaretville, ☎ 607-363-2565. **Christ Episcopal**

Church, 41 Gardiner Place, Walton, ☎ 607-865-4698.

JEWISH – Congregation B'nai Israel, Wagner Avenue, Fleischmanns.

LUTHERAN – Immanuel Lutheran Church, Andes Road, Route 28, Delhi, ☎ 607-746-2098. **Trinity Lutheran**, Route 10, Stamford, ☎ 607-652-7823.

METHODIST – Stamford United Methodist Church, Stamford, ☎ 607-652-7350. **Andes United Methodist**, Lower Main Street, Andes, ☎ 914-676-3455. **East Branch/Harvard United Methodist Church**, East Branch, ☎ 607-637-2571. **Bloomville United Methodist**, Main Street, Route 10, Bloomville, ☎ 607-538-9940. **Margaretville United Methodist Church**, Church Street, Margaretville, ☎ 914-586-4410. **Roxbury United Methodist**, Main St., Roxbury, ☎ 607-326-9366.

PENTECOSTAL – Non-Denominational Pentecostal Church, 28 E. Front Street, Hancock, ☎ 607-637-4672.

PRESBYTERIAN – First Presbyterian Church, 96 Main Street, Stamford, ☎ 607-652-7242. **Bovina United Presbyterian**, Maple Street, Bovina Center, ☎ 607-832-4889/4278. **First Presbyterian,** 4 Clinton Street, Delhi, ☎ 607-746-2155. **First Presbyterian**, Second Street, Deposit, ☎ 607-467-2559. Both the **Presbyterian Church**, Route 10, Hamden and **United Presbyterian**, Route 2, Delancey, can be reached at ☎ 607-746-3612; 607-746-6756.

REFORMED – Jay Gould Memorial Reformed Church, Main Street, Roxbury, ☎ 607-326-7101.

Campgrounds

Overview

In the Catskills, privately run campgrounds with hot showers and flush toilets far outnumber public sites. Within the 14,800-acre **Willowemoc Wild Forest**, located in the southwest corner of Catskill Park, primitive camping is allowed at sites marked with round yellow DEC markers or throughout wild forest lands at least 150 feet from any trail, road, spring, steam, pond, lake or other water source. A camping permit is required for groups of 10 or more, or for camping at the same site for more than three consecutive nights. ☎ 914-256-3000.

Woodall's, publisher of RV/camping guides, directories and magazines for over 63 years, inspects campsites annually and rates them according to facilities and recreation. Cleanliness is its most important criterion. A five-diamond rating does not necessarily mean a better park, only one that is more fully-equipped. However, those campsites listed in **Woodall's 1999 Guide** had to achieve at least a minimum rating.

A reservation service for US campgrounds can be found at www.park-net.com.

Aside from Woodall's, a more complete list can be found in **New York Campgrounds**, a free publication of Campground Owners of New York (CONY). I found my 124-page copy at Catskill Corners. Copies can also be obtained by sending $2 to cover postage and handling to CONY, PO Box 497, Dansville, NY 14437-0497. Plus, check out the CONY Web site at www.campgrounds.com/cony, which is a font of information.

Sullivan County

Sullivan County has thousands of acres of campgrounds, fertile streams, lakes to fish and mountain trails to hike. In the annual travel brochure that Sullivan County publishes, the section on campgrounds covers two full pages.

State-Run Campgrounds

*For RV sales, service or parts, try **Campers Barn** (☎ 800-724-3711). In Kingston, it's open daily and is off the Thruway's Exit 19.*

Mongaup Pond Campground in Rockland is a public campsite in the preserve, covering 275 acres with 163 sites. No hookups. A day-use fee is charged for entering the campground, which is open mid-May to December. Permits are issued on a first-come, first-serve basis or by reservation, for a maximum of two weeks. Runs a recreation program for children in July and August. ☎ 800-456-CAMP; 914-439-4233; www.park-net.com.

If you've never camped before, you might want to call the Beginner Camper Program offered from mid-June to mid-August at Mongaup. The program provides a tent, sleeping bags, mattress pads, cooking equipment and a staff member to show you the ropes. The fee is $14 per day. ☎ 914-256-3099.

Little Pond Campground, Livingston Manor, with 75 sites, offers fishing, boating, swimming and hiking. ☎ 914-439-5480.

Private Campgrounds

Kittatinny Campgrounds on the Delaware River has a fully-stocked trout steam running through its 250 wooded acres. There are 350 sites ($24.50 for two people), 90 of them with water/electric hookups. Offers rec hall, pool, boating, canoeing, fishing, playground, hiking trails, tenting, deli, snack bar, paintball. Reservations recommended. Open April 15 through October 15. Located two miles north of Barryville on Route 97. ☎ 914-557-8611; 914-557-8004; or 800-FLOAT-KC.

Covered Bridge Campsite, Livingston Manor. On the Willowemoc River; 75 sites, 50 with hookups. The rustic campground includes tenting, rec room, fishing, playground, sports field. Open May to December. ☎ 914-439-5093; www.campgrounds.com/coveredbridge.

Hunter Lake Campground, 177 Hunter Lake Dr., Parksville. Campers only; no day use. Seasonal sites available May 15 through October 15. Rustic and secluded. 93 sites, 45 with full hookups. Rec hall, lake swimming, boating, fishing, sports field, horseshoes. $22-25 for two adults with two children. Open Memorial Day through Labor Day. ☎ 914-292-3629.

Upper Delaware Campgrounds in Callicoon is a 60-acre resort that offers opportunities for canoeing, horseback riding, swimming, and touring, anywhere from one day to a whole summer season. Many of the 225 sites are located on the river's edge, and a large rustic area is set aside for tent campers. Electric and water hookups are available for RVs. The site gets lots of families, has a playground on site, and takes kids on hayrides on weekends. Open May through October. ☎ 914-887-5344; 914-887-5110.

Campgrounds

Deer Run Rustic Campground, Route 97, Narrowsburg. Large private sites for the rustic camper. Open April through October. ☎ 914-252-7419.

Woodstock on the Lake Campgrounds, Darling Road in Bethel, is on a one-mile-long 100-acre lake with 200 sites on its shore. Large pool, full hookups, tenting, hiking trails, fishing, sports facilities, modern bathrooms. Open May 15 through September 30 (weekends only after Labor Day). Fifteen minutes from Monticello. ☎ 914-583-6210; www.woodstock-on-the-lake.com.

Yogi Bear's Jellystone Park Camp-Resort at Birchwood Acres in Woodridge has 250 sites, all with hookups, that are either in the woods or in open fields. All-day activities are offered during the summer for adults and children. Pool, hot tub, playground, fishing, sports complex. Day rate: $33-38. Nine miles west of Ellenville on Martinfeld Road. ☎ 914-434-4743; www.nyjellystone.com.

Ulster County

Ulster County has 19 public campsites, many of them with full facilities. The Department of Environmental Conservation (DEC) operates the following two state-run campgrounds.

State-Run Campgrounds

Kenneth Wilson, Phoenicia. 76 sites, no hookups. Tenting, swimming, boating, canoeing, fishing, playground. Open mid-May through mid-October. For more park and camping information, consult the

Web site at www.park-net.com/usa/ny/kenn or ☎ 914-679-7020.

Woodland Valley, Phoenicia. 72 sites. Day rate is $10-$12. Fishing, hiking, coin-operated showers. Park is nestled in a scenic valley. Campground has mostly wooded sites with some campsites located along a small stream. Nearby hiking trails includes Slide Mountain, the tallest peak in the Catskills. Visit the campground's Web site at www.park-net.com/usa/ny/wood or ☎ 914-688-7647.

Woodland Valley campsites can be reached only from Rte. 28, near Phoenicia.

Private Campgrounds

Yogi Bear's Jellystone Park in Gardiner has a half-mile frontage on the Wallkill River and features 150 sites with hookups, water and electric. Tenting, pool, mini-golf, canoeing, theme weekends. 50 Bevier Road. ☎ 914-255-5193.

"Hey hey hey, Boo-Boo!"

Yogi Bear campsites are franchised (70 locations throughout the US). Both sites in the Catskills (above, and in Sullivan County, page 418) rent cabins and trailers and are open April 30 through Columbus Day. ☎ 800-558-2954; www.campjellystone.com.

Hidden Valley Lake Campground in Kingston is open all year. This no-frills campsite has no pool, planned activities or playground, only the amenities we all treasure – modern restrooms and hot showers. What it offers, according to its brochure, is "Peace, Quiet and Beauty Unlimited" on 220 wooded acres. The campground has 100 sites, some with hookups, and rental cabins. Fishing is excellent along

Campgrounds

its spring-fed, mile-long lake. A public swimming pool is nearby. 290 Whiteport Road. ☎ 914-338-4616.

Skyway Camping Resort in Ellenville has 180 sites, 149 with full hookups. Day rate is $38 for two adults and two children. It's the only campground in the Catskills with a Woodall's five-diamond rating in both facilities and recreation. Skyway isn't called a resort for nothing. It has phone hookups, romper room, workout room, library, rec hall, heated pool, spa, boating and fishing, sports field, playground, tenting and theme weekends. Luxury rentals include cable TV with VCR, refrigerator, microwave, stereo cassette player. Daily rate for a trailer is $89 for four people, with a minimum of a four-day stay. Open May 1 through Columbus Day. ☎ 914-647-5747. Its new Web site at www.skywaycamping.com features a slide show.

Rip Van Winkle in Saugerties at 149 Blue Mountain Road has 125 sites, many with full hookups, on 160 acres of secluded woodland. One-mile frontage on Plattekill Creek offers fishing and stream swimming. There's also tenting, hiking trails, two playgrounds, and hayrides. ☎ 914-246-8114; 800-246-8334. Day rate is $22-$27.60 for two adults. Open mid-May through October 15.

Oakland Valley Campground, Cuddebackville. 110 sites, 65 with hookups. Seasonal sites available. Tenting, rec hall, pool, river swimming, fishing, playground, sports field, horseshoes, volleyball. Planned activities. Mostly wooded sites beside a river. Open May 1 through October 15. ☎ 914-754-8732.

Greene County

Brookside Campgrounds in Catskill is a half-mile south of the Catskill Game Farm on Route 32. The family-owned site has mountain views, 50 sites and 22 full hookups ($25 per night for four people), tenting ($20 for parties of four), pool, hiking trails, playground and game room. Reservations suggested on holiday weekends. Open April 15 through October 15. ☎ 518-678-9777.

Indian Ridge Campsites in Leeds is in a rustic setting with all the amenities: hot showers, laundry room, clean modern restrooms. The campsite is conveniently located only one mile from Exit 21. It has a fishing pond, playground, swimming pool, hiking trail and recreation area. Of the 70 sites, 50 have water and electric. The day rate is $21-$23 for four people. Open May through October. ☎ 518-943-3516.

Pine Hollow Campsite, off Route 32A in Palenville, is situated on 30 acres of secluded woods. It has a rec hall and playground. 35 sites, 19 with hookups. $19 for two people. Open May 21 through October 14. ☎ 518-678-2245.

Whip-O-Will, Round Top. 230 sites, some with full hookups. This 88-acre mountain setting has coin-operated showers, pool, rec hall, general store, boating and fishing on seven-acre lake, mini-golf, sports field, playgrounds. Day rate is $19-$23 for two adults with two children. Open April 15 through October 15. ☎ 518-622-3277; 800-WOW-CAMP.

White Birches, Windham. 130 wooded sites, only four have no hookups. Boating, fishing, playground, sports field, rec hall. Open all year, but facilities are fully operational Memorial Day through Columbus Day. Day rate is $20 per family. ☎ 518-734-3266.

Delaware County

There are about 20 camping locations throughout the county in this region endowed with 700 miles of fishing streams, 11,000 acres of reservoirs, and miles of unbroken forests.

State-Run Campgrounds

State parks include **Bear Spring Mountain** in Walton (☎ 607-865-6989), **Beaver Kill** and **East Branch** in Downsville (☎ 607-363-7501), **Little Pond** in Turnwood (☎ 914-439-5480) and **Oquaga Creek** in Masonville (☎ 914-439-5480).

Private Campgrounds

Peaceful Valley Campsite is in Downsville, with 160 sites, 60 with full hookups, and some fully-furnished log cabins. Located on the East Branch of the Delaware River, it features bathhouses and laundromat, Olympic-size pool, mini-golf, playgrounds, canoe rentals, and hiking trails. (The site borders the Finger Lakes Hiking Trail, see page 387.)

The property includes three islands; the largest, Bear Island, is eight acres. The campsite is under new management, which has remodeled the entrance and convenience store, added some ponds, and repaired the roadway. The annual Peaceful Valley Bluegrass Festival is held here the third weekend in July, and an antique show the following weekend. ☎ 607-363-2211; www.peaceful-valley.com.

Christy's Beaver Spring Lake, Route 23, Davenport. 104 sites with hookups, RV rentals, 14-acre lake for boating and fishing, pool, camp store, arcade, bathhouses and showers. Planned weekend activities. $18 or $19 for two adults and three children. Open April 15 through November 30. ☎ 607-278-5293.

Pioneer Trails Campgrounds in DeLancey was established in 1965 and advertises old-fashion rustic camping with modern convenience (hot showers, for one thing). Eighteen acres with pool, volleyball, horseshoes. 50 sites, 15 with hookups. Open Memorial Day through Labor Day. ☎ 607-746-6789.

Catskill Mountain Kampground, Downsville, has 90 sites, 65 full hookups. Site is level and shaded on a 1,500-foot frontage of the East Branch of the Delaware. Tenting, pool, volleyball, horseshoes, playground. Seasonal hookups available. Open April 1 through October 15. Day rate is $16 for two people. Three miles south of Downsville on Route 30. ☎ 607-363-2599.

Delaware Valley Campsite has 88 sites, 80 with full hookups. $24 for two adults and two children. Family run. Located on East Branch of the Delaware with shaded sites. Sports field, horseshoes, volleyball. Open May 1 through October 15. ☎ 607-363-2306.

Ox-Bow Campsites, Route 30, on East Branch of Delaware. Fishing, hunting, river swimming, ballfield, two playgrounds, rec hall, laundry. Pets must be leashed. 100 sites, 75 with hookups. $20 for two

Campgrounds

people. May 1 through mid-October. ☎ 607-363-7141; winter ☎ 516-757-4153.

Roscoe Campsites, 80 sites, five with hookups. Campsite geared to those who wish to fish or play in the Beaverkill River. Their attitude is to let you be lazy. Tenting, hot showers (no charge), playground. On the Beaverkill, a half-mile west of Roscoe. $15-25 for two people. ☎ 607-498-5264.

Russell Brook Campsite, Cooks Falls, off Route 17 on Russell Brook Road (five-and-a-half miles west of Roscoe). 140 sites, all with hookups. Less than a mile from the Beaverkill River. Two stocked fishing ponds for kids. Hiking, hunting, fishing in forest preserve, tenting, daily hayrides, pool, rec hall, playground, basketball, camp store. Planned weekend activities. ☎ 607-498-5416.

Butternut Grove on the Beaverkill River. Old Route 17 (seven miles west of Roscoe). 80 sites with hookups. Picnic tables, tenting, hot showers (no charge). Fishing is the main event. Hiking, biking and golf nearby. $17 for four people. Open April 1 through November 30. ☎ 607-498-4224.

Farm Markets & More

The kindly fruits of the earth.
— The Book of Common Prayer

Overview

The New York State Department of Agriculture and Markets publishes a 62-page booklet entitled ***Guide to Farm Fresh Products***. It's printed in four regional editions and gives the dates open, produce sold, information as to which have farm tours, restaurants, and pick-your-own apples; includes a harvest calendar and brief description of each market. For a copy of the Metro Region edition, which includes the lower Hudson Valley (encompassing the Catskills), New York City and Long Island, contact the department at 1 Winners Circle, Albany, NY 12235, ☎ 518-457-7076, or send a self-addressed postcard requesting the guide to: 55 Hanson Place, Brooklyn, NY 11217, ☎ 718-722-2830. You can also ask for farm-stand locations over the phone at ☎ 800-355-2287. Or simply check the Web site at www.agmkt.state.ny.us.

To avoid being redundant, I have omitted the adjectives "fresh" and "homemade" from most of the entries. All the fruits and vegetables listed here are fresh-picked so I just use the word "produce." Baked goods are homemade. If you're looking for organic food, the guide mentioned above is a good source, but the best way to learn a farmer's production method is to call him or her directly. I've cited only those that emphasize their organic produce.

Come spring, farm markets spread like weeds across the counties. Those open all year are the exception. Unless you're in the area already, it's a good idea to call ahead.

To find favorite apple varieties and apple festival listings, consult the Web site of NYS Apple Association at www.nyapple-country.com.

Fruit & Vegetable Harvest Calendar

January	Apples, cabbage, carrots, onions, potatoes, squash (winter), turnips
February	Apples, cabbage, carrots, onions, potatoes, squash (winter), turnips
March	Apples, carrots, onions, potatoes, squash (winter)
April	Apples, carrots, onions, potatoes
May	Apples, asparagus, radishes, rhubarb, spinach
June	Apples, cherries (sweet), strawberries, beans, broccoli, cabbage, lettuce, peas, radishes, rhubarb, spinach, squash (summer)
July	Apples, blueberries, cherries (sweet and sour), peaches, raspberries, strawberries, beans, beets, broccoli, cabbage, carrots, cauliflower, celery, corn, cucumbers, eggplant, lettuce, onions, peas, peppers, potatoes, radishes, rhubarb, spinach, squash (summer), tomatoes, turnips
August	Apples, blueberries, melons, grapes, peaches, pears, plums, prunes, beans, beets, broccoli, cabbage, carrots, cauliflower, celery, corn, cucumbers, eggplant, lettuce, onions, peppers, potatoes, radishes, rhubarb, spinach, squash (summer), squash (winter), tomatoes, turnips

September	Apples, blueberries, melons, grapes, peaches, pears, plums, prunes, raspberries, beans, beets, broccoli, cabbage, carrots, celery, corn, cucumbers, eggplant, lettuce, onions, peppers, potatoes, pumpkins, radishes, spinach, squash (summer), squash (winter), tomatoes, turnips
October	Apples, grapes, pears, raspberries, beans, beets, broccoli, cabbage, carrots, cauliflower, celery, corn, cucumbers, eggplant, lettuce, onions, peppers, potatoes, pumpkins, radishes, spinach, squash (summer), squash (winter), tomatoes, turnips
November	Apples, pears, beets, broccoli, cabbage, carrots, cauliflower, celery, onions, potatoes, radishes, squash (winter), turnips
December	Apples, cabbage, carrots, cauliflower, onions, potatoes, squash (winter), turnips

This schedule is approximate, compiled from various sources that in some cases were radically different from one another.

What's Dear to Deer

Plants occasionally eaten by deer are pansy, sunflower, wood hyacinth, cranesbill geranium, English ivy, iris, peony, coneflower, sedum, meadow rue. What deer really like to eat are hollyhocks, impatiens, Mexican sunflower, crocus, daylily, hosta, cardinal flower, phlox, rose, and tulip.

– From *Guideline for Plants Damaged by Deer*, compiled by Cornell Cooperative Extension of Westchester Master Gardeners

Farm Markets & More

 # Farm Markets

Sullivan County

A new event designed to promote Sullivan County farms and their fresh produce is the **Fall Garden Harvest Market** held Sundays in October at the 1969 Woodstock Music Festival site in Bethel. New vendors with their fall bounty and attractions are added every weekend. This family-fun festival has featured hayrides, pony rides, petting zoo, kite flying demonstrations, antique and custom autos, stiltwalkers, and art and crafts.

BECKER'S
99 School Street
Callicoon
☎ 914-887-4633

Open daily, Easter to Labor Day; closed Sunday in winter. Greenhouse, flower shop, candies and cards.

CATSKILL MORNING FARM
138 Hardenburgh Road
8 miles south of Livingston Manor off Route 149
Livingston Manor
☎ 914-482-3984
www.morningfarm.com

Open daily April through December; closed Tuesday May through October; open November and December for long weekends. Thirty acres include gift shop, greenhouse, organic farmstand, display gardens, koi pond and farm animals. The shop carries cookbooks, honey, birdhouses, bath and body products, and everything for the gardener. The farm has grown from a single greenhouse since Maria Grimaldi, a horticulturist, founded it in 1990. In 1998 she sold it to Steven Wilkinson and Gerard Ilaria, but she remains Farmer in Residence.

DIEHL'S FARM MARKET
Route 52A and Gabel Road between Jeffersonville and Hortonville
Callicoon
☎ 914-887-4935

Open Easter to Christmas; closed Wednesday. Greenhouse, maple syrup, ice cream, eggs, jams, honey, crafts.

DUKE'S FARM MARKET
Route 52
Jeffersonville
☎ 914-482-5776

Open daily May through October. Produce, eggs, preserves.

EGG UNIVERSITY
Kaplan Farms
Glen Wild Road
Woodridge
☎ 914-434-4519

Open daily 8am-3pm, year-round. Fresh eggs. Hold your nose.

THE FARMERS MARKET
985 East Broadway
Monticello
☎ 914-794-2744

Open daily, year-round. Produce, nursery products, honey, baked goods.

Farm Markets & More

FISHER FARM
430 Aden Road
Four miles east of Liberty. Route 55E, north on
Muhlig Road, turn right at Four Corners.
☎ 914-292-5777

Open mid-September through October. Pumpkins;
pay by the piece.

GORZYNSKI ORGANIC FARM
Route 52
Cochecton Center
☎ 914-252-7570

Open Saturday and Sunday 1-5pm, June through
Halloween. Produce, mustards.

K BRAND FARMS
Glen Wild Road
Between Woodridge and Rock Hill
☎ 914-434-4519

Open daily until 2:30pm, year-round. Fresh eggs.

LILLY'S FARM MARKET
Route 17B
Monticello
☎ 914-794-5342

Open daily July through October. Produce, dairy,
honey, breads, jams, kosher products, gift items.

LM FARMS
Route 17B (next to Neves Taxidermy)
Bethel
☎ 914-583-4648

Open daily Mother's Day to Christmas. Greenhouse,
vegetables, apples, pumpkins, Christmas trees.

LOU'S PRODUCE & BAKERY
Route 209
Summitville
☎ 914-888-0027

Open daily, year-round. Produce, greenhouse.

MAAS'S FARM MARKET
Route 55, just past the village center
Grahamsville
☎ 914-985-2686

Open May to October 15. Flowers; fruits and vegetables after second week of June.

★ **DID YOU KNOW?**

New York State is the second-largest apple-producing state, but grows the greatest variety of apples of any state. New York produced just over one billion pounds in 1998, and the Hudson Valley is one of its three principal apple-growing areas. Sales of apples in Ulster and Orange counties represent more than $32 million per year.

MONTICELLO FARM HOME & GARDEN
Route 17B, less than two miles west of the raceway
Monticello
☎ 914-794-6457

Open daily, year-round. Formerly an Agway, this huge store carries everything for farmers, gardeners, farm animals, house pets, and for all the rest of us – gloves, jackets, sleds, hardware. Greenhouse open in the summer.

Farm Markets & More

MONTICELLO GREENHOUSE FLORIST
Next to farmers' market on Broadway
Monticello
☎ 914-794-2744

Open daily, year-round. Inside is a lovely shop with artificial flowers and baskets. Outside is the real stuff.

NORTH BRANCH CIDER MILL
Main Street, eight miles south of Roscoe
North Branch
☎ 914-482-4823

Open 10am-4:30pm; closed Tuesday. Working mill and country store. Honey, mustard, dressing, maple syrup, jam, fresh-ground coffee, pancake mix, baskets.

Owner Dan Sullivan presses apples as he needs them during the week. To watch him squeeze the apples into cider on a big turn-of-the-century cider press, head there on Saturdays at 10:15am, except in July and August, when good apples are not available. Look for apples and pumpkins in the fall and Christmas trees in November and December.

RIVER BROOK FARM
Route 97 and C. Meyer Road
Cochecton
☎ 914-932-7952

Open Saturday 11am-dark, May through October. Over 50 varieties of organic vegetables, herbs and flowers. Farm animals include emu, goats, sheep and chickens.

SILVER HEIGHTS FARM
275 Eggler Road
Jeffersonville
☎ 914-482-3572

Open May through December; closed Tuesday (Fridays at Liberty Farmer's Market). Petting farm with dairy goats, chickens, and turkeys. Herb greenhouse and flowering shrubs.

STEPHENSON'S GARDEN CENTER & FARM MARKET
328 Route 52E
Liberty
☎ 914-292-2301

Open daily, end of March through Christmas. Country-style market. Greenhouse, garden supplies, gift shop.

SULLIVAN COUNTY AREA FARMER'S MARKET
Darby Lane, across from the Elks Building
Liberty
☎ 914-292-6180; 914-292-5250

Open Friday 3-7pm, June through October. Open-air market has produce, baked goods, plants and maple products. Also carries locally made goat cheese, honey, jams, hydroponic tomatoes and emu meat products. Every vendor is directly involved in the production of the products and will be happy to answer questions about growing practices, etc. Special events are often held on the last Friday of the month.

WALNUT MOUNTAIN FARM
200 Ferndale-Loomis Road
Liberty
☎ 914-292-8172

Open daily, Mother's Day through mid-October (Fridays at Liberty Farmer's Market). Greenhouse. 40 varieties of vegetables grown organically.

WILD ROOTS FARM
Route 52
Youngsville
☎ 914-439-4799

Open weekends, June through November. Organic vegetables – snap peas, snow peas, lettuce, radishes, peppers and tomatoes.

◎ TIP

According to Amy Gillingham of Wild Roots Farm, certain varieties of lettuce, such as red leaf and butterheads, don't ship well – a good reason to buy from a local farm.

Ulster County

ADAMS FAIRACRE FARMS
Route 9W N
Kingston
☎ 914-336-6300

Open daily, year-round. Produce, baked goods, greenhouses and nursery, deli and cheese shop, Christmas trees, and everything for the birds.

ALYCE & ROGER'S FRUIT STAND
Route 28, 22 miles west of I-87 (Thruway)
Mt. Tremper
☎ 914-688-2114

Open April through October, 10am-6pm, closed Tuesday. Also open Labor Day to Halloween, Friday through Monday, 10am-6pm. Produce, baked goods, herbs, honey, local specialties. Fresh ground peanut butter while you wait.

APPLE BIN
Route 9W
Ulster Park
☎ 914-339-7229

Open daily at 7:30am, year-round. Produce, apples, pumpkins, herbs, cut flowers, gourmet coffees and teas, fruit pies and other baked goods.

APPLE FAIRACRE FARMS
Route 9W
Kingston
☎ 914-336-6300

Open daily, year-round. Produce, cheeses, gourmet coffees, fish, meals, bakery, garden supplies.

APPLE HILL FARM
141 Route 32S, just past SUNY Campus
New Paltz
☎ 914-255-0917

Open August through December, daily 10am-6pm. Restored 1859 barn. Produce, U-pick apples and pumpkins. Dried flowers, pies, weekend hayrides, Christmas trees.

APPLEJACK FARMS
DuBois Road
Wallkill
☎ 914-895-3564; 914-895-9284

Open Monday through Friday at 8am, September through November. Apples and cider.

BARTHEL'S FARM MARKET
Route 209, one mile north of town, next to hospital
Ellenville
☎ 914-647-6941

Open daily, April through December. Produce, pumpkins, greenhouse, nursery stock (trees and shrubs), Christmas trees.

Farm Markets & More

BILL BOICE
599 Old Kings Highway
Saugerties
☎ 914-246-2549

Open daily, April through Halloween. Vegetables in summer only; flowers in April; peaches, sweet corn.

BORCHERT ORCHARDS
Lattintown Road
Between South and Bingham streets
Marlboro
☎ 914-236-7239

Open daily, June through December. U-pick strawberries; produce.

JOE BUZZANCO'S GREENHOUSES & FARM
2050 Sawkill-Ruby Rd (Cty Road 31), off Route 209
Kingston
☎ 914-336-6528

Open 10am-5pm daily, May through October; closed July. Produce (except apples), flowering plants.

CHRISTIAN'S GREENHOUSE
Route 209
Kerhonkson
☎ 914-626-5201

Florist shop open Monday through Saturday at 9am, year-round (Sunday during holiday seasons). Bedding plants for sale April through June.

CLARKE WESTERVELT FARMS
38 Clarks Ln., off Willow Tree Rd., one mile west of 9W
Milton
☎ 914-795-2270

Open June through October; closed Monday. U-pick apples, cherries, peaches, pears, raspberries. Hayrides, tractor trailer rides during apple harvest.

CM FARM MARKET
Route 9W
Highland
☎ 914-691-5832

CM Farm Market is owned by Casa Mia Restaurant, which is next door.

Open daily 10am-7:30pm, mid-April through December. Homemade pasta sauces, pastas, breads, produce, salad dressings, pies and ready-to-eat Italian dishes such as clams, calamari, stuffed mushrooms, and lasagna.

COUNTRY FRESH FARM MARKET
On Route 9W in a small shopping plaza
Milton
☎ 914-795-FOOD

Open daily, 6am-9pm. year-round. Produce, homemade bread and desserts. Breakfast, lunch and takeout. Tables outside.

DAVENPORT'S CIRCLE FARM
Corner of Washington Avenue and Thruway Circle
Kingston
☎ 914-334-9004

Open daily, March through first week in November. Greenhouse, produce, baked goods, sweet corn.

DAVENPORT FARMS
Route 209
Stone Ridge
☎ 914-687-0051

Open daily, year-round. Full-scale market. Produce (specialize in asparagus, broccoli, apples and sweetcorn), baked goods, dairy products, pasta, sauces, bedding plants, hanging baskets.

Farm Markets & More

DOLAN ORCHARDS
Route 208, 3 miles from town
Wallkill
☎ 914-895-2153

Open daily at 9am, August through February. U-pick apples, pumpkins and cherries; vegetables, U-cut Christmas trees.

DRESSEL FARMS
271 Route 208, 2½ miles south of Main Street
New Paltz
☎ 914-255-0693

Open September through June. U-pick berries (June), apples and pumpkins (September and October). Hayrides, farm animals. Mail order.

◎ TIP

Roderick Dressel Sr., of Dressel Farms, says to treat apples like a gallon of milk – store them in the refrigerator, not in the garage.

FOUR WINDS FARMS
158 Marabac Road
Off Route 208, one mile south of Routes 44/55
Gardiner
☎ 914-255-3088 (call ahead)

Open daily, year-round. Tomatoes, free range chickens, lamb, eggs, wool products.

GALLO'S OF WOODSTOCK (formerly Mohican)
Route 212
Woodstock
☎ 914-679-4272

Open daily, year-round. Produce (much of it organic), imported cheeses, fruit and pasta baskets, coffee, four greenhouses.

GILL'S FARM MARKET & GREENHOUSE
Two locations in Hurley; one on Route 209 (☎ 914-331-8225), open daily, April through October; and the other on Hurley Mt. Road (☎ 914-338-0788), open daily, mid-July through September.

U-pick pumpkins, produce, flowers; baked goods, dairy products, homemade sauces. Fall festival every weekend in October features hayrides, maze, and pumpkin painting.

GRETA'S POTTING SHED
854 Route 212
Saugerties
☎ 914-246-9889

Bedding plants, perennials, cut flowers, produce, Christmas trees.

HEPWORTH FARMS MARKET
Route 9W, 1½ miles north of Marlboro
Milton
☎ 914-795-2142

Open daily, May through November. Organic produce, baked goods, aged cheese. U-pick sweet cherries and apples. Hayrides.

HORN OF PLENTY
Route 28, 1½ miles west of Exit 19 circle
Kingston
☎ 914-331-4318

Open daily, year-round. Produce, honey, baked goods, bread, plants, homemade ice cream, deli.

Farm Markets & More

HURD'S ORCHARDS
Route 32
Four miles south of New Paltz via Exit 18 & Rte 299
Clintondale
☎ 914-883-7818

Open weekends, September through October. U-pick apples, pears and pumpkins; hayrides, baked goods, cider, donuts, Christmas trees, woodland hiking trail, 4-H animals, 22-foot tepee, harvest festival weekends. 500-acre farm has been in same family since 1891.

JENKINS-LUEKEN ORCHARDS
69 Yankee Folly Road
Route 299, four miles west of New Paltz
☎ 914-255-0999

Open daily, August through May. Twenty varieties of apples, five kinds of pears. Honey and cider made on premises. Pumpkins, corn, preserves, Christmas trees.

KELDER'S FARM
Route 209 (new location)
Kerhonkson
☎ 914-626-7137

Open April through October. Award-winning, century-old 90-acre market, greenhouse, petting farm. U-pick berries, vegetables, pumpkins. Produce, plants, maple syrup, tours, hayrides, display of antique farm equipment, Kelderberry balloon typhoon for kids. Strawberry Festival held Father's Day weekend; Fall Festival on Columbus Day weekend.

KINGSTON FARMER'S MARKET
On the Rondout
Kingston
☎ 800-331-1518

Open Saturday from 9am-2pm, August through October. Produce, plants, baked goods, sauces, jams, crafts.

LOCUST GROVE FARM
North Road, .25 mile north of Kedem Winery
Milton
☎ 914-795-5194

Open July through December. Produce, pumpkins. View fruit groves (including quince) and small antique car collection.

MINARD FARMS
Hurds Road
East off South Ohioville Road, 2½ miles south of Route 299, .3 mile east of Exit 18
Clintondale
☎ 914-883-5755

Open weekends 9am-6pm, September through October. U-pick apples; hayrides, tours, picnicking.

MOHICAN MARKET
57 John Street
Kingston
☎ 914-338-3740

Open year-round; closed Sunday. Produce, pastas, flowers, honey, syrup, coffee.

MOWER'S SATURDAY MARKET
Maple Lane
Woodstock (one block from Village Green)
☎ 914-679-6744
www.ulster.net/~fleamarket

Open Saturday only, May through October. Continuously running for 19 years, open-air market features furniture, collectibles, estate jewelry, crafts, fresh produce, plants, toys, and Irish gift items.

Farm Markets & More

The Web site of Mower's Market is a miniguide to Woodstock.

MR. APPLE'S LOW-SPRAY ORCHARD
Off Route 213
High Falls
☎ 914-687-9498

Open August through October or November; shop is open until April. U-pick apples and pears grown without chemicals; vegetables, pumpkins, tours, farm machinery exhibit, picnic area. On a 30-acre farm started by his grandfather, Philip Apple carries difficult-to-grow Northern Spy apples. His Summer Secret tastes like a tart Mac and is unavailable in supermarkets. His Red Delicious are from the oldest strain.

◎ TIP

Philip Apple, of Mr. Apple's, says the prime time to buy Macs is the first week of September (October is too late for Macs but fine for Delicious, Empire and Winesap). Cortlands are usually ready 10 days after Macs.

PET FARE
Route 28
Shokan
☎ 914-657-2500

Open daily, late-April through November. Two-part operation (one sells pet supplies); garden shop has greenhouse and pond supplies ranging in price from 50¢ to more than $250 for fish. Among its many exotic species is imported Japanese koi at $125 apiece.

PROSPECT HILL ORCHARD
40 Clarke's Lane
Milton
☎ 914-795-2383

Open weekends 9am-4pm, August through October. This is orchard country but Prospect Hill is the only one open to the public. Thirty of the 160 acres, in the shadow of the Marlboro Mountains, is set aside for the U-pick orchard. In the Clarke family since 1817, the orchard was founded by Steve Clarke's great-great-great grandfather. A unique feature of his farm, he says, is that three-quarters of an acre is devoted to pick-your-own Bosc pears. Another is that fruit is sold by the pound. They don't require you to buy a bag.

Customers are provided with a map of the U-pick orchard and the peak varieties that weekend. All are dwarf trees so picking is easy. Dates listed are approximate, so call first. Cherry picking (mid-June to July 4) takes the longest and keeps the kids busy. Peaches are ready in August, and apples, pears and pumpkins about the third weekend in September to Columbus Day weekend. There is a picnic area beside a pond and hayrides.

Asians and Europeans are Clarke's biggest customers because they appreciate fresh produce, he says. "If you want to have a really good time and get good fruit, come up here."

Direction Info: The farm is 10 miles north of Newburgh off 9W. Take 9W to Milton and turn left at the light (Stewart's is on opposite corner). Follow Milton Turnpike (Route 10) for one mile and turn left at Clarke's Lane (right after sign for Southern Ulster Neighborhood Center).

ROBIN'S WAREHOUSE OUTLET
249 Route 32 South
New Paltz
☎ 914-255-5201

Open daily 9am-8pm, year-round. Produce, baked goods, cheeses, roasted peanuts, jams, gourmet coffee, honey, cold cuts, cookies.

SAUER FARM
640 Kings Hwy, four miles south of Saugerties
Mt. Marion
☎ 914-246-2725

Open daily 9am-8pm, year-round. Produce, raspberries, sweet corn, melons, organic eggs, raw milk.

SAUNDERSKILL FARMS
41 Garden Lane
Accord
☎ 914-626-CORN

Greenhouse open daily, April through November. Indoor market open daily, June through November. Produce, baked goods, cider, jellies, annuals, perennials, hanging baskets, U-pick strawberries, pumpkins. Hayrides in October.

SPRINGTOWN GREEN GROCERS
Near the intersection of Routes 32 and 213
Rosendale
☎ 914-658-3164

Open daily, year-round. Organic and non-organic produce, potting plants, hanging baskets, gourmet specialities, 55 varieties of beer.

STONE RIDGE ORCHARDS
Route 213
Stone Ridge
☎ 914-687-4379

Open daily at 9am, September through November.
U-pick apples.

SUNFROST FARMS
217 Tinker Street, Route 212
Woodstock
☎ 914-679-6690

Open daily, year-round. Store sells produce, herbs,
and baked goods and has a juice bar. Lunch specialties and frothy juice blend.

SUNSHINE FARM MARKET
2 Jansen Avenue
Kingston
☎ 914-338-0022

Open daily, year-round. Produce, flowers, baked goods,
deli.

SWENSON'S ORGANIC PRODUCE
Main Street
.5 mile east of Route 209, 16 miles south of Kingston
Accord
☎ 914-626-3479

Open daily, April through October. Berries, vegetables, pumpkins. "Nibble" walks to taste produce.

TANTILLO'S FARM MARKET
Traveling west on 44/55, turn left at intersection
with Route 208 (Four Corners)
Gardiner
☎ 914-256-9109

Open daily 9am-6pm (ice cream stand open daily
11am-9pm), May through Thanksgiving. U-pick apples, peas, pumpkins, cherries, tomatoes. Other pro-

duce, pies, ice cream cakes, pastries, cappuccino, espresso, coffee beans, candies and soft ice cream.

Dueling Pies

I heard two women having a dispute at lunch. One insisted Tantillo's makes the best pies and the other swore that Wright's pies are superior. The two farm stands are practically across from one another, so you be the judge.

TERWILLIGER'S FRUIT & VEGETABLE STAND
Route 209
Accord
☎ 914-626-4209

Open daily, 9am-6pm; weekends, 8am-7pm, April through November. Produce.

TRONCILLITO FARMS
275 Lattintown Road
Three miles north off Exit 10 via Route 9W, then west three miles on Lattintown Road
Marlboro
☎ 914-236-3124

Open Friday through Sunday, mid-September through October. U-pick apples, pears, grapes, pumpkins; vegetables, cider. Hayrides and tours.

TWIN STARS FARMS
155 N. Ohioville Road
.25 mi. east of Thruway Exit 18, then one mile north
New Paltz
☎ 914-255-7077

Open August 28 through October 20; closed Monday. U-pick apples, nectarines, pears. Picnic tables.

THE VERY BERRY PATCH
300 Springtown Road
New Paltz
☎ 914-255-5569

Open weekends from third week of June through August and on Labor Day weekend. U-pick raspberries, blackberries, and fall variety of red raspberries; berries also sold retail and wholesale.

VINNIE'S FARM MARKET
Route 32A
Saugerties
☎ 914-246-0908

Open daily, year-round. Produce, candied apples, homemade pasta sauces, jams, relishes and spreads, soups, canned goods, baked goods, flowers, pumpkins, gourds, gift baskets, and giant oatmeal chip cookies that Vinnie calls a whole meal. His orange muffins are to die for. Greenhouse plants in summer.

WALLKILL VIEW FARM MARKET & GREENHOUSE
15 Route 299W
.7 mile from Wallkill Bridge
New Paltz
☎ 914-255-8050

Open daily at 9am, mid-March through Christmas. U-pick pumpkins. Sweetcorn, fruits, flowers, pies, breads, ice cream. Huge Christmas tree store and Christmas ornament room converts to a greenhouse in spring with plants for sale.

WESTWOOD FARMS GREENHOUSE
On Route 375, after turning off Route 28
West Hurley
☎ 914-679-7841

Open daily 9am-7pm, April through December. Produce, plants, pumpkins, honey, Christmas trees, bait

Farm Markets & More

shop. If Nancy's pies taste as good as they smell, you're a goner! She's got peachberry, blueberry, coconut custard, cherry, and fruits of the forest.

WILKLOW ORCHARDS
Pancake Hollow Road
South of New Paltz Road, off Route 299, 2.3 miles east of Thruway
Highland
☎ 914-691-2339

Open September and October. U-pick apples and pumpkins, hayrides, picnicking, farm animals.

WRIGHT FARMS
See *Tantillo*, above, for directions
Gardiner
☎ 914-255-5300

Open daily, year-round. U-pick apples. Produce, pies, gift baskets, jams (Wright's own brand includes hot pepper jelly and quince-apricot compote), breads, cookies, candy apples, plants, tours.

Organic Farming

Seven Ulster County farms have formed a coalition to sell organic produce to members and promote farming in the Hudson Valley. In 1940 there were 2,500 farms in the county; in 1990 the number had dwindled to 529. Shareholders in these Community Supported Agriculture (CSA) farms include individuals, restaurants, and even the Culinary Institute of America. Since there is no government subsidy, the CSA farmer relies on member fees, and some also require a commitment from their shareholders to work a certain number of hours. Consumers pay in advance for weekly shares of the produce harvest, thereby creating a partnership that guarantees the farmer's income and provides the consumer with fresh, wholesome food.

According to an article in *Ulster Magazine*, there has been a 40% increase in CSAs in the past year as the demand grows for chemical-free food. Listed below are the organic farms, all open to the public.

AND-SOW-ON COMMUNITY FARM
County Route 1
High Falls
☎ 914-626-7662

Open May through November. Vegetables, herbs and flowers. Work shares are also available.

CODY CREEK COMMUNITY FARM
153 Charles Smith Road, off Route 32
Saugerties
☎ 914-246-8028; 914-246-7549

Open June through September (other times call for availability). Greenhouse, produce, pumpkins, herbs, syrup, honey. Workshops.

FOUR WINDS FARMS
Gardiner
☎ 914-255-3088

Open daily, year-round. Vegetables.

HUGUENOT STREET HARVEST
205 Huguenot Street
New Paltz
☎ 914-256-0686

Open daily, June through November. Organic vegetables and herbs; cut flowers.

Farm Markets & More

PHILLIES BRIDGE FARM PROJECT
45 Phillies Bridge Road
.3 mile off Route 208, 4.5 miles south of New Paltz
Gardiner
☎ 914-256-9108

Open June through November. This 66-acre farm, dating back to 1702, is also involved in education, internships and research.

TALIAFERRO FARMS
167 Plains Road
New Paltz
☎ 914-883-7709

Ninety varieties of vegetables. Though there is no farm stand here, the public may purchase from Sylvester Taliaferro between the second week in May and Thanksgiving.

HIGH FALLS FOOD CO-OP
At junction of Route 213 and Lucas Turnpike
☎ 914-687-7262

Another community-supported farm; open to the public daily. Organic when possible; produce, daily, herbs, spices, condiments, grains.

Greene County

ANDY'S GARDEN CENTER
Route 23A (Next to JAMS)
Haines Falls
☎ 518-589-0141; 518-589-7061

Open Mother's Day through October; closed Wednesday. Andy has just installed a new greenhouse. He also tinkers with wrought iron and sells his son-in-law's personalized sport trophies. Stop in to say hello for a good laugh. "At a retirement age, I am increasing what I have," he says with a chuckle. "If I don't, they (his four daughters) are going to put dirt on me quick."

BENNETT'S BERRY PATCH
Independence Lane
Off Route 144, .75 mile west of Route 9W
Hannacroix
☎ 518-756-9472 (call ahead)

Open daily, June and July. U-pick strawberries.

BLACK HORSE FARMS & COUNTRY STORE
Route 9W
Six miles north of Catskill; seven miles south of the Thruway, Exit 21B
Coxsackie
☎ 518-943-9324

Open Monday through Saturday 9am-6pm; Sunday 9am-5pm, March through December. On sight of famous Black Horse Inn built in 1791 by Isaac Hallenbeck and burned down in the 1930s. Five hundred acres of produce, with greenhouse, garden center, gourmet foods and country store selling gifts, chimes, pasta sauces and own line of jellies and relishes in 1864 barn. Haunted house and pumpkins part of October Festival held two weekends around Halloween.

BLACK WALNUT ORGANIC FARM
☎ 518-239-6987
Location 1: Stone Bridge Road
Cornwallville (off Route 145 in East Durham at Zoom Flume sign); open daily, June-December.
Location 2: Catskill Mtn Organic Green Market
In red barn across from the Hunter Theater
Location 3: Alpine Garden Village
Rte 296 & South St., Windham; open May-Nov.

Farm Markets & More

Organic fruits and vegetables (including acid-free cherry tomatoes, 10 varieties of lettuce and the only organic sweetcorn in the Catskills), honey, maple syrup, and a variety of cheeses. Don't be shy about approaching the proprietor, Todd Tremble, whose mission is to spread the word about organic farming. "I like to explain what it is we do here," he says.

Catskill Mountain Foundation

The Catskill Mountain Foundation's involvement in Community Supported Agriculture (CSA) differs slightly from other arrangements. Most often, the subscriber gets a bag of whatever produce is available. Here, the money paid up front is put into a credit account, enabling the subscriber to select from available produce a half-hour before the market opens to the public. This gives members the best selection.

For an application, schedule of farm demonstrations, lectures, or information on exhibits at the foundation's bookstore and gallery, call ☎ 518-263-4908; www.catskillmtn.org.

HENRY BOEHM
Exit 21B
9W to Route 81 to County Road 26
Climax
☎ 518-731-6196

Open daily, August through December. Produce.

THE BOUNTIFUL BASKET
Main Street, ½ mile west of village on Route 23
Windham
☎ 518-734-3387

Open year-round, Monday through Saturday 9am-6pm; Sunday 9am-5pm. Produce, gourmet food, baked goods, handmade gifts, plants, Christmas trees. Café, picnicking, walking paths and farm animals.

BULICH'S CREEKSIDE FARM
Exit 21, right to old Route 23B
Leeds
☎ 518-943-5739

Open daily, May through October. Pick your own strawberries in the spring, pumpkins in the fall. Summer crops in season. Sells lots of other fruit.

CARTER'S COUNTRY FARM
& ICE CREAM STAND
Route 9W, across from Short Hills Driving Range
Coxsackie
☎ 518-731-9775

Open daily 9am-10pm, Mother's Day to Christmas. Produce, greenhouse. Frozen yogurt; 24 flavors of soft ice cream.

CATSKILL MOUNTAIN GREEN MARKET
In red barn across from Hunter Theater
Hunter
☎ 518-263-4908
www.catskillmtn.org

Open Thursday through Mon at 10am, July 4th through Labor Day; weekends only Memorial Day through July 4th and Labor Day through Thanksgiving. Organic and non-organic produce, honey, maple syrup, goat cheese.

FLEECE & FROMAGE FARMS
Siam Road
Three miles north of town via Mitchell Hollow Road
Windham
☎ 518-734-5452

Farm Markets & More

Open year-round by appointment. Sheep farm; spinning, weaving and dying demonstrations for wool production.

THE GREENERY
Route 32
South of town and north of Catskill Game Farm
Cairo
☎ 518-622-9404

Open daily, March through July. Large greenhouse.

HEARTS & FLOWERS
Warrenstein Road
One mile east off Route 41 (Jerome Ave), 1.7 miles north of town
Cairo
☎ 518-622-8232

Open daily all year, 9am-6pm. Greenhouse, herbs.

KAATSKILL CIDER MILL
4953 Route 32, .5 mile south of Catskill Game Farm
Catskill
☎ 518-678-5529

Open March through November; 10am-10pm daily during season; closed Monday and Tuesday before Memorial Day. Cider mill, crafts, pumpkins, ice cream parlor.

KERN'S NURSERY
Route 23C, .2 mile west of Route 17 in village
Jewett
☎ 518-734-3543

Open daily, late-April through October; and Friday through Sunday 10am-5pm, mid-November through December or by appointment. Greenhouse; herbs; display gardens.

LADY L (same location as Beaumont Gardens)
Route 81
Five miles west of Coxsackie, eight miles east of Greenville
☎ 518-731-7788

Open July 4 through September 30, Tuesday through Saturday. Call for spring hours. Plants, herbs, nursery products. Attractive display gardens.

STORY FARM
Route 32 south of Game Farm; stand is across the road from its farm
Catskill
☎ 518-678-9716

Open June through November. Produce, dairy products, honey.

The Storys of Story Farm are distant relatives of the folks at Story's Nursery, but have no business relationship.

STORY'S NURSERY
Route 67, 17 miles west of Exit 21 via Routes 23W and 32N; just past airport
Freehold
☎ 518-634-7754

Open all year. Need a tree? Head for Story's Nursery. Huge greenhouse and nursery. Christmas trees, vines, bushes, potted plants, hanging baskets.

THE TSCHINKEL FARM
Plattekill Road, .25 mile off Route 32
Freehold
☎ 518-966-8130

Open evenings and weekends all year. Hay, dairy products and beef. Farm animals. Hayrides on request.

Farm Markets & More

Delaware County

Bishop Farms is celebrating its 58th year in business.

BISHOP FARMS
Sidney Center Road
Sidney
☎ 607-563-3741

Open daily, June through Thanksgiving. Vegetables.

BRUCE COUNTRY FARMS
Route 28
Margaretville
☎ 914-586-2643

Open daily, year-round. Trees, shrubs, flowers. Full-service lawn and garden center.

CHARLES GARLIC & PRODUCE
County Route 23 (.5 mile off I-88)
Sidney
☎ 607-563-1034
www.geocities.com/charliesgarlic

Open mid-July to end of October (daily in October; call first at other times). Garlic and produce, like its name. Look for his blue ribbons. Charlie & Bebe Bishop are members of the Cornell Cooperative Extension and the Garlic Seed Foundation. The farm has a selection of European garlic available in different varieties: German white (strong and sweet); Italian rocambole (pungent, but pleasing); Russian red (spicy and intense) and French softneck (snappy but mild).

⊚ TIP

Garlic does *not* store well under refrigeration. Keep in a cool, dry area and it will keep for months.

DAVENPORT CENTER FARM
Intersection of Routes 23 and 10
Davenport Center
☎ 607-278-6909

Open daily, May through Halloween. Greenhouse, produce. Chickens, turkeys, dogs and cats will keep the kids busy while you shop.

DELHI REGIONAL FARMER'S MARKET
Courthouse Square
Delhi
☎ 607-746-3857

Open Wednesday 10am-2pm, June through September. Produce, baked goods, gourmet cheeses, honey.

GREEN THUMB
Route 10
Five miles west of Delhi; 10 miles east of Walton
Hamden
☎ 607-746-2248

Open daily, December 20 to March 15. Greenhouses, gardening accessories, water plants, aquatic supplies.

HECTIC FARM GARDENS
Delhi Courthouse Square
Delhi
☎ 607-746-2801

Wednesdays at Delhi Courthouse Square Farm Market. Produce.

HILLHAVEN FARMS
Intersection of Routes10 and 23
Stamford
☎ 607-652-2274

Open daily, April through Christmas. Produce, fruit baskets, craftsman tables and other items, Christmas trees.

MARY LOU DECKER'S FARMSTAND
Walton/Franklin Road (Route 21)
Walton
☎ 607-865-5938

Open daily, April through December. Produce, maple and honey products, pies, jams, cheeses.

MEREDITH MOUNTAIN FARMS
Honest Brook Road
Delhi
☎ 800-828-3422; 607-746-3857
www.catskill.net/cheez

Unique cheeses and mustards (see page 403).

MISTY MOUNTAIN OPEN AIR MARKET
Bridge and Water streets
Walton
☎ 607-865-6656

Open June through mid-October. Produce, crafts.

The octagonal house next to Octagon Farm Market is a B&B with five rooms.

OCTAGON FARM MARKET
Walton (between Walton and Delhi on Route 10)
☎ 607-865-7416

Open year-round. Produce, herbs, maple and honey products, stick candies, greenhouse.

PAKATAKAN FARMER'S MARKET
Route 30
Four miles north of Margaretville/Arkville
Halcottsville
☎ 914-586-4655; 800-586-3303

Open Saturday 9am-3pm, mid-May through early-October. Located at historic Round Barn. Produce, handmade crafts, herbs, plants, baked goods. Call for special events calendar.

QUARLTERE'S GARDEN & MARKET PLACE

Route 30
Just north of the Middletown/Roxbury town line
Roxbury
☎ 607-326-4282

Open daily, year-round except January. Produce, greenhouse, wind chimes, statuary, garden supplies, gift baskets, candles, welcome signs.

Maple Sugar Farms

★ DID YOU KNOW?

The sugar maple is New York's official state tree.

At many of these farms, you can watch the tapping and "sugaring off" process of syrup making. Weather is a key factor. Generally speaking, the sap begins to flow in early March, and runs through mid-April. Many farms sell their maple products from home, so always call ahead for precise directions and hours of operation. Also, bear in mind that tours are given only on a "good sap day."

Sullivan County

ANDERSEN'S MAPLE FARM

235 Andersen Road
Long Eddy
☎ 914-887-4238; 914-887-4817

Open year-round (call for appointment). Tours in spring. Syrup, sugar, butter. Mail order. Crafts, gifts.

Farm Markets & More

Farm also raises hormone-free cattle and sells freezer beef retail.

MUTHIG FARM
1036 Muthig Road
Parksville
☎ 914-292-7838

Open all year (call first). Tours in March. Syrup, cream, maple jelly.

VAN'S FARM VALLEY SUGAR HOUSE
133 Merritt Road
West off Big Hollow Rd., south of junction 42 and 55
Grahamsville
☎ 914-985-7739

Open year-round, but call ahead. Sugar house open during the season. Maple syrup, farm tours and farm animals.

Maple Syrup Facts*

- ❖ Warm days and cool nights make the sap run.
- ❖ Maple syrup available from producers or markets must meet exacting standards for purity.
- ❖ New York Grade-A maple syrup is classified according to its color. The darker the syrup (dark amber), the stronger the maple taste.
- ❖ A quarter-cup of New York State maple syrup contains 7% calcium and 1% potassium. It contains no fat or cholesterol and has the same amount of calories as sugar (200 calories per ¼-cup).

*Information provided by the New York State Maple Producers Association

Ulster County

LYONSVILLE SUGARHOUSE & FARM
591 County Route 2 (Krumville Road)
Route 209 to Krumville Road; look for barn after
passing Lyonsville Lake
Kripplebush
☎ 914-687-2518

Open Valentine's Day through end of March, although syrup can be ordered anytime. Syrup, syrup
candies, maple cream. Tours noon to midnight. Call
first.

Both excavators when the sap isn't running, John
and Kevin operate a sophisticated operation inside a
ramshackle barn. On Valentine's Day, the men run
2,500 lines into maple trees and draw the sap through
a line into a vat where it's boiled down to syrup under high temperatures. They stop extracting sap
when buds begin appearing on the trees.

◎ TIP

Kevin says the best sap is the earliest, so be there in February if you
can. Also, syrup can be refrigerated
or left at room temperature. If left
unrefrigerated, however, it may develop mold. If this happens, heat the
syrup in the microwave and then
scrape off the mold.

Farm Markets & More

MOUNTAIN DEW MAPLE PRODUCTS

351 Samsonville Road, two miles north off
Route 209, across from City Hall Road
Kerhonkson
☎ 914-626-3466

Open daily, year-round (call first). Tours of sap house
given February through April. Syrup, cream, candies, decorative bottles.

★ **DID YOU KNOW?**

Maple cream actually contains no
cream; here it refers to the thick consistency.

CARL SWENSON

12 Markle Road
Shokan
☎ 914-657-2547

Open March through the first week in April. Syrup;
tours.

Greene County

MAPLE GLEN FARM

Scribner Hollow Road, three miles off Route 23A
East Jewett
☎ 518-589-5319

Syrup making and farm tours February through
April. Store open year-round.

MAPLE HILL FARMS

Route 23A, 9 miles west of Hunter Mountain
and three miles from Prattsville
Prattsville
☎ 518-299-3604

Open daily, year-round. Maple syrup making demonstrations in March. Syrup, cream, sugar. Mail order. Tours. Weekends, May through November, at the Malden Service Area near Exit 21. On Friday and Saturday the stand is located on the northbound side, and on Sunday and Monday on the southbound side. Proprietor Walter Cline is a taxidermist and the farm also sells genuine deerskin products.

SPRUCETON VALLEY FARM

176 Spruceton Road
West Kill
☎ 518-989-6849

Open daily, February through April and July through Christmas; closed May and September. Syrup, cream, sugar. Tours, demos in season. Crafts, gift baskets.

Delaware County

C&R FARMS

Harvard Road, 2½ miles north of town, ½ mile south of Harvard and Route 30 junction
East Branch
☎ 607-363-7450

Open year-round. Maple products primarily. Sweetcorn and other vegetables during August. Tours given. Mail order, but no credit cards accepted.

CATSKILL MOUNTAIN MAPLE

Bagley Brook Road (County Route 2)
4½ miles east of town, 7 miles west of
Andes on Route 2
Delancey
☎ 607-746-6215

Open daily, February through April (other times by appointment). Syrup, cream, maple syrup-making equipment.

Farm Markets & More

GREENBRIAR FARM
Berg Road
Stamford
☎ 607-652-7258

Open Labor Day through Thanksgiving, and late-February through Easter; closed Tuesday. Apple cider (in fall), maple syrup (in spring), honey, jams, mustards, vinegars, cheeses. Call ahead for a spring tour.

MAPLEKIN MAPLE PRODUCTS
Pine Brooks Road
Walton
☎ 607-865-6264

Open March and April. Tours, demonstrations. Syrup, cream.

RONALD O. MORSE
Route 37
Fleischmanns
☎ 914-254-4283

Open most weekends mid-May to mid-October. Syrup, cream, candy.

PAUL'S MAPLE PRODUCTS
Across covered bridge on Back River Road
Hamden
☎ 607-746-7708/6760

Open daily, February through April (other times call first). Cream, sugar, lollipops. Gift baskets, mail order, tours. Margie and Paul are holding their fifth open house (300 to 350 people have showed up each year). It's usually at the end of March, but the weather determines the date, so call first. The object is to show how syrup can be used for other foods besides pancakes. Free food is offered – all flavored with maple syrup or maple syrup mustard – macaroni salad, cookies, hot dogs and more.

SHAVER-HILL FARM
197 Shaver Road
Off Route 23, 5 miles west of Stamford
Harpersfield
☎ 607-652-6792

Open daily, year-round. Farm tours. Syrup, cream, sugar. Mail order. Gift shop, cheese, honey, flour. Farmer also sells his products at Pakatakan Farmers' Market in Halcottsville.

SWEET 'P' SAPHOUSE
Route 44
1.2 miles north of Route 357, near E. Sidney Dam
Franklin
☎ 607-369-9530

Open March through December. Syrup, cream. Garden produce in season.

Scrumptious Maple Chicken
2-3 lb. chicken, cut up
¼ cup melted butter
½ cup maple syrup
2 tsp. lemon juice
¼ cup chopped almonds (optional)
½ tsp. salt
dash of pepper
½ tsp. grated lemon rind

Place chicken pieces in shallow baking pan. Mix remaining ingredients and pour evenly over chicken. Bake covered for about one hour at 325°, basting occasionally.

– New York State Maple Producers Association

Helpful hint: ¾-cup maple syrup equals one cup of sugar. When substituting syrup for sugar, reduce liquid in recipe by three tablespoons for each cup of syrup used.

Farm Markets & More

Christmas Tree Farms

The first farm-grown Christmas trees were from the Hudson Valley. One of the earliest growers was Franklin D. Roosevelt.

Sullivan County

TED NIED'S CHRISTMAS TREE FARM
Swiss Hill Road
Jeffersonville
☎ 914-482-5341

Open November through December. U-cut and fresh pre-cuts.

For info about Christmas trees grown in New York, visit www. christmastreesny. org.

Ulster County

ADAMS FAIRACRE FARMS
Route 9W N
Kingston
☎ 914-336-6300

Open daily, year-round. Produce, baked goods, greenhouses and nursery, deli and cheese, trim-a-tree shop (both real and artificial Christmas trees), and everything for the birds.

APPLEGATE FARM
499 Band Camp Road
Saugerties
☎ 914-246-0071

Open weekends in December. U-cut blue and white spruce and Scotch pine trees.

BRIEDIS FARMS
Mountain Valley Acre Road
Boiceville
☎ 914-657-6481

Open two weeks before Christmas. U-cut spruce and other varieties.

DIGRAZIA TREE FARM
469 Pinebush Road, .75 mile west off Route 209 via County Road 2, then right 800 feet
Stone Ridge
☎ 914-687-0449

Open 9am-4pm, Nov. and Dec. Fraser and Canaan firs, farm animals, tours, hayrides, mail order.

DISTAL BROTHERS NURSERY
Route 209 (shares parking lot with Ellenville Discount Beverages)
Ellenville
☎ 914-647-4359

Open weekends in December. Blue spruce and other varieties.

DOLAN ORCHARDS
Route 208
Wallkill
☎ 914-895-2153

Open daily at 9am, August through February. U-pick apples, pumpkins and cherries; vegetables, U-cut Christmas trees.

EAST MOUNTAIN TREE FARM
County Road 46
Napanoch
☎ 914-647-5548

Open weekends in December through Christmas (call for appointment during week). U-cut blue and white spruce; Frasier fir.

GREEN TREE FARMS
Route 28
Shokan
☎ 914-657-2387

Open from Thanksgiving to week before Christmas. U-cut Douglas firs.

HARDENBURGH FARM
Hardenburgh Road
Ulster Park
☎ 914-658-8894

Open weekends from day after Thanksgiving until Christmas. U-cut and pre-cut Scotch pine, white and blue spruce, Douglas and Frasier firs; craft shop, tractor rides.

HURD'S ORCHARD
Route 32
Clintondale
☎ 914-883-7818

Open weekends, September through October. U-pick apples, pears and pumpkins; hayrides, baked goods, cider, donuts, woodland hiking trail, 4-H animals, 22-foot tepee, harvest festival weekends. 500-acre farm has been in same family since 1891. Fresh-cut Christmas trees, holiday ornaments, cider and candy canes.

MOUNTAIN FRESH FARMS
282 Orchard Road
Two miles south of village off Routes 44/55
Highland
☎ 914-795-2260

Open daily, year-round. Choose and cut your own fresh trees. Horse and wagon rides and refreshments on weekends from Thanksgiving to Christmas. Also, certified organic vegetables. Tours by appointment.

P&D FARM & NURSERY
319 Orchard Road
Highland
☎ 914-691-7854

Open daily, Thanksgiving through weekend before Christmas. U-cut Christmas trees.

QUICK'S CHRISTMAS TREE FARM
265 Whitfield Road
Accord
☎ 914-626-7321

Open weekends, first weekend in December through Christmas; weekdays by appointment. U-cut Scotch pine and white spruce.

REILLY'S CHRISTMAS TREES
Route 9W to Esopus
Right on Old Post Rd.; bear right two miles up mountain to Popletown Road; second house on right. Fire #38.
☎ 914-384-6662

Open year-round; daily November and December; otherwise after 3pm. U-cut blue spruce or Scotch pine. $3/foot.

STOVERS CHRISTMAS TREE FARM
Schoonmaker Lane, off Route 209
12 miles south of Kingston
Stone Ridge
☎ 914-687-7512

Open 9am-4pm, November and December. Blue spruce five- to six-feet tall, wreaths, wagon-rides, tours.

Farm Markets & More

ZEEH'S TREE FARM
Off Sawkill Road
Kingston
☎ 914-331-4355

Open weekends 9am-5pm, Thanksgiving to Christmas; weekdays by appointment. Douglas firs, blue spruce and pine.

Greene County

BALD MOUNTAIN TREE FARM
Route 32C
From town, two miles west to N. Settlement Road, then four miles north bearing left
Windham
☎ 518-734-4388

Open Thanksgiving to Christmas, 9am-dusk on weekends; otherwise by appointment. Choose and cut, to 18 feet. Wreaths, garlands and greens. Sixty-mile view from 2,700 feet overlooking Ski Windham. Rides for children on various types of equipment.

GASPAR'S CHRISTMAS TREE FARM
Staco Road, six miles west of Coxsackie off Route 26
Hannacroix
☎ 518-966-5766

Open 9am-4pm, December through January. Choose and cut Norway spruce and Scotch pine; any tree, one price. Hayrides every weekend in December.

Delaware County

GILEAD TREE FARM
Steinfeld Road, 7½ miles north of Fleischmanns via Halcott Road to Johnson Hollow Road
☎ 914-254-5031

Open daily, year-round. Timber and U-cut Christmas trees.

VAMOSY TREE FARM
Odell Lake Road
Stamford
☎ 607-652-4760

Open Thanksgiving to Christmas. Christmas trees.

Honey Farms

★ DID YOU KNOW?

In the Bible, honey is dubbed "the heavenly food."

Ulster County

LENNY'S SMOKED FISH & HONEY
189 Wittenberg Road
Bearsville
☎ 914-679-2653

Open daily, year-round. Old-fashioned hot-smoked trout (honey is used in their special brine). Honey and bee products; mail order.

ROWE'S APIARIES
331-343 Clifton Avenue
Two blocks from Routes 9W and 32
Kingston
☎ 914-331-4058

Open daily, year-round. Clover and wildflower honey, honey candies; mail order.

Farm Markets & More

WIDMARK HONEY FARM
Route 44/55
Gardiner
☎ 914-255-6400

Bee pollen is the only food that contains all 22 basic elements needed by the human body: enzymes, hormones, vitamins, amino acids, and others.

Honey is on sale every November. Bring your own jar and you'll pay even less. Children can feed the farm animals – lambs, goats, sheep and roosters (see page 196).

TRAPHAGEN'S HONEY
Route 23A
Hunter
☎ 800-838-9194; 518-263-4150
Open year-round

Sells honey blends (including handmade honey/goat's milk bars of soap), jams, teas, maple syrups, salad dressings, chocolate, nuts and fragrances (see page 342).

Herb Farms

Ulster County

N. BUTTERFLY HILL HERBARY
Route 52
Pine Bush
☎ 914-744-3040

Open Tuesday through Saturday, year-round. Fresh and dried herbs, jams, natural herbal remedies, teas. Classes given.

O. SHALE HILL FARM & HERB GARDENS
6856 Hommelville Road
Saugerties
☎ 914-246-6982

Open Friday through Monday, year-round. Dried herbs and flowers, wreaths, sachets. Events.

P. TWEEFONTEIN HERB FARM
4 Jenkins Lane, Route 299W
New Paltz
☎ 914-255-7024

Open Friday through Sunday 9am-5pm, end of April through July 10. Organic herbs, aromatic roses and specialty vegetables. Bird sanctuary.

Farm Markets & More